CHIUNE SUGIHARA AND JAPAN'S FOREIGN MINISTRY

Between Incompetence and Culpability
Part 2

Seishiro Sugihara

Translated by
Norman Hu

University Press of America,® Inc.
Lanham · New York · Oxford

Copyright © 2001 by
University Press of America,® Inc.
4720 Boston Way
Lanham, Maryland 20706

12 Hid's Copse Rd.
Cumnor Hill, Oxford OX2 9JJ

Library of Congress Cataloging-in-Publication Data

Sugihara, Seishiro
[Sugihara Chiune to Nihon no Gaimusho. English]
Chiune Sugihara and Japan's foreign ministry, between
incompetence and culpability.
Part 2 / Seishiro Sugihara ; translated by Horman Hu.
p.   cm
Includes bibliographical references and index.
l. Sugihara, Chiune, 1900-1986. 2. Righteous Gentiles in the
Holocaust—Biography. 3. World War, 1939-1945—Causes.
4. United States—Foreign relations—Japan. 5. Japan—Foreign
relations—United States. I. Title.
D804.66.S84 S8413   2001   362.87'81"092—dc21   [B]   2001027033 CIP

ISBN 0-7618-1971-1 (cloth : alk. paper)

Contents

Foreword

This English version of Professor Seishirō Sugihara's book vividly recalls the tragedy of World War II, and I would urge people around the world to recall these events as a way to avoid repeating the human suffering caused by war. With far-reaching insight, this book explores my husband's concerns about rescuing those Jewish refugees, and presents an original, persuasive, and accurate depiction of the events. I am especially moved as this year marks the 100th anniversary of my husband Chiune's birth.

Thinking back on the day the decision was reached at the Lithuanian consulate to issue the visas, Chiune said to me, "I'm thinking about issuing these visas, but if the Nazis find out we might be arrested. I might also be dismissed by the Foreign Ministry. If you're against it, I could reconsider."

I pictured the Jewish refugees standing in front of the consulate day after day. "Let's issue the visas," I answered. "We can't just ignore them." This was after agonizing over the situation for days. We needed a firm resolve if we were going to save the lives of a great number of people.

My husband issued visas day and night without a break. Thousands of people converged on the consulate. After the war ended and we returned to Japan, my husband was dismissed from the Foreign Ministry for disobeying orders by issuing those visas. Years later, he passed away after having to endure many hardships to make a living. Nowadays I receive expressions of gratitude from people in Israel and elsewhere, and I feel I've lived a life with no regrets.

Coincidentally, the author of this book shares our family name, and people have commented to me, "I read the book by your son, and was deeply moved." Although I cherish each of my four sons, in my heart I feel as though I've gained another. Let me extend my deepest thanks to Professor Sugihara for his efforts.

Yukiko Sugihara
August 2000

Preface

My purpose for this English-language edition is to allow easier access for people outside Japan, directly involved in diplomacy or its research, to the ideas in the original version. I would therefore like in this special preface to elaborate for their benefit on those ideas.

This book, along with my previous work *Between Incompetence and Culpability* (UPA, 1997), examines in detail issues concerning Japan's Foreign Ministry and its diplomats. I would like to clearly indicate here the significance of certain problems for Japan and the rest of the world, problems which have been brought about by the present state of the Foreign Ministry, its diplomats, and its diplomacy.

Consequently, it is my hope this may provide some beneficial reference or insight to all those involved in conducting diplomacy with other nations, and with the study of diplomacy.

The Emperor System in Japan's History

A certain level of understanding of Japan is essential before contemplating problems to do with Japan's Foreign Ministry. This requires a measured consideration of the significance of the emperor system (*tennō-sei*). The emperor system, even for Japanese people, is not easy to understand. We have become familiar with its presence, but this ironically makes it more difficult to understand; only problematic aspects and critical perspectives are discussed and considered, and often it appears that, at least on the surface, the Japanese people themselves consider only the negative aspects of the emperor system.

However, the term "emperor system" was coined by Communists at the start of the Shōwa era, and later became established in the vocabulary of the general social sciences; it is, therefore, a unique Japanese expression to refer to a system of monarchy.

From a Communist perspective, the nation-state was conventionally seen as a tool of class rule, and the emperor came to assume the essence of the nation-state to exploit and exercise authority over the people. Furthermore, it was imperative the emperor system be overthrown by revolution.

However, even an elementary review of the Meiji Restoration for instance quickly reveals that this conclusion regarding the emperor system is simplistic and unsound.

Retaining the *bakuhan* system during the Edo period (where the *baku* or shogunate was at the head of the quasi-independent *han* or domains) made it impossible to reform Japan into a modern nation like those in Europe and America. By embracing the pretext of *taisei hōkan* (restoration of imperial rule) which allowed the shogunate to restore political authority to the emperor, Japan at this time underwent a kind of revolution, and successfully survived national crisis without undue disorder.

Japan and the rest of the world today accept that Japan was never formally colonized by a foreign power, but the Tokugawa Shogunate concluded unequal treaties of commerce first with the United States in 1858, and then with others; it also accepted foreign consular exemption from local legal jurisdiction as well as foreigners' rights to determine tariffs. Arguably, these treaties raised the degree of Japan's quasi-colonization.

In the midst of this crisis, the Satsuma and Chōshu clans, under the rule of the Tokugawa Shogunate, joined forces to start a movement to topple the shogunate. Criticism of the shogunate had begun to appear across the country, and just when it seemed the combined military force of the two clans was getting the upper hand, the Tokugawa Shogunate restored administration of the country to the emperor to avoid civil chaos across Japan, and thereby managed to avoid foreign intervention while preserving unity and bringing about the rebirth of the nation. French Consul Léon Roches requested assistance from the Tokugawa Shogunate to send a punitive expedition against Satsuma and Chōshu, but Tokugawa Yoshinobu, the last shogun, refused though not because the expedition had no chance of succeeding; he voluntarily relinquished his position as shogun and restored imperial rule. The slogan "honor the Emperor and expel the barbarian" (*sonnō jōi*) was invoked to overthrow the Tokugawa Shogunate which had opened Japan to the world without the emperor's permission, but Tokugawa Yoshinobu made no effort to resist, and cooperated fully in the restoration of imperial rule and the rebirth of the nation.

During this period of national crisis, the emperor's presence wakened the pride of the Japanese people, and by deepening national solidarity, allowed Japan to completely turn itself around without conceding any further opportunities to foreign nations.

Consequently, in this sense the term "emperor system" had its own independent context unique to Japan's system of monarchy, yet remained cognizant of those from other countries.

After successfully undergoing the Meiji Restoration, Japan committed a grave error in 1910 by annexing Korea. However, we must ask whether the Yi dynasty, the Korean royal family, was at this time the focus of pride and unity for Korea and the Korean people. If it had been, would Korean annexation have been possible without first deposing the Korean monarchy? Korea was in fact a much older country than Japan. If Korea's ancient Chosŏn dynasty, founded by the mythical progenitor Tan'gun, had survived through this period, Korean annexation most probably would not have been possible without that dynasty first being toppled. Korean annexation would most likely have been impossible if that ancient dynasty had survived.

Although Korea did not experience as many dynastic changes as China, in 1392 Yi Sŏng-gye, a subject of the Koryŏ dynasty, toppled the Koryŏ and established the Yi dynasty. Moreover, this was a Chinese-style revolution carried out with the approval of the Ming, China's imperial court at the time. The name "Chosŏn" used by the Yi to designate the Korean nation, was bestowed by the Ming emperor after Yi Sŏng-gye petitioned the Ming court.

Although the Yi dynasty in many respects governed the Korean people well, it held no real authority and failed to become a focus of pride and unity for Korea and the Korean people. The Yi dynasty's relationship with the Korean people meant, ironically, that it would occasionally pursue its own interests over those of the Korean people. This was why during Korea's annexation no substantial forces emerged from the Korean people to assist the Yi.

Circumstances in Korea must also be considered in view of geopolitical conditions surrounding Korea. To ensure its continued existence, Korea had to anticipate the wishes of the Chinese imperial court. Korea was destined never to run its national affairs freely or independently because of geopolitical pressures. The opportunity to run its own affairs and surpass China economically was never possible, at least not until the present era. This is why it had not been possible for the Korean royal court or the Korean people to develop their own free and independent character.

On the other hand, although Japan also co-existed in proximity to this giant neighbor China, the geopolitical consequences of being an island nation meant Japan was not directly threatened by China, and could independently run its affairs, centered on the emperor. First unified by the Yamato court, Japan and the Japanese people were blessed with geopolitical conditions that allowed them to run their national affairs freely and independently.

Japan was an isolated island nation separated from other countries by a great expanse of water; it was too removed from China to be under its direct political influence. However, before long even places as distant as the Hawaiian islands felt the impact of China's enormous influence. This threat conversely strengthened Japan's emperor system, and helped develop Japan's unique history.

The emperor system might inadvertently have been destroyed, despite Japan's geopolitical blessings, due to the vagaries of history. Therefore, it is undeniable that the unbroken continuation of the emperor system owed something to chance. Nevertheless, its very longevity naturally formed a foundation for bolstering its continued existence. For instance, Tokugawa Ieyasu, leader of the "expeditionary force against the barbarians," founded the Tokugawa Shogunate in 1603, and conceivably had more than enough military power to crush the Yamato court. He didn't do this though, preferring instead to have the emperor confer upon him the title Sei-I Taishōgun (Grand General for the Subjugation of Barbarians), and to rule and control Japan as leader of the samurai class.

This overview shows us that Japan's emperor system was a distinct form of monarchy, and its underlying philosophy and ideas, as well as its traditions and practice, evolved independently of the ideas, theories and history of monarchies in Europe. Theories behind European monarchies, dating from the science of government since ancient Greece, were not necessarily viewed negatively. Consequently, this means Japan's theories of monarchy, which developed within Japan independent of European influence, should similarly be accorded their rightful place in the development of world history.

Japan's first encounter with Europeans was in 1543 when Portuguese sailors with hand-held firearms drifted ashore at Tanegashima to the south of Satsuma. Not long after, the Edo Shogunate which controlled the government launched Japan into a lengthy period of *sakoku* or self-imposed national isolation. However, even in this period, the emperor system was retained, the Yamato court continued to exist and, as previously noted, became the mechanism that averted the national crisis during the last days of the Tokugawa Shogunate.

Japan's emperor system developed of its own accord under favorable geopolitical conditions, and although this was achieved independent of theories of European monarchy, it was in practice quite similar in form. However, it would be instructive here to clarify some issues regarding the theories, concepts and ideas underlying Japan's emperor system with specific reference to China.

Before its first contact with Europeans in the sixteenth century, Japan existed in a world view defined by China. There was an awareness of the existence of India through Buddhism, but Japan's lack of direct dealings consequently meant that the notion of India as a state had little substance. This means that the ideas and concepts underlying Japan's emperor system were likely informed by an awareness of certain Chinese political theories. It was therefore understood that some Chinese political theories could undermine an emperor system, namely, the Chinese political concept of *yi-hsing ke-ming* or "dynastic change through revolution." If we acknowledge that Japan's emperor system was a valid home-grown political theory, it is clearly apparent that it developed and was formed as a counter to this Chinese notion of "dynastic change through revolution." Even if, for argument's sake, the emperor system originally developed on its own, at the very least its theoretical content clearly shows that exposure to the political concept of "dynastic change through revolution" conversely transformed it consciously and ideologically into an opposing political theory.[1]

China's imperial courts were based on actual military power. In other words, they were compelled to exercise military rule. Losing military power allowed the next imperial dynasty to take over. Theoretically, this meant anyone who had amassed sufficient military force could start his own dynasty, and in that sense, such dynasties could have humble beginnings. On the other hand, this form of rule was in principle militarist since authority could only be maintained through military power. And should this power be lost, the dynasty would fall. The process leading to the emergence of a new Son of Heaven from the populace was called a "revolution," stemming from the political concept "dynastic change through revolution." China would plunge into great civil disturbance because of such "revolutions," which occurred once every few decades or centuries, and they caused unspeakable suffering for the Chinese people and untold destruction of their culture.

By contrast, the Yamato court was an imperial dynasty which first unified Japan by exerting religious authority over a primitive society founded in ancient times on rice cultivation; from its very beginnings, it combined both religious and political power. This political measure of intentionally combining religion and politics became a traditional custom of the Yamato method of governance. In other words, it had its origins in rule through benevolent government rather than military force, and this became a Yamato tradition. Consequently, this imperial dynasty was founded upon, and continued to conduct, moral government. When its traditions and customs were exposed to the Chinese political notion of "dynastic change through revolution," it underwent theorization into a political system countering that notion. As a result, the Yamato court was transformed into an imperial dynasty obliged to follow the path of moral government.

What result did this produce? It meant that Japan's history developed while avoiding the chaos stemming from the notion of "dynastic change through revolution," the endless suffering of its people, and the destruction of its culture. Cultural elements were rarely violently destroyed, and new culture developed midst the accumulation of previous artifacts from ancient times; this produced extremely favorable conditions for the amassing of culture.

For instance, take the development and unfolding of Buddhism in Japan. Although with the establishment of the Tokugawa Shogunate in 1603 Tokugawa Ieyasu in essence held supreme authority over Japan, he nevertheless exercised his rule under the pretext of being appointed by the emperor as Grand General for the Subjugation of Barbarians, and did not eradicate nor suppress Buddhism, which had been introduced and cultivated by the Yamato. He was unable to do so. In conquering Japan, Ieyasu had been troubled by Buddhist influences, and it was important that he weaken Buddhism's hold on society. However, although he did in fact interfere heavily in Buddhist matters, he neither eradicated nor suppressed Buddhism. Nor did he have the ability to do so.

It would be instructive to compare this to the situation in Korea. In 1392, Yi Sŏng-gye established the Yi dynasty by toppling the Koryŏ court, and aggressively suppressed Buddhism which the Koryŏ had devoutly preserved and cultivated; he then implemented policies to eradicate Buddhist influence from Korea. As a result, Buddhism was extremely weakened in Korea, and today, unlike Japan, Korea is no longer a Buddhist nation.

The same could also be said about Japan's indigenous religion Shinto. Shinto was an animistic religion without a progenitor, premised on a culture of rice cultivation, and a similar animistic religion existed in ancient Korea. However, Korean history unfolded with the destruction of its first royal dynasty, and thereafter witnessed a number of rival dynasties competing against, and alternating power with, each other. During this rivalry and repeated alternating, Korea's animistic religion in effect ceased to exist.[2]

In Japan, there was no reason why Shinto would have disappeared, since the Yamato dynasty, which presides over this animistic religion, has survived into the present. To the contrary, Buddhism, which was introduced and cultivated by the Yamato court, has influenced Japanese Shinto and conversely refined it. Even in this computer-driven 21st century, Shinto continues to survive as an animistic religion that enriches the hearts of the Japanese people.

In other words, Japanese culture developed a pattern exemplified by the unbroken reign of the Yamato court. Political power holders hardly ever arbitrarily destroyed Japan's accumulated artifacts, and this established a pattern whereby new culture always rooted, sprouted, and grew in the accumulated substrate of older culture. Thus, culture developed in a very productive manner. For an actual manifestation of this fecundity, let us turn to the development of Japanese literacy rates.

When the Yamato court was founded, Japan had no writing system and lagged far behind China. When the Yamato first unified Japan, writing was virtually unknown. It is said that *kanji* or Han Chinese characters were transmitted to Japan via Korea around the fifth century A. D.; but in the final days of the Tokugawa Shogunate in the 1860s, Japan boasted male literacy rates of between 40 and 50 percent, and female literacy rates of around 15 percent. At the time, these outstanding rates were the highest in Asia, and compared well against those in Europe and America.[3]

In the forward to his collected works on religion and sociology, which contain the well-known thesis "The Protestant Ethic and the Spirit of Capitalism" (1904–1905), German sociologist Max Weber asked, "Why, and through what chain of events, did the cultural phenomenon of progress take expression only in the West and nowhere else, and there alone as a matter of course?"[4] However, parallel developments in Japan clearly demonstrate that one should not overlook the existence of Japan's emperor system.

The essence of Japan's emperor system, a benevolent monarchy which ruled on the basis of virtue, is demonstrated through the following actions taken by Emperor Hirohito in the closing stages of the Pacific War.

In August 1945, when Japan accepted the Potsdam Proclamation and surrendered to the Allied nations, the emperor held in check those among his subjects who opposed surrender; he persuaded them that he had to save the lives of his people, regardless of his personal fate, and decided to accept capitulation. While this should be noted as an act attributable to Emperor Hirohito himself, conceivably it was also naturally the duty of the 124th emperor in the Yamato imperial line, with its tradition of benevolent rule.

Certainly, Emperor Hirohito bears some responsibility for the fact that war between Japan and the United States was not avoided; but one might also say that, when the emperor was confronted by an unprecedented crisis in the nation's and the people's recorded history, he gambled his own existence to prevent a tragic disaster, and this demonstrated the essence of the Yamato court and its benevolent rule.

The Glory and the Failing of the Meiji Restoration

With the Meiji Restoration of 1868, Japan began its metamorphosis into a modern nation.

In ancient times, Japan underwent the Taika Reforms of 645 A.D. This signified the transformation of the state from a mere collection of powerful clans to a single formal entity under the authority of the emperor. In other words, it meant bringing together various social systems into a formal polity patterned after the state of China. In contrast, the Meiji Restoration's task was to create a modern nation by introducing a number of systems from the nations of Europe and America.

Under the Meiji Restoration, military and police systems, as well as those for the courts and education, were all introduced from the nations of Europe and America.

Thus, in 1889 Japan was the first nation in Asia to promulgate its own constitution.

Later, Japan fought in the first Sino-Japanese War (1894–1895), the Russo-Japanese War (1904–1905), and World War I (1914–1918), and joined the community of great world powers. The unfolding of this series of victories was an astonishing phenomenon in the annals of world history.

However, these miraculous results, by their very nature, set the stage for Japan's later failure and defeat.

While international circumstances at the start of the Shōwa era cannot be ignored, Japan's national leadership was then extremely arrogant and narrow-minded. Indeed, a more specific list of the qualities of Japan's leaders then would reveal they were arrogant, over-confident, hasty, obstinate, hot-tempered, and narrow-minded. The elder statesmen who brought about the Meiji Restoration were tempered by its processes, and thus retained their sense of political realism. However, succeeding generations who assumed leadership during the Shōwa era could only relive those miraculous successes in an abstract sense; they swelled with excessive conceit, lost their sense of realism, and descended into arrogance and narrow-mindedness.

Even Japan's remarkable Imperial Constitution, Asia's first such instrument, was interpreted during the Shōwa era to provide for the "independence of the supreme command," and this destroyed national unity and slowly eroded the essence of the constitution. Blame for this flaw in the Constitution, which left room for such an interpretation, could be assigned to those who drafted it during the Meiji era. However, this dangerous interpretation was not quashed as soon as it emerged, and this was surely a failing and shortcoming we can attribute to the glory of the Meiji era, a time which embraced the thinking that inspired the sacred Imperial Constitution.

Even though the newly introduced Meiji systems originated from Europe and America, their implementation was carried out by Japanese who were part of the fabric of Japan's culture and history.

While Japan's military adopted military systems patterned after those from Europe and America, those who participated in and operated these systems were part of the fabric of Japan's culture and history. People around the world should recall that, under the emperor system, Japan's military valued order, and was an outstanding force by world standards, if the outcomes of the Sino-Japanese and Russo-Japanese Wars are anything to go by. Evidence of supreme bravery by ordinary troops, even during the war in the Pacific and despite problematic actions by certain officers, is still fresh in living memory. Moreover, although Japan's three-and-a-half year control over much of Southeast Asia was brief, the professionalism and outstanding character of Japan's military should be noted in the annals of world history, because the peoples of these areas were stimulated to develop a thirst for independence and were informed of ways to achieve it.

However, Japan's military had not incorporated the notion from these Western military systems that, in the thick of battle, defeated troops could surrender to the enemy and allow themselves to be captured; in this regard, Japan's military remained thoroughly Japanese. Although they had the semblance of Western-style troops, they were not completely Westernized, and ultimately remained inherently Japanese. Consequently, this inherent nature made the war in the Pacific more tragic than was necessary. This failing can also be attributed to the Meiji era, and the pride produced by its deeply felt spiritual convictions.

Let us return to the issue of the emperor system. As previously noted, the political concept of the emperor system was developed to counter the Chinese political notion of "dynastic change through revolution." However, following the Meiji Restoration it embraced concepts from the greater world community, and with the Shōwa era it lost its realism and became an ideology of fanatic spiritualism that plunged the Japanese people further into arrogance and narrow-mindedness. In some respects, the "Greater East Asian War" during the war in the Pacific indeed had the sacred aims of defending Japan and liberating Asia, but it is impossible to evade criticism over Japan's arrogance and narrow-mindedness. Ultimately, this was probably another failing brought on by the glory of the Meiji Restoration, which had raised the people's self-respect and unity under the emperor, and allowed the nation to triumph over crisis.

Japan's Greatest Failure: The Japanese Diplomatic Training System

Let us now turn our attention to the question of the Foreign Ministry and its diplomats. The Foreign Ministry was set up during the Meiji Restoration out of necessity as an organ to interact with foreign countries, and its diplomats were the ones charged exclusively with its diplomacy. The system to train these diplomats was patterned entirely after the European and American systems.

Japanese diplomacy faced a huge task at the beginning of the Meiji era. It had to revise the unequal treaties signed at the close of the Edo period. In early Meiji, just before the outbreak of the Russo-Japanese War in 1894 and thanks mainly to the efforts of the Foreign Ministry, Japan succeeded in bringing about large-scale revisions to its unequal treaty with England, and by 1911 successfully abolished all its unequal treaties.

In general though, a broad survey of Japanese diplomacy after 1904 would reveal that, like their military counterparts, leading officials within the Foreign Ministry in charge of Japanese diplomacy also lost all sense of realism, and descended into arrogance and narrow-mindedness. A typical example of this was during World War I when, in 1915, Japan forced its Twenty-One Demands upon China.

However, the problem with the Foreign Ministry and its diplomats is not just the notion of its arrogance and narrow-mindedness. What can we conclude from its serious and fundamental blunder of not delivering the "declaration of war" at the designated time at the start of war between Japan and the United States; or from the fact that career diplomats in Washington during that period were unable to type English? Regrettably, it means that we must brand Japan's diplomats, despite having satisfied the requirements of Japan's diplomatic training system, as completely incompetent.

However, there is more. What can we conclude from the Ministry's blithe attempt to conceal its diplomatic responsibility for not preventing the outbreak of war between Japan and the United States? Understandably, it is simply human nature for people who commit gross mistakes to try to evade this responsibility. However the Foreign Ministry's cover-up of its war responsibility, as discussed in detail in this book, has been carried out nonchalantly at the expense of the prestige of Japan and the Japanese people. Even though diplomats owe their very existence to protecting the reputation of their nation and their people, Japan's diplomats have committed a crime against the nation by covering up the Ministry's war responsibility and blithely sacrificing the prestige of Japan and the Japanese people. What does this tell us about the Foreign Ministry and Japan's diplomats?

These considerations then bring us to the question of how the Foreign Ministry and its system for training diplomats were introduced to Japan, and what form they took.

At the beginning of the Meiji era when most of Asia had been colonized by Europe, and Japan alone had bravely held onto its independence and strove, with one great flourish, to develop relations with the various countries in Europe and America, few Japanese could speak these foreign languages and consequently the skills of those who could were highly prized. The ability to understand European and American customs was also valued. However, these skills are not the essential elements of a diplomat's functions. Rather, a Japanese diplomat's role should mainly involve upholding Japan's reputation, and having a strategic and well-rounded sense of the art of statesmanship and how to deal with other countries.

Although the military systems at the start of the Meiji era were introduced from Europe and America, those who participated in and operated these systems were samurai from the Edo period. Naturally, samurai were primarily skilled in the art of warfare. Therefore, while the military systems themselves were imported, the samurai used these systems to create an inherently Japanese military that was equal in quality to those in Europe and America, even though it failed to incorporate the notion that in some instances, defeated troops could surrender to the enemy and allow themselves to be captured.

This also held true for the police system introduced from Europe and America. This system, at the beginning of the Meiji era, was also operated by men from the samurai class. During the Edo period, which spanned more than two-and-a-half centuries, it was the samurai class which resolved disturbances amongst the people, maintained public order, and preserved law and order. Using their expertise and techniques for control, they reduced corruption, maintained high arrest rates, and produced a police force to rival the world's finest.

However, this was not the case regarding the Foreign Ministry, its diplomats, and its diplomatic training system. The Edo Shogunate decided on its key policy of *sakoku* or national isolation early in its rule, and for two-and-a-half centuries maintained relations only with Korea and the Netherlands to the exclusion of all other countries, and even those relations were extremely restricted. This is why Japan was unable to accrue any repository of expertise or techniques for conducting relations with other countries. Diplomacy had to be conducted without this repository of knowledge of diplomatic matters. Moreover, unlike the countries of Europe and America, Japan was additionally burdened with having to master the Western languages and protocols required to conduct such relations, and this taxed Japanese diplomats far more than their Western counterparts.

It was under such circumstances that Japan adopted foreign diplomatic systems, but because it didn't have a repository of expertise and techniques to operate these systems, it lacked personnel skilled in the strategies to properly exploit them. Of all its imported systems, only Japan's diplomatic system lacked adequate staff with the proper qualities; it was launched in the belief that it was sufficient simply to have people who could speak foreign languages and were familiar with foreign protocol. This is probably where the misconception first arose that familiarity with foreign languages and protocol alone qualified someone as a diplomat.

Seen in this light, we can now understand that the diplomatic successes in revising unequal treaties dating from the early Meiji era were not the result of expertise by Foreign Ministry personnel, that is professional diplomats, but rather were thanks to the initiatives taken by prime ministers or foreign ministers. For instance, the last shogun Tokugawa Yoshinobu, and early Meiji government leaders such as Ōkubo Toshimichi and Itō Hirobumi (who became Japan's first prime minister in 1885), all had an exceptional flair for diplomacy. However, when Japan's diplomacy was later conducted exclusively by professional diplomats, the quality of Japanese diplomacy clearly declined.

With the Shōwa era, Japanese society appeared to be a modern nation based on individual freedoms guaranteed by Japan's Constitution. It was however still a feudal society indistinguishable from the Edo period, pervaded by feudal values. Actual conditions in Japanese society were still not those of a modern nation. What was the significance of this? It meant that vigorous public debate was scarce, and what scant criticism existed had little effect on society. Furthermore, diplomats, who as a rule had little contact with the public when performing their duties, were seldom scrutinized or criticized. In other words, professional diplomats within the Foreign Ministry, a state organ, were never subjected to public scrutiny.

Not only the Foreign Ministry but all Japan's organs of state carried out their operations under these conditions, and the egotism of individuals working at each gave impetus to the development of each organization's particular sense of pride. The Japanese government soon developed into a loose coalition of agencies, each fighting and competing with the others. The Foreign Ministry too failed to operate under the premise of a unified Japanese government; diplomacy became the exclusive preserve of the Foreign Ministry, and the community of diplomats became accustomed to fervently rejecting all outside criticism.

The growth of *keibatsu* marriages, where officials advanced their careers by marrying into powerful ministry clans, further accelerated these abuses by Japan's government organs. The internal structure of the Foreign Ministry, but also of ministries created at the start of the Meiji era including the Army, Navy, Police, and Education, formed around these *keibatsu* relationships. Personnel exchanges between ministries occurred rarely, and each organ developed its own *keibatsu* arrangement. However, the Foreign Ministry outstripped all the others in the number of its *keibatsu* marriages.[5]

It was the Foreign Ministry's foreign service examinations that perpetuated its diplomats' incompetence and shameless behavior. Recently, the Foreign Ministry decided to abolish these internally administered exams; however, although ordinary public servants since the end of the war have had to sit national public service examinations conducted by the National Personnel Authority, diplomats alone have been selected through these internally administered Foreign Ministry examinations that haven't been reformed since the end of the war. It has of course therefore been simple for children from diplomatic families to become diplomats. Such offspring typically pass the foreign service examination at the age of twenty, and are practically guaranteed their fathers' diplomatic positions. Admittedly, children of diplomats are not the only ones who pass this examination; but those who don't belong to a *keibatsu* family when they pass the exam more often than not enter one by marrying the offspring of a higher-ranking diplomat. Those who don't marry into a *keibatsu* find their futures bleak.

Due to the special circumstances of working abroad, the Foreign Ministry established itself as a professional organization which, although solely responsible for the important task of the nation's diplomacy, was not aware of its incompetence and shameless behavior due to those very qualities. This organization was composed exclusively of diplomats who appear (to external observers) to embody incompetence and shamelessness, so it is unsurprising that they are unable to recognize this incompetent and shameless behavior amongst themselves. The organization bands together to ward off external criticism. This is how it has been possible for an organization of diplomats to completely forget who they are ultimately responsible to, and what they are responsible for.

It was discussed previously how many early-Meiji leaders came from the samurai class, and that these samurai were well-versed in the arts of *bushidō* (or samurai code), as introduced to the world by Inazō Nitobe in his book *Bushido* (1900). These samurai solemnly believed in certain truths (such as, "Knowing what is right yet not doing it betrays one's cowardice"; "One mustn't be mean-spirited"; and "Value one's reputation.") This was, as Nitobe indicated, similar to the European notion of *noblesse oblige* or the responsibility of persons of high birth or rank.[6] Undoubtedly, what also applies here is the Confucian teaching on the qualities required in a leader that, "In missions to the four corners of the world, carry out your master's orders with honor."

However, during the Shōwa era, not all Japan's leaders necessarily came from the samurai class. This was a result of the Meiji Restoration, a sweeping samurai-initiated revolution that abolished the privileges of the samurai class, and cultivated an egalitarian society. Unfortunately, although many Shōwa leaders from humble beginnings were certainly capable in some respects, they were unable to adhere strictly to these tenets of the samurai code. Even though they enjoyed the privileges rightfully accorded to national leaders, they developed an insatiable hunger to further their reputations and careers. Moreover, because they weren't born into high-ranking families, they were unable to build a social infrastructure that preserved the critical "sense of duty incumbent upon persons of high birth," nor were they able spiritually to live up to this themselves. As discussed in this book, the corrupt elitism that was devoid of this samurai spirit was one reason why Chiune Sugihara, who wasn't a career diplomat, was coldly dismissed in 1947 by high-ranking elite officials, even though he had saved the lives of 6,000 Jews.

However, most members of the Japanese public were not sufficiently acquainted with democratic practices to criticize the behavior of such leaders. Much less was it possible to criticize diplomats properly because they conducted their work abroad, beyond the direct scrutiny of the Japanese people.

With the Shōwa era, the Foreign Ministry's career diplomats clearly became the group in Japan most lacking in the spirit of the samurai code, even though they should have been the most faithful adherents of that spirit because of the fundamental nature of the diplomatic profession. Since diplomats worked in a prestigious profession and enjoyed certain privileges, they became even further removed from the Japanese public. As their sense of pride and hunger for prestige grew, and while they enjoyed the benefits of diplomatic privileges, they in fact became incompetent and cowardly. Even though Japan's diplomats who represented their country abroad should have observed the samurai code more closely than even the military, they became the group in Japanese society, among all other civil servants, who had most lost touch with the samurai code of ethics.

Working in a profession introduced from Europe and America, these diplomats did not risk death in their duties. Japanese culture was based on the spirit of the samurai code with its inherent danger of death, and the heart of the Japanese diplomat became derelict without this danger. In a sense, the samurai ethic persisted because of the ever-present risk of death. Even when confronting an inequitable death, the understanding that one should endure it purified any sense of ambition or pride, and this in turn activated the "sense of duty incumbent upon persons of high birth." However diplomatic immunity meant diplomats' lives were never at risk, even if during a war troops or ordinary Japanese people fought for their very lives. This lack of immediate danger set them apart as "strangers" in their own culture which originally valued the samurai code; and collectively, these diplomats came to exert total control over Japan's diplomacy.

This reveals how problematic the Foreign Ministry's employment practices and training system were. Prospective diplomats passed a foreign service examination that could not guarantee whether they possessed the proper qualities. While intensive training in foreign languages and protocol might have prepared them adequately in certain respects, it did not sufficiently give them the qualities they actually needed to be diplomats, that is, the practical skills to deal with the variety of people they would meet at a foreign posting, or the strategic expertise required to practice statesmanship, the most essential qualification required of a diplomat. In other words, they were posted abroad without having the appropriate abilities. Furthermore, they possessed diplomatic immunity. They were posted abroad even though they might indeed have been incompetent. As discussed in this book, they may have been incompetent, or have had a sense of pride not linked to the Japanese people, or felt they were not responsible to the Japanese people due to their *keibatsu* ties. This meant they were unaware of their own incompetence and shameless behavior. Even during the crisis Japan faced immediately after the war, they had neither the ability nor honesty to acknowledge their own war responsibility, and sold out the prestige of the nation and the people to secure the Foreign Ministry's future existence. Although so many Japanese soldiers and civilians died, diplomats immediately after the war nonchalantly covered up their own enormous war responsibility.

The Postwar Diplomacy of the Foreign Ministry

As this book describes in detail, the Foreign Ministry clearly covered up its war responsibility after Japan was defeated, and did so in a manner that was concealed from the Japanese people. The postwar diplomacy of the Foreign Ministry, which kept its war responsibility from the people, was ultimately a form of diplomacy enacted not on behalf of Japan or the Japanese people, but for the benefit of the Foreign Ministry and its diplomats.

An unexpected yet unambiguous example of this sort of diplomacy by the Foreign Ministry was the 1982 dispute over textbooks that was caused by false press reports, which this author has examined in a previous publication.[7]

The Japanese media inaccurately reported that the Ministry of Education had directed school textbooks to refer to the *shinryaku* (invasion) of China merely as *shinshutsu* ([military] advance) during the authorization procedure for some textbooks to be used in Japanese schools. Even though it was quickly known within the government that these reports had been incorrect, the Foreign Ministry did not publicly reveal the truth about these mistaken reports, and decided to settle the matter by apologizing to the protesting Chinese and Korean governments. People the world over would find it difficult to understand why it decided to settle the matter with an apology, even though it knew these mistaken reports had no basis in fact. The education of children is a fundamental duty of any country, and involves the sacred task of nourishing the nation's next generation. Nevertheless, although there were no grounds to back up this criticism, the Foreign Ministry decided upon a diplomatic settlement at the expense of Japanese education. Can this truly be considered diplomacy in the national interest?

Thereafter, China has raised the issue of Japan's past war responsibility at every opportunity, and has extracted "soft" financial aid from Japan. Like in the Japanese fable, China seems to have found the lucky mallet which, when struck, grants every wish. China really has found a lucky mallet, since every time China rails at Japan over past events, it is able to extract cash from Japan.

By creating an incident over mistaken reports that had no basis in truth, and by settling the matter with an apology rather than pointing out the facts regarding the mistaken reports, the Foreign Ministry allowed China later to perpetuate this sort of behavior and to adopt its arrogant diplomatic posture.

For Japan's Foreign Ministry, allowing China to perpetuate this arrogant diplomacy complements the perpetuation of the cover-up of its own war responsibility, and perversely, this suits its purposes only too well.

In 1985, the Nanking City People's Government erected a monument known as the "Nanking Massacre Memorial Hall." At its entrance was a sign claiming that Japanese troops committed the massacre of 300,000 people. As I have explained elsewhere,[8] contemporary records show that the population of the city of Nanking before the Nanking Incident was 200,000. After the Incident, the population conversely rose to 250,000. (It is believed that after order was restored, residents who fled to surrounding areas returned to the city.) How is it possible therefore that a massacre of 300,000 people occurred, given these contemporary records? Why must "soft" financial aid be given to the Chinese government when such a monument has been built, whether with private or public funds? However the Chinese government, in raising these unsubstantiated and enormous figures to criticize Japan, seems unperturbed. If the Chinese Communist Party, now in control of China's government, feels it must raise such overblown figures, it should first disclose just how many Chinese civilians were illegally killed or died under (or because of) the Party's leadership after it seized power, and apologize to the Chinese people. Let alone the number of casualties during the revolution carried out by the Party to seize power.

It is true there are past events in the history of relations between Japan and China that would warrant an apology, however these matters were closed with the signing of the Joint Communiqué of the Government of Japan and the Government of the People's Republic of China (1972) and the Treaty of Peace and Friendship between Japan and the People's Republic of China (1978). Apologies were finalized legally, and it is pointless to make further accusations. If, despite this, China continues to request an apology, Japan might similarly ask for an apology for the Mongol invasions of 1274 and 1281!

It is undeniable that the present Chinese government, under the authority of the Chinese Communist Party, is the legitimate government of China; however if it continues to blame Japan for past war responsibilities, what should we make of its past actions in gaining power by frustrating any reconciliation between the Japanese government and the Kuomintang, which then was the legitimate government of China?

After Deng Xiaoping seized control of the Chinese Communist Party, China introduced a market economy and carried out economic reforms. These economic reforms have seen some success, but from the very start, Deng should have tried to transform China into a democratic nation by enacting political, rather than economic, reforms. There should have been reforms to gradually introduce a democratic political system, and make the transition to a government based on European- or American-style democratic elections. In principle, an economy will certainly grow if the people are granted freedom and enjoy peace, so it was clearly not sufficient to merely introduce economic reforms. This is particularly so with such an industrious people as the Chinese.

Nevertheless, if only economic reforms are enacted and China retains a political system dominated by a single party, this undemocratic power structure, not surprisingly, will have a tendency to be oppressive and hegemonic in its external relations. Japan has obligingly let itself fall prey to this.

China has found a magic formula to get "soft" loans every time it criticizes Japan for its past, so Japan has become a country against whom the Chinese government can adopt an increasingly overbearing posture. Power derived undemocratically has a tendency to resolve internal power contradictions by external campaigns, and Japan has increasingly been made to serve this purpose for the Chinese government. Not only Japan, but all the countries in the region have been subjected to this harassment.

One cannot help feeling sorry for many Chinese delegates attending international forums these days, because they aren't able to exercise real responsibility for their own country. The country they represent is a dictatorship based on the absolute control of the Chinese Communist Party which disregards the democratic process, so if people representing China aren't Party members or formal government representatives, they can only express themselves as individual Chinese. Therefore they cannot make statements representing or defending the Chinese government. Much less are they free to criticize the Chinese government. Nowadays, when democratically ruled countries are in the overwhelming majority, individuals in many countries are free to defend or criticize their own government. Nevertheless, individuals representing China are ultimately forced to remain silent; and I am probably not alone in thinking that they appear to feel totally isolated.

China under the totalitarian rule of the Chinese Communist Party is, even today, dominated by the political concept of "dynastic change through revolution."

What if the Foreign Ministry had Clarified its War Responsibility?

It is worth reiterating that the Foreign Ministry must bear some responsibility for the war between Japan and the United States, as well as for the war between Japan and China that occurred during the same period. As this book makes clear, if we see the act of war as the final step in the diplomatic process, then the Foreign Ministry has more responsibility for those wars than even the Army and the Navy.

Let us focus upon the general responsibility of the Foreign Ministry, which was charged with carrying out Japan's diplomacy, for prewar diplomatic moves that ultimately led to the outbreak of war between Japan and the United States, and upon its very elementary blunder that had very serious consequences. We can then understand that the Foreign Ministry's responsibility for the overall war was greater than that of the military. If during the postwar period the Foreign Ministry had clearly acknowledged its indisputable war responsibility and had unambiguously apologized to the Japanese people, events in Japan and the world in the postwar era would have been more straightforward.

Yet as this book makes clear, after the end of the war and at the start of the Occupation, the Foreign Ministry falsely reported to Emperor Hirohito that Hideki Tōjō had planned the "sneak attack" at Pearl Harbor. It also promoted to the highest administrative positions available within the Foreign Ministry the two diplomats at the Washington embassy who were directly responsible for failing to deliver the "declaration of war" at the designated time; it concealed the problem of the blunder which led to the "sneak attack" at Pearl Harbor; and it rendered public discussion of this impossible.

Not only does the Foreign Ministry have responsibility for Japan's wars with the United States and China, it also committed the crime of betraying the nation by concealing this responsibility from the Japanese people.

However, if the Foreign Ministry had instead taken the initiative to clarify its past war responsibility, and had unambiguously apologized to the Japanese people, what consequences would this have had for postwar Japan? What consequences would this have had for the rest of the world? In the following sections, I would like to examine this issue separately as it relates to Japan, the United States, East Asia, and the rest of the world.

1. Consequences for Japan

In the postwar era, Japan and the Japanese people, who should have expended the most effort in considering and reflecting upon the war, were unable to do so properly because the Foreign Ministry, which depending on one's perspective may have been most responsible for the war, concealed its war responsibility. Japan's military was abolished after the war by the Occupation, and the Foreign Ministry was permitted to continue. If the Ministry had accepted that its responsibility was greater than that of the military, and had acknowledged its own war responsibility, the Japanese people most likely would have been able to reflect upon these wars and consider them more frankly. If it had done this, the Japanese people would probably have been able to discuss more frankly what Japan's reasons were for waging war, even if such discussions included subjective viewpoints.

Even if we must generally conclude that these wars mainly resulted from the arrogance and narrow-mindedness of the military, it is almost certain that franker discussion about Japan's rationale for waging them might later have been possible, a rationale that prompted Japanese troops to fight so fiercely and which led Japanese people to lose their lives. By concealing its own war responsibility, the Foreign Ministry made it impossible for the Japanese people to discuss even subjectively the rationale that spurred them to fight. People around the world today recognize that the so-called Tokyo Trial, convened by the Allied nations during the Occupation, cannot be considered a proper court because it tried to place the entire blame for the war upon Japan. However, it can also be said that, during this Trial, Japan's Foreign Ministry made little effort to protect the reputation of Japan or the Japanese people. This is evident from something this book has made clear, that Chiune Sugihara who saved the lives of 6,000 Jews in World War II was dismissed during the Tokyo Trial. Thus it is undeniable that the Foreign Ministry, after the Occupation was lifted, imprisoned the Japanese people in a "warped linguistic space," and built a social infrastructure tainted by the decision of the so-called Tokyo Trial.

This book is dedicated to both Chiune Sugihara and Joseph C. Grew, the U. S. ambassador to Japan at the outbreak of war. However, if Grew had not conceived the framework for the Potsdam Proclamation that gave Japan the opportunity to capitulate, there was a real chance that Japan may have been occupied by the Soviet Union and then later partitioned. Grew was aware of the danger Japan faced of being partitioned and ruined by the Soviet Union and the United States, so before this could happen he tried to give Japan the chance to surrender, by doing his utmost to conceive and realize the framework for the Potsdam Proclamation. The Japanese people today have all but forgotten this man to whom they owe such a debt, and this is also something that probably wouldn't have occurred if the Foreign Ministry had unambiguously clarified its past war responsibility.

As will be discussed below, Grew is a figure who deserves much greater recognition, even by the American people. If we accept that the Japanese people do indeed owe Grew the aforementioned debt, then the American people would be welcome to criticize the Japanese people for not remembering the great debt he is due. Indeed, they should be critical. However, it is not that the Japanese people are deliberately showing ingratitude. The Japanese people only appear to be ungrateful because of the Foreign Ministry. It is because the Foreign Ministry, by pursuing its own interests, has imprisoned the Japanese people in a "warped linguistic space." It is inevitable that the Japanese people would appear ungrateful.

It should be mentioned in passing that the Korean issue received very little attention because there was no-one within the American government who showed concern over Korea as Joseph Grew had done for Japan; Korea was quickly partitioned and occupied by foreign powers, and the Korean people are still suffering the tragedy of being at war with each other.

Clearly, there were wrongs which postwar Japan should have reflected upon, so it is conceivable that these wrongs may also have been more frankly acknowledged and discussed if Japan had been able to frankly discuss why it had gone to war.

Although so many Japanese troops fought and so many Japanese people died in these wars, there has been no proper debate about why war was waged, and this has brought about the decline of the spirit of the Japanese people. It is like a cancerous growth on the body. While the Foreign Ministry (the cancerous growth) steadily weakened Japan (the body), it conspired to secure its continued existence.

2. Consequences for the United States

Since Japan's Foreign Ministry is so fond of making apologies, many might think it has probably made a point of apologizing to the American people for the "sneak attack" at Pearl Harbor. However, to the present day the Foreign Ministry has not apologized once to the people of the United States for this "sneak attack."

As this author has noted in a previous publication,[9] the Foreign Ministry could not have apologized to the American people yet, because it only made an apology of sorts as late as 1994 to the Japanese people for the blunder in delaying the delivery of the "declaration of war."

The fiftieth anniversary of the attack on Pearl Harbor came in 1991. Then-President George Bush gave a speech at a ceremony to commemorate the anniversary, where he more or less forgave Japan for the attack. However, Foreign Ministry statements gave every appearance that the Ministry had no responsibility whatsoever, as is revealed for example in the statement by Foreign Minister Michio Watanabe, who remarked,

> We feel a deep remorse about the unbearable suffering and sorrow Japan inflicted on the American people and the peoples of Asia and the Pacific during the Pacific War, a war that Japan started...because of the reckless decision of our military.

Although the "sneak attack" at Pearl Harbor was the direct focus of attention during this anniversary, the Foreign Ministry instead expressed its regret for the issue of the overall war between Japan and the United States.[10]

This compounded existing distortions in the American people's understanding of the war. In general terms, the war between Japan and the United States was due to Japan's arrogance and narrow-mindedness, but this was a war which at first Japan did not want. It was one which Japan would have avoided if possible. This war, which broke out despite it having been unwanted, was fundamentally due to the ineptness of Japan's diplomacy. Nor can any excuse be made for the fact that the "declaration of war" was not delivered at the designated time.

If the Foreign Ministry had apologized to the American people by forthrightly acknowledging these facts and frankly admitting its responsibility for the "sneak attack" at Pearl Harbor, it may have become possible to recognize more candidly the errors committed by the American people and the American side. One could theorize that Roosevelt's stubborn insistence upon the "unconditional surrender" formula to end the war was an error. This "unconditional surrender" formula gave the enemy no terms for surrender, even when the outcome of the war was practically decided, and it forced the enemy to capitulate "without conditions." The defeated side is given no chance to give up, and ultimately the war can be pursued until the enemy's bitter end. The enemy nation is thus destroyed, its land turned to smoldering ashes, and war ceases only with the installation of total military occupation.

This formula meant that war would be fought to the bitter end, even if it was clear the enemy faced certain defeat. In a sense, it increased the number of war casualties meaninglessly. Originally, international laws regarding war were formulated with the aim of minimizing the number of these meaningless war casualties. From the American perspective regarding the war with Japan, the Japanese Navy had in effect been destroyed, and any further victims on the American side resulting from fighting a Japan devoid of offensive capabilities would have been, in a sense, meaningless war casualties. Continued fighting would have been unavoidable if the enemy had refused to give up despite being given conditions for surrender; but to continue fighting without offering any such conditions was intrinsically not in the public interest.

Consequently, after the *Yamato* was sunk during the battle for Okinawa, the Japanese Navy was in effect destroyed and no longer able to launch any sort of attack on the American side, so it was not essential to force Japan to surrender by dropping the atomic bomb. The atomic bomb was dropped because Japan did not accept the Potsdam Proclamation, but from practical considerations, it was probably not really necessary.

Clearly though, American government and military leaders felt then that dropping the atomic bomb to force Japan's surrender was unavoidable. Roosevelt's formula for "unconditional surrender" encouraged these government and military leaders to consider this their only option. They felt duty bound to carry out the formula which Roosevelt had put in place. While this author certainly cannot condone their way of thinking, it must be conceded that they felt they had no other option.

The Pearl Harbor "sneak attack" at the start of the war provided the psychological impetus for the American people's support of this "unconditional surrender" formula, and they affirmed their government and military leaders' way of thinking. Initially, the American people had not wanted war. However, the Japanese Navy launched its "sneak attack" at Pearl Harbor during negotiations to avert war between Japan and the United States. Therefore, the American people believed throughout the war that Japan had actually deliberately and systematically launched a "sneak attack" at Pearl Harbor, although it could be argued that President Roosevelt skillfully finessed events to give that impression. That is why psychologically the American public supported Roosevelt's "unconditional surrender" formula.

Eventually the war came to an end. Later, it was revealed that the "sneak attack" at Pearl Harbor had not in fact been deliberately planned by Japan, but rather was due to an administrative blunder at Japan's Washington embassy; so if the Japanese side, that is, the Foreign Ministry, had taken the initiative to acknowledge its responsibility and had sincerely apologized to the people of the United States, the American public may have been able to frankly acknowledge the failings of the "unconditional surrender" formula that had galvanized their rationale for fighting the war. Furthermore, it could be argued that Japan was driven into the war, even though the Japanese side clearly must bear a certain amount of war responsibility because it made the first move. However, this "sneak attack" precipitated a war that magnified the American public's distrust and hatred of the Japanese people out of all proportion. If, when the war ended, the Foreign Ministry had taken the initiative to acknowledge that this "sneak attack" had been caused by an administrative blunder and sincerely apologized, and had also acknowledged that the Ministry had actually been just as arrogant and narrow-minded as the military, it may conversely have been easier to focus attention on why the Japanese side felt compelled to go to war. If the Foreign Ministry had taken the initiative to acknowledge its war responsibility, frank discussion of deeply held beliefs on the

Japanese side regarding the war may have been possible, even if these discussions included subjective views. Furthermore, if the Ministry had taken the initiative to admit that its administrative error had made the war between Japan and the United States unavoidable and greatly expanded its scale, the American side may also have more frankly recognized that this "unconditional surrender" formula had its failings. They would have then been able to better understand the circumstances on the Japanese side that made it feel compelled to wage war.

Viewed from this perspective, we can see that the American people should also have a greater appreciation of the achievements of Joseph C. Grew, the American ambassador to Japan at the outbreak of war. The "unconditional surrender" formula put in place by Roosevelt meant continuing the war to the bitter end. This probably also means that the number of American troop casualties was increased unnecessarily. Moreover, if the Soviet Union had invaded the Japanese home islands, the subsequent Cold War would also probably have been more deeply entrenched than the sequence of historical events that eventually unfolded. If Grew had not produced the framework for the Potsdam Proclamation, the damage caused to the American people would certainly have been magnified. We should come to a new awareness that Grew's achievements were also of extremely great value to the American people.

Grew's recommendations for the Potsdam Proclamation called for a clear indication that the emperor system would be retained, however this was dropped under the advisement of Cordell Hull, America's secretary of state at the outbreak of war and throughout its duration. As a result, Japan's capitulation was delayed, the atomic bombs were dropped, and the Soviet Union joined the war against Japan.

The case was made above that, subjectively at least, the dropping of the atomic bomb may not have been necessary. However, because of the importance of this issue, let me make the following remarks to eliminate any possible misunderstanding.

The very opinion itself that dropping the atomic bomb to force Japan to surrender was unnecessary has even become more widely accepted in recent years in the United States.

However, there are vast differences between this author's interpretation from a Japanese perspective of the notion that dropping the atomic bomb was not needed to force Japan to surrender, and similar interpretations that have developed in the United States, especially concerning how such conclusions have been formed, and what significance these historical facts have been accorded.

Having grappled with the issue of the atomic bomb since high school, Gar Alperovitz argued in 1995, in *The Decision to Use the Atomic Bomb and the Architecture of an American Myth*, that it was unnecessary to drop the atomic bomb to force Japan to surrender. He thoroughly examined historical materials declassified to that date and summed up current arguments in the United States about dropping the atomic bomb. "Quite simply," he writes, "it is not true that the atomic bomb was used because it was the only way to save the 'hundreds of thousands' or 'millions' of lives as was subsequently claimed. The readily available options were to modify the surrender terms and/or await the shock of the Russian attack. Three months remained before a November Kyushu landing could even take place in theory...."[11]

However if we pursue this line of argument to its ultimate conclusion, allowing the Soviet Union to invade and occupy Japan's home islands to force Japan to surrender presumably meant there would be no American military casualties, and the war would be won without having to drop the atomic bomb. From a Japanese perspective, Japan itself would have been devastated, to say nothing of preserving the emperor system. Furthermore, if the United States and Soviet Union had partitioned Japan, Japan would undoubtedly have become a divided nation; and in the worst-case scenario, it is conceivable that Japan may have been plunged into circumstances where, as in the Korean War, the Japanese people similarly waged, or were forced to wage, a war amongst themselves.

This author [Seishirō Sugihara], a native of Hiroshima, lost an elder brother in the atomic blast, and had many relatives who perished because of the bomb. However, dropping the atomic bomb hastened Japan's surrender, and brought this about before a Soviet invasion of Japan's home islands (that is, before Japan could be partitioned or totally destroyed), so I have no qualms about acknowledging its significance. The victims of the atomic bomb certainly didn't die in vain. Put simply, in the desperate circumstances the Japanese side then found itself, if the Japanese military itself had taken the initiative to surrender unconditionally, there would clearly have been no need to drop the atomic bomb nor for the Soviet Union to join the war against Japan; but of course, the military was psychologically unprepared to simply give up a war that the Japanese side also felt justified in pursuing. If their roles had been reversed, the American side would surely have felt the same. It was already obvious that the United States had virtually won the war, and that Japan no longer had the offensive capability to pose any threat to the United States. Yet psychologically, the American side could not unilaterally cease hostilities, nor give priority to an early end to the war. The United States too had just causes for fighting the war, and a framework from which it could not deviate.

In other words, Alperovitz employs the scenario of the Soviet Union joining the war against Japan to support his reasoning that dropping the atomic bomb was not necessary to force Japan to surrender. From Japan's perspective, this argument has certain unacceptable aspects. Even if this scenario was employed, why weren't steps first taken to have the Soviet Union try to persuade Japan to surrender? If after such attempts at persuasion Japan had still refused to comply, then one could well conclude that having the Soviet Union join the war against Japan was unavoidable. However, why was no consideration then given to restricting the Soviet Union's role to that of persuading Japan to surrender? Why was that never contemplated? Fifty years later, why did Alperovitz likewise not consider this in his research on the dropping of the atomic bomb?

As Alperovitz indicates, it is unmistakable that, if the preservation of Japan's emperor system had been guaranteed, or if the Soviet Union had been prevailed upon to try to persuade Japan to surrender by advising that rejecting such counsel might trigger its own entry into the war, then dropping the atomic bomb would have been absolutely unnecessary, and Japan would most likely have surrendered. This is surely self-evident.

There is certainly an element of truth to some of Alperovitz's assertions about dropping the atomic bomb, namely that in order for the American people to rid themselves of any feelings of regret, they came to believe that dropping the atomic bomb saved the lives of many American troops, and that this mistaken assumption was deliberately cultivated by those who were then responsible for dropping the bomb. From a Japanese perspective, his principled stand certainly deserves respect, but Alperovitz's assertions are, nevertheless, somehow lacking when seen from Japan's point of view. This is because they don't get to the core of why this mistaken assumption was cultivated, nor do they begin their explanation there. The core reason lies with President Roosevelt's involvement in how war between Japan and the United States broke out. Any examination of this issue must consider whether war broke out due to inevitable yet natural causes, or artificially contrived ones.

In April 1941 Japan and the Soviet Union signed a neutrality pact, just before the outbreak of war between Germany and the Soviet Union. Consequently, the Japanese side faithfully observed the neutrality pact during the German-Soviet war and did not invade the Soviet Union. This meant that the Soviet Union was able to redeploy troops stationed in Siberia to its war against Germany, win that war, and avoid a national crisis. In effect, one might say that by observing the neutrality pact, the Japanese side had a hand in the Allied nations' defeat of Nazi Germany. Therefore, it would probably have been more ethical to first prevail upon the Soviet Union to try to persuade Japan to surrender, before inviting it to join the war against Japan in 1945 while the Japan-Soviet Neutrality Pact was still in effect. If the Japanese side had still refused to comply with this advice, then the Soviet Union's joining the war against Japan would have become morally defensible.

Nevertheless, on August 9, 1945, even though the Japan-Soviet Neutrality Pact was still in effect, the Soviet Union abruptly declared war on Japan and launched its invasion without prior warning. In fact, the United States encouraged the Soviet Union to enter the war against Japan in this manner. Things developed this way because of President Roosevelt's direct overtures to Stalin at Yalta. Considered in this light, the Soviet Union's entry into the war against Japan was not the simple option suggested by Alperovitz. Moreover, one must question whether any study of the rights and wrongs about dropping the atomic bomb is actually complete without scrutinizing the miscalculations behind issues like this.

It's true that dropping the atomic bomb had a dimension beyond simply bringing about Japan's surrender, such as providing a demonstration of postwar American power, and it is recognized that this increasingly pricked the conscience of the American people. It is also known in Japan that, because this was the first time the atomic bomb had been used, there were deep concerns and expectations about its experimental nature. Moreover, Alperovitz is probably correct when he points out there was room to strive harder to find an alternative to dropping the atomic bomb, and that U. S. leaders at the time did not make that effort. However, it can be ruled out that some people schemed to drop the atomic bomb while believing there was no need to do so. American leaders at the time certainly didn't take any pleasure in their decision to drop the atomic bomb, but circumstances at the time called for bringing an end to the war, and it was believed and decided that dropping the atomic bomb was unavoidable. It is more important to consider instead why this situation came about. If we focus attention on this question, we must also consider not only the situation that prevailed at the time, but also the overall background, causes and reasons that brought about the circumstances where this train of thought and decision-making process was considered unavoidable. Without considering the matter in this light, no definitive conclusion about dropping the atomic bomb can be drawn.

As for the outbreak of war between Japan and the United States, Japan's "declaration of war"—delivered after the attack on Pearl Harbor began, even though it was intended to have it delivered thirty minutes beforehand—explained that, "the American Government, always holding fast to theories in disregard of realities, and refusing to yield an inch on its impractical principles, caused undue delays in the negotiations. It is difficult to understand this attitude of the American Government."[12]

This "declaration of war" was delivered late, clearly after the attack on Pearl Harbor commenced; and U. S. Secretary of State Cordell Hull, upon receiving it, chastised the two Japanese ambassadors with the pre-prepared and thoroughly calculated statement that, "In all my fifty years of public service I have never seen a document that was more crowded with infamous falsehoods and distortions." As such, the content of the Japanese statement was not given even a cursory examination by the American public. However, the passage from the "declaration of war" quoted above could be paraphrased as follows: "Even though we were conducting critical negotiations to decide between war and peace, the United States perversely stuck to its talk of principles. Would any responsible government in the pursuit of actual international relations do this: not yield an inch? This is what the Japanese government, which made every possible effort and repeatedly offered concessions, simply cannot understand."

In August 1941 the United States halted oil exports to Japan, and with no source other than the United States for replenishing its oil, every passing day saw Japan's oil reserves diminish and its military strength decline. If reconciliation with the United States could not be reached within a certain deadline, Japan would have no alternative but to strike out in war. Japan found itself thrust into a situation where, if it was to go to war, it had to strike quickly while sufficient stocks of oil still remained. Although with the benefit of hindsight one might question whether war was the only alternative if no reconciliation could be reached, the Japanese side at the time, under enormous pressure and with its military growing weaker by the day, came to believe that this was indeed the only option. American government leaders, from Roosevelt down, knew fully well through intercepted cables that the Japanese side held this belief. Although the Japanese side tried to bring about a reconciliation and came up with a number of compromise proposals, the American side stuck to its talk of principles and was unprepared to yield an inch. Viewed in this light, one can only conclude that it is apparent the American side tried to provoke Japan to start a war.

Furthermore, there is also the so-called foreknowledge theory which maintains that, even though Roosevelt had prior knowledge of the Japanese Navy's Pearl Harbor operation, he failed to pass this information on to local military authorities in Hawaii. This "foreknowledge theory" has recently been examined in Robert B. Stinnett's *Day of Deceit: The Truth about FDR and Pearl Harbor* (New York: Free Press, 2000), and if we assume this theory has now largely been substantiated, we can then understand the significance of why President Roosevelt so stubbornly adhered to the "unconditional surrender" formula. Undeniably, Roosevelt used the lives of Allied and American troops, not to win a victory over Japan, but to crush Japan. In other words, the issue of dropping the atomic bomb is connected to the significance of Roosevelt's stubborn adherence to the "unconditional surrender" formula to end the war, and no definitive explanation for this issue nor the issue of dropping the atomic bomb is possible without examining this connection.

Clearly, dropping the atomic bombs, which brought instant death to tens of thousands of civilians in a single explosion, was morally indefensible. Some Americans felt pangs of guilt after dropping such bombs, and it is admirable that by exercising their consciences they were identifying broadly with the humanity of others; they were also identifying with a Japan that suffered the bombing, and understood however marginally the pain of the victims of the bombing. However, it should be recalled that air raids on Japan's cities, such as those over Tokyo, had indiscriminately killed defenseless civilians long before the dropping of the atomic bomb, and were routine occurrences.

In the June 11, 2000 edition of the *Daily Yomiuri*, Ted Van Kirk, a navigator aboard the B-29 bomber *Enola Gay* that dropped the atomic bomb on Hiroshima, claimed, "Till this day, the four people on the plane still living all say it was the right thing to do." He also believed that "casualties would have been far greater—to Allied soldiers, prisoners of war, even the Japanese citizenry—if the bomb had not been used and World War II had continued." Conceivably, such statements naturally reflect the circumstances which prevailed when the atomic bomb was dropped, and the perspective of a soldier carrying out orders in a highly structured organization like the military. Indeed, if war had continued, and a desperate battle for the home islands had ensued, the number of casualties would probably have far outstripped the number of victims produced by the atomic bombs. In this sense, Van Kirk's statements are accurate because, although dropping the atomic bomb stiffened the resolve of Japan's government and military leaders not to surrender, it did indeed have the desired effect of stopping the war.

Van Kirk's testimony notwithstanding, this author believes that, at the very least, it serves little purpose to criticize the B-29 crewmen regarding the issue of dropping the atomic bomb. At that time and under those circumstances, the ones who deserve criticism are not the soldiers who actually dropped the bombs, but rather those in the military and government who made the decision to do so. Upon further reflection though, it seems inadequate to merely restrict criticism to only those directly involved in the decision to drop the bomb. Without asking who was responsible for the circumstances that led them to make such a decision, or reexamining the engineered causes that plunged them into these circumstances, it is impossible to have a correct interpretation of the issue of dropping the atomic bomb. The manner in which war broke out between Japan and the United States conceals something even more significant than the dropping of the atomic bomb.

But let us return to the issue at hand. It must be pointed out that the question of the outbreak of war between Japan and the United States, discussed at length in this book and which is profoundly related to the issue of dropping the atomic bomb, is closely connected to the Foreign Ministry's cover-up of its responsibility for the war between Japan and the United States. If the Foreign Ministry had clarified its war responsibility for the outbreak of this war, and had not continued to conceal that responsibility, we would have a simpler, clearer understanding of world history regarding *why* war between Japan and the United States broke out, *who* was responsible, and *what* the ensuing consequences were. Because the Foreign Ministry has not clarified its own war responsibility, and has continued to conceal it, examination of these *three* aspects of the outbreak of war between Japan and the United States has remained inconclusive, and accounts of world history have also remained unclear. It has to be acknowledged that the consequences of the Foreign Ministry's cover-up of its war responsibility have extended beyond Japan to reach the United States and the history of the world, and even extend to the issue of dropping the atomic bomb.

3. Consequences for Asia

The Foreign Ministry, which concealed its war responsibility and was unable to explain Japan's reasons for fighting the war, was certainly unable to explain these reasons to the peoples in the countries of Southeast Asia who achieved independence after the war. The Ministry decided to consign to oblivion the important issue of what had influenced these countries' moves to rid themselves of their former colonial status.

Regarding diplomacy towards China, the Chinese Communist Party, China's present government, has also forgotten some of its past actions to gain power by frustrating attempts at a peaceful reconciliation between Japan and the Kuomintang regime, which formerly ruled China. Because the Foreign Ministry adopts an unnecessarily servile diplomacy, it needlessly allows the Chinese government, a dictatorship which today is still influenced by the political doctrine of "dynastic change through revolution," to become increasingly domineering. It is hard to see why Japan has to reflect upon the arrogance of its past diplomacy, when clearly Chinese diplomacy, while enjoying Japan's diplomatic support, consistently ignores international rules and courtesies. Furthermore, this servile diplomacy towards China is not only bad for Japan, but also encourages China to adopt a domineering stance towards other countries in China's vicinity, and harms the countries of Southeast Asia.

4. Consequences for the Rest of the World

The Foreign Ministry's incompetence, and its shameless cover-up of its war responsibility, has global consequences when compared with Germany's postwar treatment of issues related to World War II.

The American people, for whom anger over the "sneak attack" at Pearl Harbor represented a psychological turning-point, lent their support to Roosevelt's "unconditional surrender" formula, as noted above. Because of this, Germany which was not directly involved in the "sneak attack" also suffered enormous harm. The first time Roosevelt ever mentioned the term "unconditional surrender" was at Casablanca in January 1943 when Roosevelt and British Prime Minister Winston Churchill held a press conference.[13] Soviet leader Stalin raised doubts about forcing the "unconditional surrender" formula on Germany. He felt it would only further unite the German people, prolong Germany's surrender, and increase the number of casualties on both the German and Allied sides.[14] However, Roosevelt insisted upon forcing the "unconditional surrender" formula upon Germany, and in fact the war with Germany dragged on until Germany had been completely reduced to "scorched earth," Hitler had killed himself, and the Nazi regime had been wiped out. This resulted in the deaths of even greater numbers of

German troops and civilians, Allied troops, and Jews interned in concentration camps.

The above sections allow us to understand the wider ramifications of the Foreign Ministry's incompetence and shameless behavior, obviously not only for Japan, but also for the United States, Asia, and Europe. This normally inconceivable diplomatic blunder, where a "declaration of war" could not be delivered properly at the designated time, clearly had global significance. However, even if the postwar Foreign Ministry's actions to cover up its war responsibility and its refusal to take the initiative to admit this blunder had not had such deep consequences for Japan, it would still have had global significance for America, Asia, and Europe, and would have distorted global perceptions of the war. The incompetence and shameless behavior of Japan's Foreign Ministry had an inordinate effect upon World War II, where so many soldiers and civilians throughout the world fought bitterly and died.

A variety of reforms were enacted in Japan after it lost the war and was placed under Allied occupation. However, viewed in this light, not drastically reforming the Foreign Ministry was clearly a great mistake. The foreign service examinations, rather than being reformed, were overlooked and left intact. Even though the Ministry had had so much war responsibility, the matter was closed without any reforms being carried out at all. It might generally be argued that, to the contrary, the Ministry's enormous war responsibility may have rendered self-reform quite difficult. Therefore, it might actually have been better if the occupying forces had also abolished the Foreign Ministry. Had this been done, the war responsibility of the prewar Foreign Ministry might have been clearly assigned to an abolished organ of state, and conceivably views throughout Japan and the rest of the world might not have been distorted in the way they subsequently were. Arguably, it was disastrous that the Foreign Ministry was not dismantled, obviously not only for Japan, but also the rest of the world. This may have been the largest policy failure of the occupying forces.

The Dangers Posed by Marxism And Communism

Without an appreciation of the threat posed to Japan by Marxism and Communism with the arrival of the Shōwa era, people around the world can only develop an imperfect understanding of the history of Japan during this period and the processes by which Japan went to war.

As examined at the beginning of this preface, Communists first started using the term "emperor system" during the early Shōwa era.

The emperor system was then considered to be a negative structure that had to be destroyed. If one believed the emperor to be at the core of a state apparatus for class control, then naturally the emperor system would be viewed negatively. But to what extent was this way of thinking mistaken?

Marxism and Communism proposed to build a non-exploitive, egalitarian society, but the emperor system encompassed a similar viewpoint, namely "one sovereign and equality for the whole nation" (*ikkun banmin byōdō*). Nevertheless, if we accept that, in practice, the emperor was the key element of a system that had throughout Japan's history condoned unwarranted discrimination against certain people, even if they were Japanese, and that national order was maintained without addressing this contradiction, then arguably the emperor system was imperfect, at least in a historical sense. It must therefore be recognized that the step-by-step unfolding of history sets limitations on all cultures.

However, when the emperor system was exposed to influences from the outside world with the arrival of the Meiji era, the concept "one sovereign and equality for the whole nation" undoubtedly became incorporated into it.

Most troops serving in Japan's Army and Navy came from the peasant class. Officers in leadership positions felt that inequality in Japanese society had to be addressed, and exploitation was not permitted. According to their espousal of the emperor system, inequality and exploitation were no longer to be tolerated. Young officers in particular believed in the emperor system, but took their understanding of this belief to extremes. This is what caused the military insurgency of February 26, 1936. In a sense, there was a chance that the Japanese military would draw closer to Marxism and Communism. In other words, and in social theory terms, Japan's military might have adopted Marxism and Communism. Nevertheless, this was actually highly unlikely. That is, Marxism and Communism saw the emperor, who was revered by the military, as an enemy of the people, and were determined to destroy him. Therein lay a tragedy unique to prewar Japan.

After the war, the Soviet Union, even though it sent no troops to join the Allied occupation of Japan, did indeed participate as a member of the Allied side. It should be recalled that the Soviet Union was perhaps saved from certain crisis when Japan, at the outbreak of the war between Germany and the Soviet Union in 1941, upheld the Japan-Soviet Neutrality Pact. However, the Soviet Union joined the war against Japan anyway during its closing stages, in violation of that

Neutrality Pact. Notwithstanding, criticism of the Soviet Union was not permitted because it was a member of the Allied nations, and this was enforced by the censorship imposed by the occupying forces during their strict Occupation. Paradoxically, the Soviet Union too joined the forces investigating Japan's war responsibility.

Under these circumstances during the Occupation and thereafter, Socialism and Communism, which in theory aspired to an egalitarian, non-exploitive society, were freed from their prewar and wartime restraints, and became a strong force in society.

Socialism and Communism naturally considered Japan's past in a negative light. Therefore they concurred with Occupation policy which was based on the notion that Japan had systematically launched a "sneak attack" at Pearl Harbor, that is, the Occupation policy which placed all the blame for the war on Japan, and condemned Japan's past.

Hence in the postwar period, societal conditions were created whereby those elements of Japan's prewar history worthy of recognition could no longer be recognized. The Foreign Ministry's cover-up of its war responsibility further entrenched those conditions. This cover-up by the Foreign Ministry imprisoned the Japanese people in a "warped linguistic space," and rendered proper assessment or discussion of that extremely damaging war impossible. Thus, resolving this issue was no longer possible, despite the objective shared by Socialism and Communism to totally repudiate Japan's past on the one hand, and by Occupation policy to push all the blame for the war onto Japan on the other. Indeed, it entrenched the situation even further. If the Foreign Ministry wanted to make sure these societal conditions became entrenched, it had to place its own war responsibility beyond public scrutiny. The Japanese people were unable to disparage past excesses committed by the occupying forces or the faulty past of Socialism and Communism, because the Foreign Ministry, a state organ, had covered up its own war responsibility, and had implemented foreign policy so that the Japanese people were able to see only a distorted past.

Incidentally, with the collapse of the Soviet Union in 1991, the Cold War in effect came to an end. It has turned out that, historically, Marxism and Communism were clearly not the social theories that would bring happiness to humanity. Which means that, conceivably, the social sciences in Japan today might well be lumped together with Marxism and Communism.

Produced over a period of more than fifty years, it is highly unlikely that the distortion of postwar Japan, caused by the Foreign Ministry's acts of self-preservation, can easily be rectified. However, some contrition by the Foreign Ministry for its past transgressions might help make way for a new history for Japan and the world. Since diplomacy involves developing the national interest from many different perspectives, there can be no fixed or simplistic approaches. However, it is obvious that, in any country, diplomacy should primarily protect the prestige of that country and its people. Therefore, the same must apply to Japanese diplomacy: it should primarily protect the prestige of Japan and the Japanese people. This is precisely where the essence of Japanese diplomacy should lie. The Foreign Ministry must no longer stifle the spirit of the Japanese people.

Protest by Diplomat Naoya Nakano

The death of the young Japanese diplomat Naoya Nakano is discussed in the epilogue to the Japanese version of this book. With his parent's permission, I can disclose here that he committed suicide in a Foreign Ministry building on July 8, 1996. Apparently his death was meant as a protest against the Foreign Ministry.

As discussed in a previous publication,[15] my first interaction with Naoya Nakano was on October 15, 1992, when, accompanied by a magazine reporter, I delivered a question sheet entitled "Questions Regarding the Delay by Japan's Embassy in the United States of the Notice for the Attack on Pearl Harbor Fifty-One Years Ago" to the Foreign Ministry's Domestic Public Relations Division. The section head who came out to handle my inquiry glanced briefly at the sheet, immediately flashed a look of displeasure, and blurted out an "expletive." For a moment, I couldn't quite believe my ears. This was the first time I had ever officially met with a Foreign Ministry employee qualified as a diplomat. It is understandable that the Pearl Harbor issue is not something which Foreign Ministry officials would want to deal with. However, it is incredible that someone paying a formal visit to the Ministry and lodging a request for information would be subjected to such vulgarity. My first experience with Japanese diplomats taught me how little training these diplomats receive in dealing with people.

The person who then persuaded the section chief to hold his tongue and formally accept the question sheet was Naoya Nakano, who had accompanied him. Eventually, I received a formal reply from the Foreign Ministry. Developments in this matter then progressed further: historical materials related to an internal Foreign Ministry investigation into the blunder which had delayed the delivery of the "declaration of war" and led to the "sneak attack" at Pearl Harbor, and which hitherto had been classified, were finally released to the public. This meant that, for the first time, the Foreign Ministry was expressing its regret over this matter. Nakano's efforts at this time had yielded real results.

In 1995, I presented him with a copy of my book *Japanese Perspectives on Pearl Harbor: A Critical Review of Japanese Reports on the Fiftieth Anniversary of the Pearl Harbor Attack* (trans. Theodore McNelly; Hong Kong: Asian Research Service, 1995). He complemented me on my efforts, saying that he hoped this book, among others, would help to "provoke objective and profound reflection, and liberate public debate in Japan from the two extremes of 'self-destructiveness' and 'defiance.' " Never a truer word was spoken.

Nakano passed the foreign service examination and entered the Foreign Ministry in 1988 at the age of 23. He apparently made a conscious decision then not to marry into the Ministry's *keibatsu* families. As he carried out his duties he gradually found himself sidelined to less-important positions, and sadly was in fact being forced out of the Ministry. Although he passed the admittedly flawed foreign service examination at 23, before long his future was bleak because he refused to marry into a *keibatsu* family.

Diplomats are sent early in their careers to work abroad, and it is difficult to acquire professional experience at home office. Compared to other ministries, there are relatively fewer opportunities for contact with supervisors, and evaluations are based on impressions formed during these sporadic contacts, and through *keibatsu* ties.

Ironically, after the war those with any commonsense at all were shunned within the Foreign Ministry, a state organ that started the postwar era by concealing its war responsibility and was riddled with harmful practices. Since the young diplomat Naoya Nakano had felt that one should avoid both "self-destructiveness" and "defiance," then he too would ultimately have been pushed out.

The Foreign Ministry's present diplomatic system is far too problematic. It isn't just that Nakano is not recognized as a patriot, in the context of the *bushidō* ethical code. Although Japan's Overseas Development Aid, said to be the largest in the world, is apparently being improved somewhat at present, there has however long been criticism over its enormous waste and lack of results. Aid is normally given to encourage "self-reliance and effort," but apparently in reality observance of this principle is far from ideal. Occasionally, aid is given without a word of thanks, is totally wasted, or precipitates corruption and bribery. Such aid should be used to advance and spread knowledge, an assertion I make not simply because my chosen field is pedagogical studies. It could be spent for instance on scholarships for gifted students, or on building libraries. For the latter, as in the example set by the founder of the Carnegie Foundation, aid could go to library infrastructure and fixtures; and by enlisting the efforts of local personnel, it could also be used to buy and collect books and other materials. Aid should not only be used to build libraries, but the origin of the donation should be clearly indicated somewhere on site so that visitors will not overlook where that aid came from. Wouldn't this ensure that aid can be given without it getting caught up in waste, corruption, or bribery? Isn't this the only way to ensure that aid from rich countries to poor ones remains sound?

In any case, there are many other problems with the Foreign Ministry's diplomacy. When Diet members travel abroad, locally posted diplomats are expected to behave like tour guides, which is unacceptable given their weighty diplomatic responsibilities. Diet members should try to avoid this practice, and make an effort not to impede routine operations.

These problems, along with others not necessarily within the province of diplomacy, mean that the Foreign Ministry's diplomatic training system, in use since the Meiji era, must be fundamentally reexamined. The Foreign Ministry and its diplomats must be "reborn" with the understanding that their raison d'être is to protect the prestige of Japan and the Japanese people.

Although Naoya Nakano's protest against the Ministry ended with his death, perhaps the fact that someone like him could emerge means there is indeed some hope of reforming today's Foreign Ministry. Perhaps there is a chance that a community of diplomats can be fostered which understands the tenets of *bushidō*, and is "firmly rooted in the soil of their own country." On the other hand, is Nakano's death merely proof that diplomats of his caliber will continue to be shunned forever? I would like to believe that, despite Nakano's unfortunate death, his presence was the first sign of an ethical future for the Foreign Ministry. This author has learned that Nakano's young colleagues have vowed his death must not have been in vain.

The Achievements of Chiune Sugihara

Although this book is about Chiune Sugihara, little has been said about him in this preface.

However, as has been explained in great detail, Chiune Sugihara was a Japanese diplomat in Kaunas, Lithuania, who, not long after the outbreak of World War II and in violation of home office instructions, issued a large number of visas in 1940 to Jewish refugees fleeing from Poland, and as a result saved the lives of 6,000 Jews. Although Sugihara was not a career diplomat, he was extremely capable; and in June 1941, about a month before war between Germany and the Soviet Union actually broke out, he sent valuable intelligence predicting that such a war was likely.

After Japan's defeat, Sugihara returned to Japan in 1947 following a lengthy period of incarceration, but was dismissed from the Foreign Ministry for not following orders. This happened at a time when an investigation of the Nanking Incident was being conducted at the Tokyo Trial, and when Sugihara's acts of kindness would have shone at their brightest. As this book reveals, incredibly the Foreign Ministry sacked him even though (or perhaps precisely because) it knew the value of his actions.

Afterwards, the Foreign Ministry both formally and informally did all it could to obstruct recognition of Sugihara's benevolent deeds. The Foreign Ministry, which secured its own future at the expense of the prestige of Japan and the Japanese people, and which dismissed Sugihara in an act consistent with its aforementioned self-serving nature, had no option but to place Sugihara's acts of kindness beyond public scrutiny.

This was the result of what amounts to the "crime" perpetrated by the Foreign Ministry against the Japanese people and the people of the world, namely, concealing its war responsibility. Chiune Sugihara's admirable and shining achievements, during what for Japan was a ridiculous war, have endured in no small measure around the world; and for the Foreign Ministry to recognize these achievements means having to frankly admit its prewar incompetence, and its war responsibility for not being able to evade a clearly avoidable war brought about by that incompetence. As such, the postwar Foreign Ministry consigned Chiune Sugihara's achievements to oblivion, and had to continue obstructing populist moves to honor Sugihara. In other words, the series of actions the Ministry took to conceal Sugihara was a quintessential and concrete example of its criminal behavior in concealing its own war responsibility, namely, the "crime" perpetrated by the Foreign Ministry against the Japanese people and the people of the world.

Although somewhat overdue, Japan's Foreign Ministry henceforth will probably have to honor Chiune Sugihara's achievements and follow in his footsteps, and this may mean it will clarify its responsibility for its prewar incompetence, and for the war it was unable to avoid because of that incompetence. Individuals who were particularly responsible for those failings should be identified, as should those in the postwar era who played an active role in concealing the Ministry's war responsibility.

If Chiune Sugihara's achievements had been recognized soon after the war, the prewar Foreign Ministry's war responsibility might have been unambiguously placed into the historical record in a manner transparent to all. With this new beginning, the Ministry would probably not have gone on to deceive the people of Japan and the rest of the world. There presumably wouldn't have been any reason for deceit. Thus, this is why the assertion can be made that Chiune Sugihara and his achievements are clearly linked to the postwar Foreign Ministry's crime of concealing its war responsibility.

In the same vein, Joseph C. Grew, the American ambassador to Japan at the outbreak of war, and his achievement of preventing Japan's partitioning, aren't recognized either. To recognize Grew's achievements, the prewar Foreign Ministry's war responsibility would have to be clearly explained. It would be impossible to allow the Ministry's war responsibility to remain undeclared, and at the same time recognize Grew's achievements. This is why the postwar Foreign Ministry has constantly encouraged the Japanese people to forget Grew's achievements. This author has called for the recognition of the achievements of both Chiune Sugihara and Joseph C. Grew, not only in this book but also its prequel *Between Incompetence and Culpability*. It is my fervent hope that readers outside Japan will also take this wish to heart.

Translator's Note

In September 1939, the partition of Poland by the Soviet Union and Nazi Germany forced thousands of Jews to escape anti-Semitic persecution by fleeing to Lithuania. With the assistance of two men, acting Dutch consul to Lithuania Jan Zwartendijk and Japanese vice consul Chiune Sugihara, these refugees had a brief window of opportunity to exploit an unlikely escape route across the Soviet Union to Japan. Among them were approximately 300 members of the Mirrer Yeshiva, an academy of higher Jewish studies, the only European yeshiva to survive the Holocaust in its entirety. Although Japan was ostensibly a transit point before proceeding to Dutch-controlled Curaçao, many refugees were able to travel on to other safe havens. Interest in what happened at the Japanese consulate in Lithuania during those troubled months has grown steadily since Sugihara's death in 1986, and has produced a body of literature reflecting diverse and sometimes conflicting perspectives on what Sugihara represented, and what he tried to do.

Yad Vashem, the Israeli institution pledged to the study and commemoration of the Holocaust, has dubbed non-Jews who saved the lives of Jewish refugees "righteous gentiles." Frequently the movement to honor these individuals has been driven by the persistent efforts of close-knit families, dedicated and loyal friends, and not least by those who were saved by their humanitarian efforts. The lives of diplomats so honored were often ruined by the very authorities whose orders they either outright disobeyed or delicately finessed. Portugal's Aristedes de Sousa Mendes was a typical example of one such diplomat who could not ignore the suffering of the refugees, nor their fate "should they fall into the hands of the enemy." Acting upon his "feelings of altruism and generosity" Sousa Mendes followed his conscience and issued visas to Jewish refugees in Bordeaux, despite explicit orders to the contrary from the Salazar government which, one biographer observed, subsequently condemned him to financial ruin.[1] Sousa Mendes was posthumously declared a Righteous Gentile by Yad Vashem in 1967.

Chiune Sugihara, by contrast, was rather late to join this group of honored individuals. Unlike the Portuguese government, the Japanese Foreign Ministry never explicitly banned the issuing of visas to Jews during World War II; it was therefore long thought that Sugihara was acting within government-sanctioned parameters when he issued transit visas to Jewish refugees. Nevertheless, Sugihara like Sousa Mendes was punished after the war as a direct consequence of his humanitarian efforts, and this disciplinary action left him broken and demoralized. After the war, Sugihara spent many years in Moscow working to develop Japanese trade links with the Soviet Union, but seemed somewhat embittered by his prewar and wartime experiences and rarely discussed the turn his life had been forced to take. One year before his death, Sugihara was honored by Israel in 1985 with the "Righteous among the Nations" award for saving the lives of Jews in 1940. He also received the Raoul Wallenburg Award posthumously in 1990, and even had a street in Lithuania named after him the following year. Meanwhile in Japan though, little was known about Sugihara's heroic actions for more than five decades. Ironically, in the early 1980s a German journalist living in Japan was the first to alert many Japanese to Sugihara's achievements. It was only recently that Sugihara finally received a modicum of recognition in his own land, notably the Nagasaki Peace Prize in 1992, and a plaque at the Diplomatic Records Office in Tokyo in 2000. Why was he consigned to virtual obscurity for most of his life?

Until recently, the role Sugihara played in saving Jewish refugees had generally been treated as a minor episode in the overall analysis of prewar Japanese policy towards Jews. Tokayer and Swartz's *The Fugu Plan* (Paddington Press, 1979) typifies initial mainstream attempts outside Japan to pay serious attention to Sugihara's efforts. The authors placed his contribution in the context of the so-called Fugu Plan. This "plan," with its genesis in a 1934 "trial balloon" article by Yoshisuke Aikawa, hoped to exploit Jewish potential and resources to develop Manchuria. Its benefits would be threefold: direct application of Jewish skills, an influx of Jewish capital, and perhaps most importantly, goodwill and support from America's "influential Jews" that would indirectly create new economic possibilities. Support for this overly-optimistic strategy came from leading figures in the Japanese government, including Foreign Minister Yōsuke Matsuoka. Indeed, Jews fortunate enough to reach Tsuruga with documentation irregularities—obviously forged visas, and in some cases no visas or even passports—were shown remarkable leniency by immigration officials. This accommodating policy was attributed to Matsuoka, who supposedly turned a blind eye if such discrepancies were handled at a "local level." Sugihara's humanitarian acts were presented here in the context of Japan's national policy towards Jews, emphasizing his feelings of patriotism and imperial fealty, as well as his sense of moral obligation. Sugihara weighed the risks to his career, but accepted that an administrative punishment was worth saving so many lives. The plight of the refugees reminded him that, "Even a hunter cannot kill a bird which flies to him for refuge." [2]

It was not until the early 1990s, with the appearance of a loving and intimate portrait by Chiune's widow Yukiko Sugihara, that a movement began to try to distance his actions from official Foreign Ministry policy. Her Japanese bestseller showed the Sugihara family was well aware of what was happening to the Jews in Eastern Europe in the late 1930s. Yukiko revealed they had heard rumors of the "Jew Hunting" campaign of terror, but readily admitted they had no inkling of the eventual Holocaust that was to engulf those unable to escape. Her husband learned first hand of the horrors being perpetrated against Jews from a five-man committee delegated to represent the hundreds who had thronged the consulate seeking visas. The Sugiharas were no longer dealing with abstract rumors or mere hearsay: they were now being confronted by real people pleading for compassionate treatment. Aware of possible German reprisals should he help these refugees, he consulted Yukiko on how to proceed. Although ordered several times to issue transit visas only to those who had firm ongoing entry permits to final destinations beyond Japan, Chiune realized that strict adherence to such orders would in effect condemn many who could not meet this requirement to certain death. He decided therefore to issue visas to anyone who requested them, regardless of the state of their claim. Furthermore, he clearly exceeded his authority as vice consul by continuing to issue visas even after he had closed down the consulate, and handing out blank visa forms from a train window as his family departed Lithuania as ordered.[3]

Yukiko described her lingering resentment towards the Foreign Ministry because of its hostile treatment of her husband. Chiune was summarily sacked after the war for "that incident in Lithuania."

Subsequently, the couple rarely discussed the "incident" and she recounts their "bitter suffering in our homeland." Not only had Chiune at the age of 50 been deprived of all prospects for a diplomatic career and forced to find a new livelihood to support his family, shortly after returning to Japan their young son Haruki died. Yukiko attributed his death to the "countless hardships of the previous ten years" the family had spent outside Japan while Chiune served his country. To add insult to injury, rumors emerged at the Foreign Ministry that he had taken money for issuing visas to the refugees. Not surprisingly Chiune was thoroughly embittered by his experience, and spent the remainder of his working years abroad. Yukiko surmised that her husband probably found his self-imposed "exile" in Moscow preferable to remaining in Japan. When he learned years later of the thousands of survivors who owed their lives to his visas, he reflected that his decision had been worth every hardship he had endured. Although he conceded that disobeying his country's orders "may have been wrong," he had been unable "in good conscience" to ignore the Jews' pleas for help and had done only what "any decent human being would have done."[4]

This image of Chiune Sugihara as a "tragic" and "rule-flaunting" hero was somewhat qualified in 1996 by Boston University professor Hillel Levine. His *In Search of Sugihara* dismissed as banal Chiune's postwar reflection that he had simply acted "out of love for mankind," because it does little to unravel the complexity of his actions or motives: "His act is so full of light, his motives are so full of shadows." What was behind the "conspiracy of goodness" Sugihara triggered which brought about the extensive yet improbable "underground" railroad out of Lithuania? For Levine, the answer lay in the nature of the vice consul's original brief: As Japan's "new eyes" in Eastern Europe, Sugihara had to ascertain whether Germany planned to attack the Soviet Union, and if so, when. Suspicion that Hitler was not being completely straightforward with his Axis ally made Sugihara's intelligence reports vital for his superiors in both Berlin and Tokyo. Levine believed that Sugihara's resolve for his "desperate and principled moral act" only crystallized when the *kind* of refugees appearing at the Kaunas consulate changed from the well-heeled and well-organized to the desperate and miserable. While recognizing Tokyo may have granted Sugihara "a certain amount of leeway in signing dubious visas" to accommodate influential Jews like Victor Sassoon, Levine seemed more convinced that Matsuoka tolerated Sugihara's disobedience (which was gradually coming under fire within the Ministry) because his continued intelligence gathering on the German-Soviet front was of "great value."

This is also why, he argued, Sugihara "inexplicably" survived the so-called Matsuoka Purge.[5] Single-handedly, Levine believed, Sugihara could not have achieved such worthy results, but this did not diminish his dramatic gesture.

What gradually emerges from Levine's account is the portrait of an elusive intelligence operative covertly spying on German ally and Soviet foe alike, but who unwittingly found himself in a disturbing situation that demanded a personal and principled response. Sugihara weighed the substantial risks from all sides: the Nazis (who might have objected to his aiding the refugees), the Soviet Union (where capricious rivalries might have brought a backlash), and the Foreign Ministry (whose punishment might have entailed, according to Levine, summary execution). Sugihara's association with "un-*deutschfreundlich*" (un-German-friendly) Polish spies, with their link to a London-based government-in-exile, must have vexed German observers, but Sugihara strangely enough employed an ethnic German, possibly a Gestapo mole, as consulate secretary. This paradox prompted Levine to ponder "*what* was going on in Sugihara's consulate?" He attributed the internal contradictions in Sugihara's infrequent postwar recollections of those distant events to the workings of "old spy instincts." In Levine's view, Sugihara projected the "careful falsehood" of himself as a "tragic hero" while glossing over less savory aspects of his espionage activities, yet this in no way detracted from the love of life that was evident in his courageous act. If anything, Levine found more irksome the criticism of steadfast Sugihara supporters who responded to his thesis with "a disappointment bordering on the hostile!"[6]

Indeed, it is puzzling why the memory of an honorable man like Chiune Sugihara elicits such strong antithetical feelings between would-be custodians of the Sugihara legend. Detractors in Japan have discounted several of Levine's claims. These critics include Katsumasa Watanabe, member of a *kenkyūkai* (study group) on Sugihara, who alleged Levine made "more than 300" mistakes and distortions in his book. His laundry list included everything from errors about Chiune's personal life and Japanese culture, to more serious charges of academic dishonesty. Another vocal critic is Hiroshi Matsuura.[7] Whatever one might make of these challenges, the tone these critics adopted was clear: Chiune Sugihara never made false claims on heroism as Levine asserted. To hypothesize, as Levine did, that the Sugiharas tried to recast Chiune as a "tragic hero" was to fundamentally misunderstand the "essence (*shinzui*) of Sugihara's visas." Instead, Watanabe for instance is happy to accept Sugihara's claims of humanitarian philanthropy at face value.[8]

What then is one to make of this bitter exchange? In a climate where fierce battles over modern Japanese history are regularly waged between "progressives" (for whom candid historical reporting is more important than preserving a tidy image of Japan) and "revisionists" (who want to preserve "a national history" of which Japan can be proud), some might despair that this "brawling" has drastically reduced the number of genuine modern-day Japanese heroes.[9] This yearning perhaps explains the widespread popular enthusiasm for the Sugihara story since it first broke in Japan in the 1980s. Here at last was a home-grown hero who seemed beyond reproach, and who, for all the "right" reasons, showed compassion and mercy during a bitterly disputed period of recent Japanese history. Casting aspersions on that hero, warranted or otherwise, does not sit well with those whom Levine maintains are busily at work writing the legend of a bigger-than-life "candidate for sainthood."[10]

Lack of attention to detail, and speculation about Chiune's postwar reticence (certainly open to interpretation), has probably done more harm than good to Levine's worthwhile attempt to differentiate between the inherent good in Chiune's act on the one hand, and postwar characterization of that act by both rescuer and rescued on the other. It may even have reinforced his critics' resolve to cultivate the very image of an idealized Sugihara he rejects. More prudent observers may in the long run produce greater rewards. Pamela Rotner Sakamoto, in her survey of the Foreign Ministry's approach towards the Jews from around the mid-1930s to the attack on Pearl Harbor, assiduously avoided forming any conclusions about Sugihara's motives in 1940 or his reflections on life after the war. Rather than being drawn into the near-impossible task of pinning down Sugihara's state of mind, she restricted herself to examining his actions and came up with a vital observation: Sugihara's act was exceptional because although "many Japanese diplomats issued visas that saved Jews...only a few like Sugihara saved Jews by issuing visas." Sakamoto's careful approach revealed that Sugihara clearly broke with Ministry policy; she documented the finesse with which Sugihara tried to justify his acts, and appear, ex post facto, to be following orders while "liberally interpreting them," a euphemism surely for knowingly breaking the rules. The steady trickle of Sugihara refugees reaching Japan without ongoing destinations nor sufficient funds grew to unexpected proportions, and obviously caught the Foreign Ministry by surprise. As early as April 1941, the Ministry singled out the Kaunas consulate for admonishment in its report "Situation of European Refugees Coming to Japan." This drew a sharp line between

Sugihara's actions and official Ministry policy. In the end, Sakamoto shows that Sugihara stands out because, unlike "bystanders" who were content to obediently follow orders, or were indifferent or even openly anti-Semitic, he was one of the few diplomats in the field, Japanese or otherwise, to heed a powerful human imperative and *act* on his sympathy with the refugees.[11]

Readers familiar with the present monograph's prequel *Between Incompetence and Culpability: Assessing the Diplomacy of Japan's Foreign Ministry from Pearl Harbor to Potsdam* by Seishirō Sugihara (no relation to Chiune), will be aware of the author's attempt to hold the Foreign Ministry accountable for a long line of scandalous blunders and cover-ups that have plagued it in the twentieth century. These include its failure to deliver the December 7, 1941 note breaking off diplomatic relations with the U. S. at the time designated by Tokyo, ultimately leading to the Pearl Harbor operation being stigmatized as a "sneak attack"; and the postwar promotion to vice foreign ministers of the two officials responsible for that blunder. The author argues that while Japan's military was abolished during the Occupation, the Foreign Ministry secured its own future at the expense of Japan and the Japanese people, and deliberately and systematically placed Chiune Sugihara's acts of kindness beyond public scrutiny.

The author's passionate denunciation of the shabby treatment of this "rescuer of souls" demonstrates how the postwar (and prewar) Foreign Ministry worked against the national interest. He takes issue with official explanations: Sugihara's dismissal was not due to staff cuts during administrative reorganization under the Occupation, and was not a result of the extensive purges of Japanese officials from public service. Nor was Sugihara dismissed for being incompetent, since he was one of the Ministry's most talented experts on Russian affairs, and would have been useful during the Occupation because the Soviet Union, a signatory to the Potsdam Proclamation, was one of the key nations allied against Japan. The Ministry not only forced Chiune to resign, but also treated him shabbily. Rumors were spread that "Sugihara should have enough money because he took payment from the Jews when he issued those visas," but this misrepresentation was later denied by those who had received visas. The author argues this rumor was used to erase positive impressions of Sugihara who had indeed saved the lives of several thousand Jews, and thereby suppress both criticism over his dismissal and any support or sympathy for him.

Postwar efforts by survivors like Yehoshua Nishri to find Chiune Sugihara were frustrated by Foreign Ministry officials on technicalities to do with the pronunciation of his name. The author concludes the Ministry was determined to keep quiet about Sugihara and ignore him. Exasperated, Chiune had to sit back and watch many colleagues, mostly mid-ranking officials responsible for a prewar diplomacy resulting in war with the United States, rise to positions of authority within the Ministry. The author also blames the Ministry for the fact that no widespread movement to publicly honor Chiune arose until after his death on July 31, 1986, thus allowing it to avoid honoring Sugihara's achievements during his lifetime. It consistently ignored Chiune; and "when ignoring him was no longer an option, it tried to diminish his stature in every conceivable way." It was as though rehabilitating Chiune, who had saved lives by disobeying orders, would somehow discredit all the officials who had obeyed those orders.

The author does not doubt Chiune Sugihara had an innate sense of kindness, and argues that he also needed to exercise mental resolve and a great deal of care because he knew issuing visas to Jews could ultimately bring misfortune to himself and his family. Chiune definitely did not allow his wife Yukiko to assist with issuing the visas, as a precaution against implicating her in this activity. The author attributes Chiune's goodness to a Mencian ethic, and claims that compassion for human life was the key to his benevolence. Chiune had no other ulterior motives: How could he "refuse to issue them visas on the pretext that their travel papers were not in order, or that they were a threat to public security? Did this really further the national interest?" He notes that Chiune indeed attracted attention to himself by conspicuously issuing so many transit visas to refugees, and deserves to be honored because he jeopardized his own future to save their lives. Chiune Sugihara didn't even want to be a "hero," which is why his good deed has struck a chord in the hearts of the Japanese people.

Another important aspect of the present study is the question of war responsibility. The author squarely confronts the Foreign Ministry for its failure to acknowledge the part it played in guiding Japan down the road to war with the United States. Mainstream journals and newspapers (such as the British weekly, *The Economist*) continue to assert that, "After the surrender in 1945, Japan jettisoned *all the vestiges of its militaristic past* and built a modern democracy that laid the foundations for its emergence as an economic superpower 30 years later."[12] However, the author emphatically questions this assertion. It is well known that Japan's naval organization was completely dismantled during the Occupation, and reorganized in consultation with progressives like Admiral Kichisaburō Nomura, who in the prewar period cautioned strongly against challenging the forces of the United States.[13] But the author contends that the Foreign Ministry escaped any comparable overhaul, and continued its flawed existence into the postwar era around the very individuals who had shepherded Japan down the path to war.[14] One such individual, Toshikazu Kase, established a paradigm for prewar Japanese diplomatic history that glossed over and diverted attention away from what the author believes to be the Ministry's obvious and glaring failings.

The author highlights several episodes that demonstrate the "incompetence and culpability" of the Foreign Ministry during the twentieth century, and argues passionately that, for the postwar Ministry which continues to conceal its war responsibility, "Chiune Sugihara is precisely the sort of 'witness' who threatens its existence and attests to its deplorable past." He calls on Ministry officials to finally address the wrongs perpetrated against Chiune Sugihara, not only to rehabilitate the reputation of one of modern Japan's noblest heroes, but also as the first step towards a moral and ethical diplomacy.

Norman Hu

Chapter 1

The Pearl Harbor "Sneak Attack" Cover-Up and the Foreign Ministry's Responsibility

On October 26, 1997, during a state visit to the United States, China's President Jiang Zemin stopped in Hawaii at Pearl Harbor to lay a floral tribute at the *Arizona* Memorial. Ostensibly a demonstration of Sino-American friendship, it was obviously done out of spite against Japan. Some nerve, I thought.

The subsequent identification by Tokai University professor Takeo Iguchi of a long-lost "declaration of war" (in the December 1997 issue of the magazine *This is Yomiuri*[1]) also provoked much public debate in Japan about the question of the "sneak attack" at Pearl Harbor.

On December 8, 1941 (Dec. 7, U. S. time), Japan went to war against the United States by attacking Pearl Harbor. Japan had originally intended to deliver (thirty minutes before the attack began in Hawaii) a final notice to U. S. Secretary of State Cordell Hull that would serve as a "declaration of war." However, due to blunders in Japan's Washington embassy, charged with processing the diplomatic cables and delivering them to Hull at the designated time, the note was instead delivered about an hour after the attack began, thereby turning the Pearl Harbor offensive into a "sneak attack." United States

President Franklin Roosevelt exploited the resultant "sneak attack" to rally support for the war effort, and until war's end the American people invoked the slogan "Remember Pearl Harbor!" and expressed their hatred for Japan. Dropping the atomic bomb and the Soviet Union's entrance into the war were felt to be justified, and Japan was held in contempt. It could therefore be said that the blunder in delaying the "declaration of war" brought Japan into extraordinary disrepute, and caused enormous human suffering.

Incidentally, Professor Iguchi is none other than the son of Sadao Iguchi, the former Washington embassy counselor, who bears crucial blame for this blunder. Sadao Iguchi neglected to implement emergency procedures at the embassy despite receiving orders from the Foreign Ministry's home office to "make every preparation,"[2] thereby contributing to the delay in delivering the "declaration of war." Although Professor Iguchi insists that the home office must also bear some blame for the "sneak attack" at Pearl Harbor, this does not in any way absolve his father of responsibility. The Foreign Ministry, humiliated by Sadao Iguchi's blunder, has consistently avoided this issue through the postwar era; nevertheless, the Foreign Ministry must surely feel further embarrassment since Sadao Iguchi's son is raising this issue again.

"Postwar" Era Began by Deceiving Emperor on Pearl Harbor

On September 27, 1945, shortly after Japan's defeat, Emperor Hirohito and Supreme Commander of the Occupying Forces General Douglas MacArthur met for the first time.

Before all else, the emperor raised the question of the "sneak attack" at Pearl Harbor. However, the person appointed to interpret between the emperor and MacArthur was none other than Katsuzō Okumura. Not only had the aforementioned Sadao Iguchi failed to implement emergency procedures at the Washington embassy, but Okumura (who was charged with typing out Japan's diplomatic cables) had shirked his duties on the eve of war between Japan and the United States, and was at a friend's place playing cards or some such activity; Okumura was therefore directly responsible for the final notice not being delivered at the designated time.

Since the emperor was unaware at this time of the real circumstances surrounding the "sneak attack," he stated that it had been arranged by Prime Minister Hideki Tōjō, but that nevertheless he (the emperor) accepted full responsibility for it. The emperor's total acceptance of responsibility is often remembered for the deep impression it left on General MacArthur, but pinning the blame for the "sneak attack" on Tōjō is clearly problematic.

In records assembled by MacArthur's political consultant George Atcheson from his personal recollections of MacArthur, the emperor allegedly stated he had been "tricked" by Tōjō. Given his mild-mannered nature, it is inconceivable the emperor would have made such a blunt statement, but clearly he made some statement that was indeed interpreted this way.[3]

In fact, the emperor had met two days earlier on September 25 with *New York Times* reporter Frank Kluckhorn. He responded to the reporter's written questionnaire regarding the "sneak attack" issue with a prepared statement that he had not intended "to have the war rescript used as General Tōjō used it."[4]

For the Japanese side, it was unclear at the time whether to put Tōjō's name forward regarding the "sneak attack" at Pearl Harbor issue, a pressing question for the occupying forces. When the meeting between the emperor and MacArthur was being considered, then-Foreign Minister Mamoru Shigemitsu claimed, "If blame is shifted to a former leader…and it is publicly declared that His Majesty had no personal responsibility for the attack on Pearl Harbor, then the preservation of Japan's national polity will be destroyed from within."[5] This was to become an important reason why he was later forced to resign as foreign minister.

To announce, however, that the attack on Pearl Harbor was not a "sneak attack" ordered at the national level and sanctioned by the emperor, it was probably decided that putting Tōjō's name forward was unavoidable, and it was likely that a prepared answer sheet bearing Tōjō's name was substituted at the last minute.

Thus the "sneak attack" at Pearl Harbor became the starting point of the war between Japan and the United States, and was the reason the war became so tragic; and Japan's "postwar" era began with the emperor being deceived and forced to give untruthful responses regarding this "sneak attack," perhaps to protect the reputation of the Foreign Ministry.

Toshikazu Kase Must Bear Witness

Incidentally, the emperor's interpreter when Kluckhorn received this prepared statement was Katsuzō Okumura, the same person who had interpreted at the first meeting between the emperor and MacArthur. Okumura's own negligence had directly caused the "sneak attack," yet ironically he was present when the statement naming Tōjō was handed to Kluckhorn, and also at the meeting between the emperor and MacArthur when it was asserted that Tōjō had organized the "sneak attack."

Here I would like to pose an open question to former Foreign Ministry official Toshikazu Kase who, despite his advancing age, remains in good health.

Kase had the rank of secretary under Foreign Minister Yōsuke Matsuoka; later, he also worked concurrently as a key division chief and secretary under Foreign Minister Shigenori Tōgō during the climax to negotiations between Japan and the United States in late 1941. Under Tōgō, in the period which Professor Iguchi has called into question, Kase occupied a key post with enormous responsibilities. After the war, Kase worked as third department chief in the Cabinet Information Bureau.

In his memoirs, Shigemitsu records that he was surprised to find the emperor had been unaware of plans for the Pearl Harbor attack, and "because of the gravity of the situation, I summoned Kase and ordered him to investigate it."[6] This clearly attests to Kase's direct involvement. And Frank Kluckhorn, whose audience with the emperor took place when Shigeru Yoshida was foreign minister, reported in the *New York Times* that Kase told him Yoshida had approved the prepared statement given to him by the emperor.[7]

It cannot be said that Kase at this time was unaware of the true circumstances of the "sneak attack" at Pearl Harbor. Despite Okumura's imperfect grasp of the American dialect, and his lack of personal acquaintance with Yoshida, Okumura later observed that, surprisingly, he was appointed by Yoshida himself to interpret for the emperor.[8]

In other words, although fully aware that the "sneak attack" at Pearl Harbor had been caused by an administrative error at Japan's Washington embassy, someone in the Foreign Ministry planned for the emperor to falsely claim Tōjō had organized a "sneak attack." This person was either Kase, or some official whom Kase would have been able to observe closely. Kase has a responsibility to bear witness to the truth regarding these grave facts of history.

In any event, how were the people of Japan informed of the "sneak attack" at Pearl Harbor that brought Japan into such disrepute and caused so much human suffering? During the intense atmosphere of the war itself, the Japanese public and military naturally were unaware that the war with the United States had been started by a "sneak attack" at Pearl Harbor. Nor did they know that American soldiers were consumed with revenge when attacking Japanese troops and civilians.

The Japanese people gleaned some information about the "sneak attack" at Pearl Harbor during the Tokyo Trial. Shirōji Yūki, special assistant to Ambassador Saburō Kurusu who had been sent to the United States in November 1941, testified on August 19, 1947, regarding the circumstances of the delay of Japan's final notice. For the first time, the Japanese people learned that the war between Japan and the United States had been started by a "sneak attack," and that this was caused by an administrative blunder at the Japanese embassy in Washington. However, it wasn't possible to determine exactly who was responsible for it, nor what consequences the "sneak attack" had. That is, due to strict censorship rules imposed at the time by Occupation authorities, the Japanese people were not at liberty to debate the issue. It was impossible to report anything about the Tokyo Trial except literal courtroom proceedings.

On the other hand, when Occupation authorities discovered that the "sneak attack" at Pearl Harbor had merely been caused by an administrative blunder, there was no further need to pursue the matter. It was felt that the significance of this issue for Japan was beyond the scope of the Tokyo Trial. Furthermore, when it was understood at the trial that the "sneak attack" at Pearl Harbor had been the result of an administrative blunder, there was indeed no further investigation.

Since the Japanese people were not at liberty to discuss the matter, and no importance was attached to it by the Tokyo Trial, it was as though for Japan this issue had been resolved, and time subsequently slipped away.

The problem arises after the Occupation was lifted. The "sneak attack" at Pearl Harbor, which could not be discussed during the Occupation, should have then been explored, and a deeper understanding of its importance reached. However, even if the will to discuss it had existed, certain measures were taken to make this discussion impossible.

Shigeru Yoshida, prime minister during the closing stages of the Occupation and in four other postwar cabinets, reinstated Sadao Iguchi to vice foreign minister even though he was no longer a ministry employee. It will be recalled that Iguchi was responsible for not implementing emergency procedures at the Washington embassy on the eve of the attack on Pearl Harbor, despite receiving instructions to "make every preparation"; he was therefore one of the officials most to blame for the delay in delivering the final note. Furthermore, soon after the Occupation was lifted, Yoshida also reinstated Katsuzō Okumura to the same rank, even though he was no longer a ministry employee. Okumura, it will be recalled, failed to type the final note when he was supposed to but had been at an acquaintance's place instead, and directly caused the delay in its delivery. Not only did the Foreign Ministry fail to question their responsibility for delaying the final notice to the United States, it perversely promoted them to the highest positions within its organization.

The Foreign Ministry was therefore obliged to use all its energies to prevent the public from discussing this serious issue. Some have denounced certain historical perspectives on postwar Japan as mimicking those established at the Tokyo Trial; and it was of course very unfair that the Allied nations single-mindedly and unilaterally, under the peculiar circumstances of the Occupation, used the Tokyo Trial to place the blame for starting the war squarely upon Japan. However, after the Occupation was lifted, the Japanese people were still unable to discuss the war freely and objectively, and the Tokyo Trial verdict became the accepted version of history promulgated among the Japanese people. The "sneak attack" at Pearl Harbor was surely an important point essential to any objective discussion of the war, but because proper debate of this issue was stymied, discussions regarding Japan's war inevitably became distorted. Arguably, the Foreign Ministry had imprisoned the Japanese people into a "warped linguistic space."

Roosevelt's Death Came Like Divine Wind

What would have become of Japan in the closing stages of war with the United States, started by a "sneak attack" at Pearl Harbor, if President Roosevelt had lived on and continued to lead the war effort?

Roosevelt succeeded in pushing all the blame for starting the war onto Japan. Before the war started, if Roosevelt had really wanted to avoid war, there were several courses of action and ample information available to him to prevent it. Even without prior knowledge of the Pearl Harbor attack, he still had the information and means to prevent the war. Nevertheless, war broke out between the two nations, and in practical terms Roosevelt must also bear great responsibility for starting the war.[9] Although extant historical records deceptively retain only those documents favorable to the United States, and successfully thrust the entire blame for starting the war upon Japan, the "sneak attack" at Pearl Harbor contributed additional and decisive impetus to this "success." Though Roosevelt knew the "sneak attack" had actually been caused by an administrative error, he claimed to the American people that Japan had deliberately launched a "sneak attack" and thereby fanned hostility against Japan.

For Roosevelt it was imperative that, in any peace talks to end the war, no room was left to claim that Japan and the United States were both responsible for the outbreak of war.

In 1943 in Casablanca, Roosevelt outmaneuvered British Prime Minister Winston Churchill by demanding that Japan as well as the other Axis powers surrender unconditionally.[10] This was done to deny the Axis any way to end the war by suing for peace. He also urged the Soviet Union to enter the war against Japan. This meant though that Moscow would have to abrogate the Soviet-Japanese Neutrality Pact, a treaty whose observance by Japan during the 1941 Nazi campaign against Moscow had probably saved the Soviet Union from a crisis.

Viewed in this light, Japan would most likely have become partitioned like Germany or Korea if Roosevelt had lived on to lead the war effort. Roosevelt would have ensured that the "destruction" mentioned in the last part of the Potsdam Proclamation would have become Japan's postwar fate. Naturally, the "sneak attack" at Pearl Harbor would have played a decisive factor in this destiny.

On April 12, 1945, President Roosevelt passed away suddenly at his retreat in Warm Springs, Georgia. His sudden death reversed Japan's fate from "destruction" to one of liberation. Japan escaped the worst possible outcome thanks to Roosevelt's death, and for Japan it was as though the *kamikaze* (Divine Wind) had blown.

Japan was to benefit from another fortunate development. When Roosevelt died, Joseph C. Grew, who had been the United States ambassador to Japan at the outbreak of war, held the position of under secretary of state. Grew firmly believed that war between Japan and the United States would benefit neither side, and as ambassador he had exhausted his powers to avoid war. But he was unable to prevent it because Roosevelt was already determined upon war. Grew returned to the United States roughly nine months after war broke out, but continued to be concerned about the future of Japan, which found itself caught up in a senseless war.

Soon after Roosevelt's death, Grew became acting secretary of state under President Harry Truman, and not long afterwards, on May 7, Nazi Germany surrendered unconditionally.

The next day, War Secretary Henry Stimson had a private word with Grew and revealed two important secrets.[11] A secret accord had been signed at Yalta calling on the Soviet Union to join the war against Japan; and work developing the atomic bomb was progressing. Japan was surely headed towards "destruction." We can only speculate as to the extent of Grew's shock.

Before inflicting this "destruction," surely an opportunity to surrender could be given to Japan, and for this Grew had the Potsdam Proclamation in mind. Announcing surrender terms before Japan's "destruction" was complete would give Japan the chance to give up, thereby avoiding the resultant enormous sacrifices and allowing Japan to end the war while leaving the emperor system and government intact.

Ultimately, the Potsdam Proclamation was put together by a group headed by Stimson, but it was Grew who persuaded Stimson to adopt this approach. Several days after learning about the secret Yalta agreement from Stimson, Grew approved and handed to Stimson a memorandum calling for a reassessment of the secret accord. After reading Grew's memo, Stimson noted that he was "very glad that the State Department has brought [these issues] up and given us a chance to be heard on them."[12] Government leaders in the United States at that time were totally committed to Roosevelt's policies, so Grew's proposal for an explicit statement to Japan was of special significance.

Thus, the Potsdam Proclamation was announced on July 26. Stimson's draft regarding the postwar Japanese government allowed that it would "not exclude a constitutional monarchy under her present dynasty," but unfortunately this was removed at the behest of Secretary Hull who had headed the Department of State since the outbreak of war.[13] The removal of this guarantee was the reason Japan was unable to immediately accept the Potsdam Proclamation. As a result, atomic bombs were dropped on August 6 and 9 upon Hiroshima and Nagasaki respectively, and the Soviet Union joined the war against Japan on August 9. Later, at an imperial conference, Emperor Hirohito stated that, "Regardless of what happens to me personally, I must save the lives of my people."[14] Nothing less than the beginning of a dramatic new phase for Japan's emperor system had allowed Japan to surrender without suffering "destruction." Although the Soviet Union joined the war, Japan was able to surrender before the home islands were invaded, and before the Soviet Union could carry out a partitioned occupation of Japan. Unfortunately, Korea was partitioned and occupied, and later suffered the further tragedy of the Korean War. Although later faced with the problem of the Northern Territories, and having to accept an Allied occupation, Japan was ultimately able to conclude the war and yet keep its national polity intact.

Let Us Not Forget Grew's Accomplishments

Japan escaped "destruction" thanks to Grew's timely efforts, but after the war his work was soon forgotten. Indeed, from the apparently harsh conditions of the Potsdam Proclamation, it is not easy to discern Grew's covert attempts to rescue Japan. However, as research on this period of history advances, and further significant elements embedded in the Potsdam Proclamation are revealed, the Japanese public will become more familiar with Grew's contributions, and a statue to his memory may one day be erected at the Imperial Palace. Further historical research can contribute to unearthing those hidden significant elements.

Nowadays though, Japan has more or less forgotten Grew. When Japan surrendered on August 15, Grew felt his mission was over and he resigned as under secretary of state. He refused to return to Japan after the war, saying that he didn't want to meet with Japanese friends in the position of victor. Nevertheless, Grew kept up with many activities to boost Japan's recovery.

One such activity was raising funds to build the International Christian University. Established through the generosity of many American donors, Grew was chair of the fund-raising committee in the United States, and worked hard at collecting funds.[15] This author visited the campus expecting that this university at least would have erected a monument to Grew's memory because of his efforts to establish the ICU. But university staff seemed unaware of who Grew was, except for someone in the historical materials editorial office. I am not singling out the ICU for particular criticism, but simply pointing out that, like this university, the rest of Japanese society also seems to have forgotten Grew. One book that celebrates Grew's achievements was published in Japan in 1996 by Kikuya Funayama, the son of Grew's former valet Sadakichi Funayama, but this book has generally been overlooked.[16]

What caused this sorry state of affairs? Clearly, the Foreign Ministry's extensive efforts to block any resolution of the Pearl Harbor "sneak attack" issue is largely to blame. Recognizing Grew's contribution would force it to publicly examine the "sneak attack," an event that resulted in more tragedy during the war than was ever necessary. It is therefore impossible for the Ministry to ever appraise Grew's contributions positively, nor do anything but encourage others to forget Grew.

Shigeru Yoshida, on intimate terms with Grew before the war, published his memoirs between 1957 and 1958; and a record of Grew's efforts was readily available at the time because Grew also published his memoirs in 1957. Yet Yoshida barely mentions Grew's contribution at all in his memoirs. He was clearly not at liberty to discuss Grew's efforts, because Yoshida had promoted those responsible for the "sneak attack" at Pearl Harbor to vice foreign ministers.

In 1960, to commemorate the centennial anniversary of relations between Japan and the United States, the Japanese government sent medals of honor to many Americans. General Douglas MacArthur received the Grand Cordon of the Order of the Rising Sun, with Paulownia Flowers, while Joseph Grew received the Grand Cordon of the Order of the Rising Sun, a slightly lower yet nonetheless impressive honor. At first I thought Grew's efforts had been publicly acknowledged in full, but I was soon taken aback. In fact, all previous American ambassadors to Japan had received honors of the same rank as Grew. In other words, the grand honor bestowed on Grew was not to acknowledge Grew's contributions to Japan at the end of the war, but simply for his service as ambassador before the war.

Culpability for Producing "Warped Linguistic Space"

Shigeru Yoshida also visited the United States in 1960, as head of a special goodwill mission to commemorate the centennial anniversary of Japan-U. S. relations. When Yoshida passed through Hawaii, the place where war had broken out, the press were expecting him to make some sort of statement, but Yoshida issued none. Indignant reporters requested a press conference but Yoshida refused, saying instead that he was "old and tired." (Nevertheless, he was quite able to attend a hula dance after dinner.)[17]

In the end, if Yoshida had made any statement at a press conference in Hawaii, the place where war had begun, he would have had to raise the issue of the "sneak attack." That would have meant going into the blunder by the Washington embassy on the eve of war, so this is probably why he made no statement and refused a press conference.

Then in 1991, as the fiftieth anniversary of the Pearl Harbor attack approached, the United States designated December 7 as National Pearl Harbor Remembrance Day; and on the day itself, President George Bush flew to Pearl Harbor and presided over extensive ceremonies.

In contrast, what happened in Japan? There were no activities whatsoever to mark the day. Even as late as 1991, the Foreign Ministry had not declassified the partial findings of an internal investigation (conducted during the Occupation) into the blunder made at the

Washington embassy that caused the "sneak attack" at Pearl Harbor.[18] Upon closer scrutiny, the Foreign Ministry clearly had still not publicly acknowledged this blunder. It is therefore not surprising that the Ministry made no public gestures to commemorate the fiftieth anniversary of the Pearl Harbor attack.

However, it was impossible for the Ministry to let the day pass without any action at all. Or rather, it was impossible to ward off questions by American reporters as the fiftieth anniversary of the Pearl Harbor attack approached. Foreign Minister Michio Watanabe gave the following response to a reporter from the *Washington Post.*

> We feel a deep remorse about the unbearable suffering and sorrow Japan inflicted on the American people and the peoples of Asia and the Pacific during the Pacific War, a war that Japan started...because of the reckless decision of our military. [19]

This answer had of course been prepared by an administrative bureau within the Foreign Ministry. Although both Japan and the United States were focusing on the fact that the war had been started by a "sneak attack" at Pearl Harbor, and even though President Bush was to make an official statement forgiving Japan for the Pearl Harbor issue, Watanabe evaded the point entirely, and responded instead with a comment about the overall war between Japan and the United States. More misleadingly, he pushed the entire blame for the war on the former military, and avoided apportioning any responsibility to the Foreign Ministry. Perhaps it bears remembering that since the Meiji era the Foreign Ministry had often committed Japanese diplomacy to a wrong-headed course, even before any military aggression had been taken in the field. It could be argued that the Foreign Ministry was indeed more responsible than the military. Watanabe's statement could be seen as the "distillation" of five decades of continued secrecy about the Pearl Harbor issue.[20]

Emperor Akihito paid a state visit to the United States in mid 1994, during which there had been plans for a visit to Pearl Harbor. This author promptly published an article in the May 1994 issue of *Shokun!* titled "The Emperor's Pearl Harbor Visit Cannot Become the Foreign Ministry's Apology by Proxy," arguing that the visit be prevented, and appealing for it to be canceled.[21]

If Emperor Akihito had visited Pearl Harbor before the administrative blunder by the Washington embassy over the "sneak attack" at Pearl Harbor had been publicly acknowledged to the Japanese people, or before an apology had been made to the Japanese nation, or even before the relevant historical materials had been declassified, this would have been tantamount to using the emperor's visit as a proxy apology for the blunder committed by the Foreign Ministry, and having the emperor take part in concealing the responsibilities of the Foreign Ministry.

Fortunately, proponents of this line of argument were able to hold sway, and the emperor's visit to Pearl Harbor was canceled at the last moment.

In November the same year, the Foreign Ministry resolutely declassified certain historical materials related to the "sneak attack" at Pearl Harbor. It was in effect apologizing to the Japanese public, fifty-three years after the fact, for its administrative blunder regarding the "sneak attack" at Pearl Harbor.

However, the Foreign Ministry has not shown any sign of regret for concealing the facts for so long and virtually fabricating history, nor for shutting the Japanese people into a "warped linguistic space."

The foregoing text in this chapter appeared in my article in the January 1998 issue of *Shokun!* titled "Open Question to Mr. Toshikazu Kase" regarding the Pearl Harbor issue. Apart from minor changes to reflect the passage of time, it remains as it appeared when published.

I sent a copy of the article, along with a cover letter, to Mr. Kase requesting a response, and I did receive a reply of sorts. His son, Hideaki Kase, published an article in *Shokun!* in March 1998 titled "For the first time! Toshikazu Kase's Testimony: Answering Questions about Pearl Harbor." Unfortunately, this was for the most part an answer to the piece published the previous month by Professor Iguchi on the misplaced "declaration of war"[22] and devoted very little space responding to my article.

This author has always had the utmost respect for Hideaki Kase and his activities in the press and in society. In 1998, he was editorial advisor for the film *Pride–The Fateful Moment* which was critical of the Tokyo Trial, and he is to be commended for those efforts too. He should also be shown due respect for his loyalty in writing this article on behalf of his now elderly father.

Nevertheless, the problem here is one of social science.[23] What follows is my rebuttal to Toshikazu Kase.

Rebuttal to Toshikazu Kase

Hideaki Kase writes that "although some people appear to claim that my father while in the Foreign Ministry played a pivotal role in concealing responsibility for the delay of the final notice, which lead to the outbreak of war between Japan and the United States, their arguments are extremely weak, and cannot be substantiated." The evidence is also weak, he continues.[24]

Certainly, this author has never claimed categorically that Toshikazu Kase played a pivotal role in any concealment efforts. It is clear though that he had an important part to play, and afterwards never discussed these critical facts; this is the issue I raised, and for which I urged an explanation.

Toshikazu Kase was the key official who transmitted to Washington the "final notice" that was supposed to be delivered before the attack on Pearl Harbor. As such, he knew from the outset that Tōjō was not to blame for the "sneak attack." He can reject with complete impunity the arguments made by Professor Iguchi, son of the former Washington embassy counselor Sadao Iguchi, that there had been "no mistakes made at the embassy to the United States."[25] However Kase, then third department chief of the Cabinet Information Bureau, told *New York Times* reporter Frank Kluckhorn that Foreign Minister Shigeru Yoshida had approved the spurious statement scripted for Emperor Hirohito on September 25, 1945, that the emperor had not intended "to have the war rescript used as General Tōjō used it."[26] Clearly, Kase played an important part in concealing the Foreign Ministry's responsibility for the "sneak attack" at Pearl Harbor. Moreover, until the evidence surrounding these historical facts was thrust upon him, Kase remained silent on these historical facts for more than fifty years. This in itself brings his responsibility into question.

Next, let us examine why the emperor was made to deliver the spurious statement that he had been tricked by Tōjō. Hideaki Kase's explanation in the aforementioned *Shokun!* article is far from adequate. According to Kase, "All attention was then focused on how to protect the emperor system, and no thought was given to such frivolous notions as concealing the responsibilities of the embassy in the United States on the day war broke out."[27] Certainly, Japan was desperate then to preserve the emperor system. Japan surrendered and accepted the Potsdam Proclamation, and its greatest wish was to protect the emperor system; therefore desperation may very well have produced this spurious answer. For the Allied nations too, from the start of the Occupation it was of great importance why Japan made a "sneak attack" at Pearl Harbor, and how this "sneak attack" had been carried out; so any initial Japanese claim that it had resulted from a blunder at the Washington embassy may have been dismissed as a mere lie. It is not inconceivable that a tentative statement implicating Tōjō was given, because broadly speaking it could have been taken as part of Tōjō's overall strategy for starting the war. Any explanation that such a critical incident was due to an administrative error might have been less persuasive, indeed considered ludicrous, and thus all the more unbelievable. Such fears may have existed at the time. Hideaki Kase's article argues that it was imperative then to preserve the emperor system, but he makes no attempt to explain why it was necessary to come up with a statement that contradicted the facts.

Moreover, no explanation has ever been given for the circumstances surrounding the scripting of this spurious statement, nor of Shigeru Yoshida's involvement.

There is another question that remains unanswered by Hideaki Kase's article. Why was Katsuzō Okumura, the person directly responsible for the blunder at the Washington embassy, appointed as interpreter at the first meeting between the emperor and MacArthur? The Foreign Ministry, as previously mentioned, selected Okumura to interpret at the September 25, 1945 meeting between *New York Times* reporter Kluckhorn and the emperor, and also two days later at the meeting between the emperor and MacArthur. It will be recalled that Okumura was the one who, rather than typing the final note on the eve before war broke out, instead shirked his duties and went to an acquaintance's place, thereby directly causing the "sneak attack." Even Okumura was curious why he had been selected.[28] He was the last person who should have been selected as interpreter. Why then was Okumura chosen? Hideaki Kase's article doesn't refer to this issue at all. Even though the Foreign Ministry was determined to protect the emperor system, there was clearly a deliberate attempt to conceal the responsibility of the Foreign Ministry, and to somehow finesse the issue. Despite the important role he played in these events, Kase remained silent until the evidence surrounding these historical facts was thrust upon him. Nor does the article written by his son (cited above) provide any explanation whatsoever regarding this point. He has yet to give a satisfactory response to open questions posed by this author.

Toshikazu Kase was a key participant in these events, yet has also been, in the postwar era, an influential historical researcher on the prewar negotiations between Japan and the United States. The perspectives adopted by a researcher must be different from those of a participant. The researcher is responsible for presenting a fair interpretation of history. Therefore, as a researcher privy to certain facts, isn't Kase duty bound to bring together these facts and make them public?

There is therefore one thing I would like to suggest to Toshikazu Kase who is both participant and researcher. According to Kase's 1951 memoir *Journey to the Missouri,* he conscientiously kept a diary. The fact that today's Japan began the postwar period on such a bad footing (and that this bad start had such a troubling impact) must be of great concern, even to someone like Kase. We must therefore reexamine the course of events at the start of the war, and those at the start of the postwar era. This is why I urge him to make his diaries public. Naturally, diaries are private and he has no formal obligation to disclose them. However, Kase's diaries would be an invaluable historical source in any reexamination of these important historical events. They would undoubtedly trigger a reappraisal of that period in history.

Making these diaries public may reveal numerous inconsistencies with statements Toshikazu Kase has made so far. But this is surely not such a bad thing. Such an act of personal sacrifice, to ameliorate what even Kase would consider to be the troubled state of Japan today, would be admirable. Rather than leaving behind a reputation tarnished by acts of deception, he would do well in the days that remain to him to reveal the truth for the first time in his life about things that were done for the nation, and thereby bequeath a legacy of truth to posterity. I cannot urge Kase strongly enough to make his diaries public.[29]

Chapter 2

Teaching about Japan's War with the United States

Why Did Japan and the United States Go To War?

Teaching children about the outbreak of war between Japan and the United States must begin by posing a very simple question: "Why did Japan and the United States go to war?" Otherwise, it is impossible to realistically convey the true significance behind the start of the war between Japan and the United States.

Children know that in Japan's ancient Yayoi period (200 B.C.–A.D. 200), trenches were built around the perimeter of villages. They should, however, also be made to understand that these were not defenses against attack by wild animals, but primarily against attack by fellow humans. Understandably, in these ancient times when food production was low, villages with dwindling food supplies would raid those with abundant provisions. The formation of states in these ancient times should be thought of partly as an effort to reduce such conflicts between rival villages.

In any event, it is important for children to have a general understanding that humanity's beginnings are linked to a history of conflict over the struggle for existence.

We might say that, with the arrival of "modern" times, states developed extensive police forces to subdue domestic threats. It can also be said, however, that armed conflicts (namely, war) would easily break out between states, and that there was no mechanism to prevent it. Armies became the preferred method to forcefully resolve conflicts between states. These conflicts were not struggles for existence in the ordinary sense, but were generally battles for existence between people with the state as the unit of battle; there was no unequivocal method for states to avoid war, and war became instead routine behavior between states. Children should learn that, broadly speaking, strong states used war to defeat and colonize weak ones, and in earlier times they would have enslaved the inhabitants of these defeated states. In such times, no single state could strive unilaterally for peace, nor could it be the only one without an army.

Children must be made fully aware that this became the fortune of the modern state. The League of Nations, established after World War I, was the first international organization set up to prevent war; but it wasn't until the founding of the United Nations following World War II that this structure gained any degree of clout. Moreover, they must also learn that this international structure was only established after the world experienced, and reflected on, the tragedy of a Great War of global proportions, rather than in peacetime through reasoned negotiations by the nations of the world. In today's world, the nuclear deterrent means it is no longer so easy to start a war. However, as the media constantly report, there is practically always a small-scale war occurring somewhere in the world. The world has yet to reach the stage where all nations can peacefully discuss and settle issues without the use of force. At present, no country can in principle remain totally unarmed.

For children to have this understanding of war, they must learn that human history has developed gradually and in stages. Otherwise, there can be no realistic answer, which children themselves would find satisfactory, to the simple question, "Why did Japan and the United States go to war?"

Historical Trends and the Role of Individuals in Wartime

For a genuine understanding of the nature of war, we must grasp the relationship between the great historical trends that reverberate between countries at war, and the role of the individual.

First, conflicts between countries don't arise solely because of decisions and actions made by designated leaders, such as presidents and prime ministers.

For example, let's consider the Russo-Japanese War (1904–1905). Thanks to then-U. S. President Theodore Roosevelt's generous mediation, the matter was settled on terms favorable to the Japanese side. However, the subsequent retreat of Russian influence from China and Korea left a power vacuum, and led to a struggle between Japan and the United States to assert authority over the region. In broad terms, the resolution of the Russo-Japanese War meant the mutually cooperative relationship that had existed between Japan and the United States became an unavoidable rivalry where national economic interests collided. We must therefore understand that conflicts between nations don't arise solely because of the decisions and actions made by individual leaders, but rather through great and inescapable historical trends.

Nevertheless it should be pointed out that, even regarding the war between Japan and the United States which resulted in such tragic consequences, the decisions and actions of some individuals may have produced vastly different results. After the Russo-Japanese War, Japan rejected American rail tycoon Edward H. Harimann's proposal to jointly operate the South Manchurian Railway, because of Japanese plans to fill the power vacuum in Manchuria and offset sacrifices Japan made during the war. This decision has largely been attributed to the individual efforts of then-Foreign Minister Jutarō Komura. Although patriotic, Komura's decision was flawed and only deepened the conflict soon to develop between Japan and the United States.

The implementation of flawed diplomatic policies, such as Japan's Twenty-One Demands in 1915 on a newly emergent China, also exacerbated Chinese antagonism and strengthened the bonds between China and the United States. Any balanced appraisal of history must make people aware of Japan's successively mistaken policies toward China. The conflict that developed between Japan and the United States was therefore also due to the buildup of flawed decisions and actions by Japan. Merely stating that militarism reared its ugly head during the early Shōwa period does not satisfactorily address the issue. It is probably more profitable to point out that circumstances were created which permitted the rise of militarism. Rather than making simple judgments about militarism, we must also consider the accumulation of mistaken Japanese policies, and the international conditions when militarism emerged.

Japan and the United States consequently became embroiled in a great conflict. But even in 1941, to lure Japan into war then-President Franklin Roosevelt made decisions and took actions which led directly to the outbreak of war. From Japan's perspective, it was unable to use important opportunities to avoid war with the United States, and this also greatly contributed to why war resulted. To a certain extent, war broke out because of decisions and actions taken by individuals in the Japanese military and diplomatic corps responsible for the negotiations with the United States.

Let me introduce a more concrete example from the Japanese side. A great opportunity to avoid the war arose when hostilities between Germany and the Soviet Union broke out in June 1941. Then-Foreign Minister Yōsuke Matsuoka, who had signed a non-aggression pact with the Soviet Union, was just back from a tour of Europe. Roosevelt urged Matsuoka to visit the United States, and British Prime Minister Winston Churchill advised him how unprofitable Japan's continued association with Germany was. They desperately wanted to prevent Japan from mediating between Germany and the Soviet Union at a time when hostilities seemed imminent between the two, and also from attacking the Soviet Union if there was a German-Soviet war. If Japan had then grasped the situation, identified the importance and potential of cordial ties with the United States, and taken appropriate action, it could easily have achieved a friendly relationship with the U. S. If Japan had done so, although war with the United States may have broken out at some other time and on a different scale, the war that began in December 1941 could definitely have been avoided.

Also, Japan's response may have been different if any of its policy makers had recognized the United States was actually using the notorious Hull Note of November 1941 to provoke Japan to attack the United States; we should appreciate that here too was a chance to avoid war.

For a more intimate understanding of the Japanese government's response to the Hull Note, we must reexamine Roosevelt's reelection to a third term of office in the fall of 1940. During that election Roosevelt solemnly swore to the American people never to take the nation to war. This means that even if the American side wanted to enter the war, it couldn't do so if it appeared the United States had started it. In which case, when the American side eventually did enter the war, it had to look as though war had been thrust upon the United States. And there was ample scope for this to happen. The Foreign Ministry's inability to interpret that challenge highlights its long accumulation of years of incompetence. Examining the Ministry at this time alone reveals the incompetence of its entire staff, including its ambassadors, ministers, counselors and secretaries dispersed around the world.

Discuss Responsibility for Starting the War in Equal Terms

Historically, the war between Japan and the United States came about because of deep trends of conflict between Japan and the United States. Children should be taught that, while the war would have been difficult to avoid, decisions and actions taken by individuals involved might have prevented it from occurring then, and in that manner. We must encourage the straightforward study of the responsibility of policy makers for starting the war, by producing an accurate historical picture of the decisions and actions taken by those individuals responsible for deciding those policies.

As for the actual outbreak of war between Japan and the United States, children must first be taught that it began with the surprise attack on Pearl Harbor by the Imperial Japanese Navy.

The following day (Dec. 8, U. S. time), Roosevelt declared that Japan had unexpectedly attacked the United States in the middle of peace negotiations, that it had unilaterally started the war, and that it had launched a "sneak attack" at Pearl Harbor. Japan, he claimed, bore sole responsibility for starting the war.

It must be made clear to children that Roosevelt may have known beforehand about Japan's plans for a surprise attack on Pearl Harbor, even though most people in the United States shy away from this foreknowledge theory because it remains unsubstantiated by explicit evidence.[1] However, even without prior knowledge of the Imperial Japanese Navy's surprise attack at Pearl Harbor, Roosevelt had read practically all of Japan's important diplomatic cables, and had accurately surmised Japan's intention to launch a war; we must therefore revisit the facts and make it clear that Roosevelt knew precisely what he himself could have done to avoid war.[2] Clearly, we are forced to conclude that Roosevelt was prepared to stand up to Japan if attacked, that is, the American side in substance was also prepared for the eventuality of war.

In August 1941, the United States suspended oil exports to Japan. This amounted to a military embargo because Japan, unable to produce oil, was almost completely reliant upon the United States for imports. With only two year's worth of oil reserves, Japan's tanks, planes, and battleships would have been brought to a standstill within those two years, and Japanese military power risked automatic and complete ruin. It would have meant Japan's total defeat without even firing a single shot. Children need to learn that, if a compromise with the United

States couldn't be reached and conflict was unavoidable, then war had to be launched quickly to gain even the slightest possible advantage.

December 8 (Japan time) was chosen as the date for starting the war because Japan's southern campaign through Southeast Asia had to be completed before the end of winter, to exploit the dry period before the monsoons. It was clear even then however that the German campaign against the Soviet Union was floundering, and the December 8 starting date was extremely poorly timed. (Junior high school students can also be taught that scant days before the start of war, Roosevelt's "secret war plans" had been exposed by the press, and Roosevelt was in difficulties with the largely non-interventionist American public. The attack on Pearl Harbor in effect extricated Roosevelt from this predicament.) Moreover, it must be made clear that the war started in a manner contrary to the Japanese government's original intention: Due to a blunder at Japan's Washington embassy, the final note (declaration of war) was not delivered thirty minutes before the surprise attack as intended, and the attack at Pearl Harbor thus inadvertently became an unannounced "sneak attack."

Teach that the Pearl Harbor "Sneak Attack" Made WW II More Tragic

Teaching history means not just identifying individual facts, but clarifying what influence a particular historical fact had. The most significant question regarding the war between Japan and the United States is probably the "sneak attack" at Pearl Harbor.

The table below shows the animosity felt by American soldiers towards the Japanese military during the war. The study, conducted mainly between February and April 1944, was done at a time when the war's outcome had virtually been decided. The Imperial Japanese Navy arranged for a "declaration of war" to be made before the surprise attack on Pearl Harbor, but because of a blunder at the Washington embassy, the declaration was not delivered on time, and the strike became a "sneak attack." From Japan's diplomatic cables, Roosevelt essentially knew beforehand that the delay in delivering the note was caused by an administrative error, but as noted earlier, he did not advise the American public of this. By declaring that there had been a "sneak attack," he roused animosity against Japan, and even as late as 1944 American troops had no idea that the "declaration of war" had been delayed by an administrative error. They assumed the Imperial Japanese Navy had launched a "sneak attack." According to the survey below, troops

Table
Vindictiveness toward Japan by U. S. Troops

Location and Rank of United States Troops	Percentage Who Would		
	Wipe Out the Whole Nation	Make the People Suffer Plenty	Punish the Leaders Only
A. Europe			
Officers	44 (15)	16 (18)	37 (64)
Enlisted men	61 (25)	9 (6)	26 (65)
B. Pacific			
Officers	35 (13)	19 (20)	43 (63)
Enlisted men	42 (22)	9 (8)	47 (68)
C. United States			
Enlisted men	67 (29)	8 (4)	23 (65)

NOTES: Surveys conducted in November 1943, and February–April 1944; Number of divisions surveyed: Europe, 2; Pacific, 3; United States, 3; Parentheses indicate percentages with respect to Germany.
SOURCE: Stouffer, *The American Soldier* (Princeton, 1949), p. 158

stationed in the Pacific who had actually fought against Japanese soldiers and whose war buddies had been killed, were less antagonistic towards Japan and the Japanese military than those who had no actual experience fighting Japanese troops, let alone set eyes on a Japanese soldier.[3]

As mentioned previously, Roosevelt had accurately surmised beforehand the Japanese government's intent to launch a war, but he kept this strictly secret from the public. The American people only learned after the war that Roosevelt had read all Japan's important diplomatic cables.

The American people, through the end of the war, fought under the assumption that Japan did indeed launch a "sneak attack." Together with deeply held racist prejudices, they attacked Japan and its soldiers with the fury of "devilish embers" under the assumption that Japan had committed an act of cowardice. They did not ease up on these attacks, even when Japan had lost the capacity to resist. Air raids over Tokyo, the battle for Okinawa, and the dropping of atomic bombs on Hiroshima and Nagasaki, were carried out remorselessly because of that assumption.

If not for the Potsdam Proclamation which was made possible by the efforts of Joseph Grew, U. S. ambassador to Japan at the outbreak of war, Japan would have had no opportunity to surrender as the war ended. The war would have continued, and like Germany and Korea, Japan would have risked becoming partitioned. When trying to comprehend how tragic this war was, we must recognize that Japan too might have ended up divided. Children must learn that this was another potential tragedy caused by the "sneak attack" at Pearl Harbor.

In short, children should be taught that the Potsdam Proclamation was instrumental in saving Japan.[4] They will thereby learn that some Americans, through their decisions and actions, were sympathetic towards Japan. Conversely, it should also be taught that regrettably Korea, without a champion like Joseph Grew, was partitioned and later suffered a tragic civil war.

When and How Historical Facts are Made Known

History isn't just a matter of bringing facts together. It's also important to know when and how these facts are made known to the public.

Only after the war did the American public learn, albeit in a haphazard way, the little-known facts about the "sneak attack" at Pearl Harbor. This "sneak attack" had made the war between Japan and the United States more tragic than was necessary. During the war, they weren't properly aware of the complete context of the frequently shouted slogan "Remember Pearl Harbor!" They only learned the whole story, in a piecemeal fashion, when the Joint Congressional Committee on the investigation of the Pearl Harbor attack was convened between November 1945 and May 1946, and when the report of the findings of that investigation was made available.

This problem was mirrored on the Japanese side. Or rather, the facts were transformed and became even further warped in Japan's case, under the particular circumstances of the Occupation.

The Japanese public knew that the war with the United States began with the Imperial Japanese Navy's surprise attack at Pearl Harbor, but had no idea during the war that the Allied forces had finessed this into a "sneak attack." They only learned this after the war during the proceedings of the Tokyo Trial. It was, however, impossible at the time to discuss questions related to the "sneak attack," questions such as what significance the "sneak attack" had, or under what circumstances it had occurred, or whether any particular individual was responsible for it. They only learned about it indirectly and in a piecemeal fashion through the Tokyo Trial, and not directly from the Foreign Ministry that had been directly responsible for this blunder. In fact, it was as late as November 1994 before the Foreign Ministry formally recognized the "sneak attack" as a blunder, and in effect apologized to the Japanese public. Until that point, the Foreign Ministry had made no formal apology at all to the Japanese public.[5]

History is the task of interpreting the past, but the Japanese government's more-than-fifty–year silence over its responsibility for this tragic blunder, and how the war began by a "sneak attack," is highly abnormal. The government has distorted the truth, and the Japanese people have been forced to accept a truth distorted by their own government.

Therefore, interpreting history does not just mean correctly knowing historical facts, but must also include knowing when and how these facts were discovered and made known.

Postwar America's Goals for the Occupation

The study of history, as previously noted, means having a sound interpretation of the past; and this is particularly true regarding World War II, which produced so many victims. It is also an obligation for later generations, so the teaching of history in our schools plays an important role in achieving that objective.

The war between Japan and the United States ended with Japan's acceptance of the Potsdam Proclamation, at the same time the Soviet Union entered the war. Though not a participant in the war against Japan when the Potsdam Proclamation was issued, the Soviet Union shortly thereafter joined the Allied nations against Japan. Children must learn that the Soviet Union, by entering the war against Japan, was in violation of the Japan-Soviet Neutrality Pact. That is, the Neutrality Pact (concluded April 13, 1941) was in effect for five years, with the possibility of extension. Even though the Soviet Union notified Japan on April 5, 1945, that it would not renew the pact, the agreement nonetheless remained valid until April 1946. Despite this, the Soviet Union invaded Japan on August 9, 1945.

Furthermore, in June 1941 when war between Germany and the Soviet Union broke out, Japan upheld the Pact and did not attack the Soviet Union at its most vulnerable time. It should be made clear that the Soviet Union, confident in 1941 that Japan would not attack, diverted troops from its Siberian front to the war against the Germans; as a result, it categorically waged a more effective war against Germany.

The Soviet Union's participation in the war against Japan was not, however, entirely its own idea, but was also done at the request of President Roosevelt. It could in fact be said that the "sneak attack" at Pearl Harbor had some influence here.

Thus the war ended, and Japan was occupied by American troops. What was the goal of that occupation? While difficult to achieve at the elementary school level, children at the junior high school level must learn what the United States's goal for the Occupation was. Otherwise, there is no way to properly understand postwar Japan. The Occupation's goals were expressed in the State Department's "United States Initial Post-Surrender Policy Relating to Japan" dated September 22, 1945, and subsequently delivered to Supreme Commander of the Occupying Forces General Douglas MacArthur. The ultimate goal was "to insure that Japan will not again become a menace to the United States or to the peace and security of the world." However, because of deep regret over the failure to deal properly with Germany after the end of World War I, the actual policy was to psychologically disarm the Japanese so they would no longer be hostile towards the United States, while ensuring the permanent military superiority of the United States over Japan.

On the one hand, it was correct to psychologically disarm the Japanese people, and remove Japan's militaristic tendencies that supported the use of force to achieve national goals. However, one tangible corollary to this was that Japan would never again become a military threat to the United States, and that military retaliation against the United States under any circumstances would be unthinkable.

In other words, it was thought that Japan and the Japanese people would never again engage in warfare even in extreme cases for a just cause, or even more extremely, for self defense and self preservation. The United States itself would never entertain such pacifist attitudes towards war, but it nevertheless steered a defeated Japan in this direction.

A similar problem arises regarding the issue of Japan's democratization. While the idea of democracy is plain enough, and deals with the ordinary issues of people's lives and their relationships, defeated Japan was made to embrace the "democracy" determined by the Occupation, which included the goal of psychologically disarming the Japanese people. However, although democracy in the United States had little to do with militarism, neither did it include any notion of disarmament that absolutely excluded fighting for a just cause. Logically it follows therefore that the democracy Japan acquiesced to was somehow incomplete, and that Japan's democratization was flawed.

The forces of the Occupation saved the Japanese people from starvation and democratized every social system, not for any ulterior motive but as a worthy humanitarian policy; it would therefore be inappropriate to suspect that the United States, known for its humanitarian character, had any other motives. However, children must be taught that these humanitarian policies and the democratization of Japan also resulted in the psychological disarmament of the Japanese people. Put another way, the Occupation also had other goals apart from saving the Japanese people and democratizing Japan.

The Japanese people must understand that the Occupation's humanitarian policies, such as rescuing the Japanese from starvation and Japan's democratization, caused confusion as to why they had fought so hard against the U. S. in the first place, and what the war really meant. Generally, the inhabitants of defeated nations are condemned to harsh and tragic lives. However, Japan's defeat in this war paradoxically resolved many problems in Japan, beginning with the more immediate need for food and humanitarian assistance, but also long-standing social issues such as female suffrage and agricultural reform. Little wonder then that the Japanese people were confused why they had fought so hard against the United States.

The way in which the occupying forces carried out Occupation policies was ingeniously devised. While carrying out numerous humanitarian measures, war criminals were also thoroughly investigated under the terms of the Potsdam Proclamation. A strict censorship system was enforced, and the Japanese were not permitted to freely debate the meaning of the war with the United States or who was responsible for it.

Furthermore, the American interpretation of who was responsible for the war and who had started it was forced upon Japan, and soon permeated the nation.

In other words, the Occupation promulgated the interpretation that Japan was totally to blame for the war, and this interpretation spread. At the root of this evil was Japanese militarism. To prove this the United States, which had persuaded the Soviet Union to abrogate the Japan-Soviet Neutrality Pact in the closing stages of the war, even though Japan had upheld it earlier and thereby spared the Soviet Union from a crisis, was happy to portray Japan as an evil nation. And the embodiment of this evil was "militarism."

The Tokyo Trial can be interpreted in many ways, but ultimately Japan was forced to assume total responsibility for starting and pursuing the war; it is clear from the prevailing world environment that the Trial was merely an international showcase to announce to the world that the root of this evil was Japanese "militarism." It also explains why death tolls for the Nanking Incident, and other events, were misstated.

Foreign Ministry's Cover-Up of War Responsibility

Let us now look at how the actions of the Occupation forces are related to the Foreign Ministry's cover-up of its war responsibility.

The fourth article of the Potsdam Proclamation stated, "The time has come for Japan to decide whether she will continue to be controlled by those self-willed milita[r]istic advisers whose unintelligent calculations have brought the Empire of Japan to the threshold of annihilation, or whether she will follow the path of reason." This was the U. S. government's official view and interpretation of why Japan went to war with the United States and other nations in Asia.

Obviously, in historical terms, "unintelligent calculations" is an extremely simplistic observation. MacArthur's statement to the U. S. Senate on May 3, 1951, that "[Japan's] purpose...in going to war was largely dictated by security" has been totally overlooked.[6] He made this observation upon returning to the United States after being relieved of duty as supreme commander of the occupying forces. While it can be argued that militarism itself was undesirable, and that overall conditions in prewar Japan leading to its emergence were less than sensible, it can also be said, objectively, that such conditions were nevertheless present and made its emergence easier, or inevitable.

The United States's interpretation of the origins of the war, as stated in the Potsdam Proclamation, also benefited Japan. If "militarism" was the source of evil, then Japan as a whole was not "evil." However, by shifting the entire blame for the war from Japan and the Japanese people to militarism, and by turning militarism into a scapegoat for all problems concerning the war, those who were indeed responsible for the war could easily evade their responsibility.

At the beginning of the Occupation, the occupying forces regarded the Imperial Japanese Army and Navy as the main proponents of militarism, but also saw the Foreign Ministry, which administered Japan's foreign policy, in the same light. They had, in those early days, also considered dismantling the Foreign Ministry.

Respect for the national integrity of Japan was partly responsible for preserving the Foreign Ministry. This was because after Japan surrendered by accepting the Potsdam Proclamation, a small vestige of Japanese sovereignty had to be maintained. However, the Foreign Ministry also avoided dismantlement by persuading the occupying forces that it could assist in smoothly implementing Occupation policies, and by showing full cooperation with the Occupation's absolute authority.[7]

As soon as its continued existence was approved, the Foreign Ministry became an organ of the occupying forces rather than the Japanese people. Although originally targeted for dismantling, the Foreign Ministry owed its preservation entirely to the occupying forces, and would have ceased to exist had it not cooperated with those forces. The Foreign Ministry no longer existed for the Japanese people, but only to transmit the will of the occupying forces to the Japanese people. In other words, the Foreign Ministry considered cooperation with the occupying forces on their policies to be more important than what it thought of the Japanese people. The Foreign Ministry indeed excelled in this function, and lost the chance to reflect on its role as a major proponent of militarism during the war.

When the United States Joint Congressional Committee was convened between November 1945 and May 1946 to investigate the Pearl Harbor attack, great progress was made towards clearing up the circumstances surrounding the start of the war. For the first time, the American public learned that President Roosevelt had read every important Japanese diplomatic cable before the war started. They also discovered that the war had not begun in the manner which Japan had intended. It was demonstrated, albeit indirectly, that Japanese diplomacy had not wanted to challenge the United States; rather there was a strong desire to avoid war, and the onset of war was a fundamental error in Japanese diplomacy.

Seeing Japan's miserable state after it surrendered, representatives of the occupying forces and the American government must have wondered in amazement how such a poor country could ever have challenged the United States with its enormous resources. The American people, too, must have wondered about this.

Gordon T. Bowles, the State Department's representative in the first education mission to Japan, arrived in Japan in March 1946 and was a key figure in writing the mission's first "Report." Bowles, who sympathized with Japan, set about developing the State Department's Occupation policy. Many years later, this author met with Bowles and asked him directly about this issue. Bowles replied that, at the time, many people in the State Department went about their work "but had no idea why Japan went to war, nor why Japan thought it could win."[8]

Likewise, the American people had no idea about the circumstances of the start of the war. When more details about conditions in Japan emerged during the Congressional investigation of Pearl Harbor, and during the Occupation, some became somewhat sympathetic. The Foreign Ministry used this sympathy, along with its own clever machinations, to escape its past as a major proponent of militarism. Even though the occupying forces knew the Foreign Ministry was just as responsible for the war as Japan's military, they tacitly agreed to overlook the Ministry's militarist past; this was partly due to a general sympathy for Japan, but also because of the Ministry's zeal in carrying out Occupation wishes without antagonizing the occupying forces.

Viewed in this light, by cooperating with the occupying forces in this way the Foreign Ministry enjoyed enormous benefits under the Occupation system.

How was the Pearl Harbor issue, a fatal disgrace for the Foreign Ministry, dealt with during the Occupation?

The United States's motive for investigating the Pearl Harbor issue was to determine how an enemy was able to launch such a damaging assault, regardless of whether it was a surprise attack or a "sneak attack." On the other hand, Japan should have examined this issue to determine why the Pearl Harbor campaign became a "sneak attack" contrary to the Japanese government's original intention, what influence it later had on the war with the United States, and how the issue was dealt with after the fact. However, the Japanese public were unable to debate this issue at all under the strict censorship of the Occupation. It was impossible to independently investigate, examine, or discuss this issue in any way.

What little the Japanese knew about the "sneak attack" which had started the war with the United States, they learned indirectly through the Tokyo Trial. Although they found out it had been caused by an administrative error at the Washington embassy, they didn't know from this fragmentary information whether anyone was directly responsible.[9] Under the Occupation's strict censorship, it wasn't possible to freely report on the "sneak attack." The "sneak attack" issue was neither resolved nor debated, the Foreign Ministry made no apology, and time elapsed as though the issue had been cleared up.

The Foreign Ministry thus cooperated with the occupying forces while enjoying tangible benefits under the Occupation system. Conversely, when the Ministry tacitly agreed to ignore its past support of militarism, it used the Occupation, under which the Japanese people were unable to debate things freely, to guide Japanese public opinion into redirecting all the Ministry's war responsibility onto the military and militarism. In other words, with the tacit understanding of the Occupying forces, the Ministry blamed everything on the military and militarism, effectively erased its past support of militarism, and evaded its own responsibility.

Many Japanese nowadays believe some amorphous and vaguely defined "militarism" caused the war. This phenomenon can be directly attributed to the perspectives and interpretations held by the occupying powers during the Occupation. However, another reason is that the

Foreign Ministry took advantage of the Occupation system to spread these perspectives and evade its own war responsibility.

One might even argue that the Foreign Ministry ought to have been dismantled. Because the Imperial Japanese Army and Navy were abolished, there was more than enough justification to do the same to the Foreign Ministry.

The Foreign Ministry must bear more war responsibility than the military because it let militarism emerge, indeed was an active proponent of it, and then allowed the critical negotiations with the United States in 1941, originally a diplomatic matter, to end in failure with the outbreak of war. Apart from the general conclusion that it bungled these negotiations, it is also responsible for failing to acquaint prewar America with Japan's position, so much so that the postwar American public would be puzzled why Japan under such pitiful conditions would challenge a powerful nation like the United States. It is also guilty of failing to infer the hidden intentions in Roosevelt and Hull's proposals. In addition, the delay in delivering the "declaration of war" magnified all these misunderstandings by the American public in an unprecedented manner. Even the Japanese people would have agreed that the Foreign Ministry should have been dismantled because of these enormous mistakes.

The occupying forces had ample grounds for dismantling the Foreign Ministry, as they had done with the Imperial Japanese Army and Navy, because of the Ministry's responsibility for militarist diplomatic policies. Indeed, the Japanese public would have been furious had it been aware of its bumbling diplomacy. The Foreign Ministry, which by rights ought to have been scathingly criticized by the Japanese people, used the Occupation system to escape criticism. By cooperating with the Occupation, the Ministry faced no criticism for its betrayal of the Japanese people from the occupying forces either.

The Foreign Ministry's charmed existence under the Occupation reached a final phase. When the Occupation was lifted, the Ministry was installed into Japan's government apparatus with its propensity to distort the facts fully intact. That is, as the Occupation was being lifted, the Ministry deliberately recalled and promoted to vice foreign ministers the two officials at the Washington embassy who were directly responsible for the blunder which caused the "sneak attack" at Pearl Harbor.

Promoting these two men after all the mistakes they had made to such high positions would be unimaginable nowadays. Without a doubt, it would be impossible. However, Japan had then just emerged from a seven-year period of occupation, and although the Japanese people knew the facts of the "sneak attack" through the Tokyo Trial, they had been unable to debate it and assumed the issue had been completely resolved. In less than seven years, Japan's "linguistic space" had been totally distorted. It was under these conditions that the two men directly responsible for the "sneak attack" were openly promoted to vice foreign ministers. One might even say that the Foreign Ministry ensured its continued existence by selling out the honor of the Japanese people and nation, and clinching its own security.

The Foreign Ministry and the Fiftieth Anniversary of Pearl Harbor

The Foreign Ministry's behavior and influence in the years after the Occupation are also clearly problematic. During the Occupation, it froze and perpetuated, domestically, the transference of its war responsibility onto the military. Then it created a biased, distorted and unfair critique of militarism, and perpetuated this in Japanese society also.

Naturally, the Foreign Ministry probably didn't want the Japanese people freely discussing its past war crimes. However, by promoting the two officials directly responsible for the "sneak attack" to vice foreign ministers, the Ministry not only showed how much it wanted to avoid any discussion of its war responsibility, it revealed its absolute desire as a national institution not to allow any such discussion. In other words, the Foreign Ministry pooled the resources of its staff, regardless of their individual convictions, to trap the Japanese people into the "warped linguistic space" created during the Occupation; it blamed militarism completely for the war, conducted distorted critiques of militarism, and would not brook any discussion of the Ministry's war responsibility. After even the briefest debate about this war responsibility, the Japanese people would surely have identified soon enough the scandal of promoting the two officials directly responsible for the "sneak attack" to vice foreign ministers.

In fact, the following examples clearly illustrate how the Foreign Ministry tried to manipulate the Japanese people in this way.

In 1991, during the fiftieth anniversary of the attack on Pearl Harbor, the Foreign Ministry took great pains to avoid marking this fifty-year milestone. Nevertheless, the foreign minister and others were finally unable to avoid the questions put to them by foreign media, and it is in their responses that we observe a continuation of the Ministry's manipulative behavior. Then-Foreign Minister Michio Watanabe's statement was dealt with in the previous chapter, so let's look at the statement by then-Prime Minister Kiichi Miyazawa. He admitted that the Japanese are "deeply aware of the responsibility [for entering] World War II with the attack on Pearl Harbor, and we inflicted unbearable damage and sorrow on the peoples of the United States, the Pacific and Asia."[10] As Watanabe had done, Miyazawa ducked the issue and addressed the question of the overall war, at a time when attention was focused on the "sneak attack" at Pearl Harbor. Watanabe even went as far as explicitly raising the military's war responsibility.[11] The normally apologetic Foreign Ministry had still not apologized to the United States regarding the "sneak attack" issue. Quite the reverse is true: rather than apologize, the Ministry to that day had not publicly acknowledged that the Pearl Harbor "sneak attack" was caused by an administrative blunder at the Washington embassy. To the Japanese people, this acknowledgment and an apology of sorts did not come until November 20, 1994, 53 years after the fact.[12]

Furthermore, the Foreign Ministry encouraged Japan to forget the accomplishments of Joseph Grew, U. S. ambassador to Japan when war broke out, and whose efforts to draw up the Potsdam Proclamation surely prevented Japan from being partitioned. It did this because honoring Grew's achievements would have meant allowing the Japanese public to examine the diplomatic blunder that lead to the outbreak of war. As discussed in the previous chapter, Grew was awarded high honors in 1960 during the centennial anniversary of friendly relations between Japan and the United States. The Ministry surpassed itself though by bestowing the same rank of honors on all former American ambassadors, rather than allowing Grew's honors to stand out.

As will be discussed in more detail later in this book, Chiune Sugihara, who saved the lives of 6,000 Jewish refugees, was dismissed in June 1947 at the peak of his career for disobeying orders. The Foreign Ministry probably did this to demonstrate its cooperation with the Occupation forces who were focusing their efforts on the Tokyo Trial, and as part of its distorted critique of militarism. The Foreign Ministry publicly acknowledged the merit of Sugihara's actions only after he passed away. For the first time, on November 3, 1991, Parliamentary Vice-Minister for Foreign Affairs Muneo Suzuki met with Sugihara's widow, Yukiko, at the Iikura Government Building. (Strictly speaking though, it is unclear whether this meeting rehabilitated Chiune's damaged reputation.) In 1969, Sugihara received a medal of honor from Israel's Minister of Religion Zorach Warhaftig; in 1985, he received the "Righteous Among Nations" award from the Israeli government, and the city of Jerusalem erected a monument to honor his achievements. However, Japan's Foreign Ministry continued to ignore these awards, even when Sugihara passed away in 1986. In 1991, a memorial to Sugihara was erected and a street named after him in Lithuania, the place where he had issued the visas, and the matter gained global exposure. It was then that Vice-Minister Suzuki, who could no longer ignore the problem, met with Yukiko Sugihara. Reportedly, there was even then great resistance within the Ministry to Suzuki's meeting with Yukiko. This alone shows how the Foreign Ministry, which during the Occupation sold out Japan to arrange its own security, was working against the people's interest, and was conducting diplomacy not on behalf of the people, but rather on its own behalf.

This demonstrates how the Foreign Ministry, even after the Occupation, continued to imprison the Japanese people in the "warped linguistic space" it created during the Occupation, and went on leading Japan in the wrong direction and manipulating history. Under Shigeru Yoshida's initiative, the Foreign Ministry's tendency to work against the people's interest became fixed and was perpetuated through the promotion, around the time the Occupation was lifted, of the two officials directly responsible for the Pearl Harbor "sneak attack."

As foreign minister, Shigeru Yoshida met immediately after the war had ended with Kantarō Suzuki, the prime minister at the time of Japan's surrender. Yoshida was deeply saddened when told to "put a brave face on defeat."[13] However, for Yoshida to "put a brave face on defeat" was like throwing the baby out with the bath water. It was nothing unusual for Yoshida, who started his career in the Foreign Ministry, and became foreign minister and later prime minister.

What has resulted from this foolishness? The Japanese people's understanding of history has been warped, they have become satisfied with the Ministry's distorted critique of militarism, and they continue to live in a "warped linguistic space." Under these conditions, creating a new national identity is impossible.

Senior high school students who take an interest in history must be treated as adults, and must be guided beyond their present understanding of the war with the United States and the war in Asia. Treating history as a social science can only lead to a broader education.

Japan's War Crimes

Although the interpretation held in the United States that militarism made Japan morally corrupt was not totally without foundation, children should learn that in the era when the Occupation unilaterally forced this interpretation upon Japan, nations could legitimately use war as the means to resolve international disputes. In "modern" times, war is generally considered an extension of diplomacy, which is why there are international laws covering it, and why it was considered a suitable method to resolve disputes between nations. Furthermore, war was an ethical course of action. Strictly speaking, the notion that war was a crime didn't exist before World War II. The occupying forces considered Japan to be morally corrupt because of militarism; to unilaterally force this interpretation upon Japan, it had to redefine the act of waging war as a crime.

Children will be unsure why this way of thinking about war was accepted before World War II. Nowadays, war is generally not condoned. Any history lesson which doesn't explain this in a way that children can properly understand is somehow deficient. The study of history must include present-day views, but would not be complete without some understanding of the perspectives and ways of thinking from the period in question.

One way to help children understand this issue is to ask them to imagine a time when fighting and taking revenge were commonplace in society. When police organs and court systems were unable to deal with disputes within a society, it was accepted that those who suffered damages or were drawn into a conflict over personal interests would settle their own disputes by fighting or taking revenge. Similarly, before international organizations like the League of Nations existed, war was the recognized method of resolving disputes between nations.

However, simply recognizing the right to wage war did not mean sanctioning every action taken in a war. In ancient times, war was practically a free-for-all; but rules for waging war were eventually developed which strictly defined what was acceptable wartime behavior. Acts which were considered unacceptable were designated as "war crimes." War crimes recognized under international law, at the time Japan went to war against the United States in 1941, concerned behavior such as the ill treatment of prisoners, and so on.

Let's take a moment to put the German massacre of Jews into context. During that era, a national plan for the organized extermination of a particular race was not considered a conventional "war crime," nor would it have been considered a normal crime of war. Although this lapse itself was indefensible, those nations who committed such massacres were nevertheless surely criminal.

Japan joined the Tripartite Pact with Germany and Italy, but never had a national plan for the extensive massacre of a particular race of people. To the contrary, there were Japanese like Chiune Sugihara who saved the lives of 6,000 Jews. If Sugihara's courage had been announced in Japan and abroad during the Occupation, suspicions about Japanese militarism may have been somewhat allayed. However, although it knew about Sugihara's achievements (or precisely because it did know), the Foreign Ministry, which pushed all war responsibility onto the military and took pains to hide its own responsibility, made no use of this information.

It is worthwhile to compare the organized German massacre of the Jews with the Nanking Incident of 1937. Although the violent excesses of Japanese troops clearly caused the illegal deaths of Chinese troops and civilians, there is now ample evidence to show there was no so-called organized slaughter campaign by the Japanese military.[14]

Moreover, while it is widely known that the Japanese military conducted research into biological warfare, Hideki Tōjō never recognized this for use in ordinary campaigns.[15] It must be understood that research on biological warfare was conducted at a critical stage of the war, and was considered legitimate. No-one knew if the enemy was also engaged in this sort of research, so Japan had to do likewise and produce counter measures to resist the enemy in case the other side used what it had developed; although experimentation on live human subjects should not have been condoned, the research itself was legitimate. It was a situation comparable to when the United States suspected Germany was developing its own nuclear bomb, and worked on developing one; after successfully completing it, the U. S. actually used it on Japan.

The Importance of Properly Reviewing and Understanding the War's Outcome

However, we cannot stop here if we want to teach children about the significance of the war between Japan and the United States. They should also learn the war provided the conditions that determined the nature of Japan's postwar existence, including the period of postwar economic prosperity.

Let's consider the following. Troops from the United States are presently stationed in Japan due to the Treaty of Mutual Cooperation and Security between Japan and the United States, and Japan has consequently enjoyed freedom from external threats. Although postwar Japan has not maintained adequate military forces, it has never been concerned about being drawn into a conflict with any other country. Japan has maintained self-defense forces to protect itself in case of attack, but these alone could never wholly guarantee its security. National security could only truly be secured by taking into consideration massive numbers of troops stationed by the U. S. Furthermore, this military relationship has never been an equal one. The United States did not station troops in Japan solely for Japan's defense; they could also be deployed at any time to the region surrounding Japan, in accordance with American objectives.

Japan was the first country to suffer a nuclear attack on its population, and it does not possess nuclear weapons. However, it would be specious to claim that Japan does not enjoy nuclear capabilities. The threat of nuclear attack upon Japan is considerably lessened thanks to the United States's nuclear umbrella. Therefore, Japan is no less dependent on nuclear weapons simply by not possessing them. At the same time, if Japan was to renounce nuclear research, it would never possess nuclear weapons, and would have to recognize American nuclear superiority over Japan in perpetuity. To that extent, Japan would have to always recognize a bilateral relationship in which it could never resist the United States.

Could the sort of relationship Japan has with the United States have been possible if Japan had not gone to war, been defeated, and then been occupied? Could it have arisen through peaceful negotiation? To explore this issue, children could be asked to think through the following exercise. For instance, could Japan and Korea have concluded an agreement like the Japan-U. S. Security Treaty, with Japanese defense forces stationed in Korea? Or vice versa: could Korea and Japan have concluded a bilateral security treaty allowing Korean troops to be stationed in Japan, and would Japan have immediately accepted Korean troops, upon Korea's request and after due consultation? Disregarding for the moment Japan's relationship with the United States, would Japan immediately accept a request from China, another military superpower, that it be allowed to station troops in Japan? If none of these scenarios seem plausible, why was it possible then that such a relationship was constructed with only the United States? The postwar Japan-U. S. relationship was only established because of the war. If Japan's postwar economic prosperity was also based on this relationship, then it too was a consequence of the war between Japan and the United States.

Let's consider some other aspects of this economic prosperity. While Japan's postwar economic development was largely due to the diligence and exertions of the Japanese people, we should also be aware of other conditions produced by the war that made this economic development through hard work possible.

When the United States was at war with Japan, it probably did not anticipate that postwar Japan would make such remarkable economic progress. As the Cold War deepened though, it had to accept Japan's speedy economic growth so as not to undermine the stability and strength of the American camp, as well as to maintain the prestige and superiority of the liberal economic system. Consequently, the United States actively supported Japan's economic growth. Although the waters around Japan had once isolated it like an endless barrier, commercial shipping developed dramatically after World War II; the oceans now linked nations, ushering in an era of ever cheaper shipping routes.

Another important condition was the worldwide disappointment over the economic malaise produced by trading blocs during the war. A liberal world trade system subsequently emerged after World War II, which made free trade possible despite international political differences. It was indeed a peaceful global trade system based on structures which emerged for the first time as a result of this tragic war.

In any case, children should learn that Japan's postwar economic development was possible because of these various factors. They will then come to appreciate that Japan's postwar economic prosperity is intimately tied to the war. The statement made by General MacArthur to the U. S. Senate on May 3, 1951, that "[Japan's] purpose...in going to war was largely dictated by security," raised an issue of critical importance concerning Japan's survival.[16]

Of course despite Japan's economic development, it would have been preferable if Japan had never gone to war. It would obviously have been better if Japan had attained its present level of economic prosperity without going to war. However, could this have been realized through peaceful negotiation, without any sort of conflict with the United States? It bears remembering that the present amicable relationship between Japan and the United States which brought about Japan's economic prosperity, and the peaceful international climate that Japan now enjoys, came into existence precisely because of this military confrontation between Japan and the United States. It should also be remembered that, when this Japan-U. S. war broke out, war was generally accepted as unavoidable when resolving international conflicts. Taking these aspects into account, war between Japan and the United States may well have been inevitable. This alone further demonstrates that human history unfolds gradually in stages.

With these issues in mind, we must develop a proper understanding of the war, clarify who was responsible, and eliminate mistaken and half-baked assessments. This is how children in future should be educated about the war. It should be possible for junior high school students, after patient explanation, to have a complete understanding of the war between Japan and the United States.

For junior high students, it might also be good to raise the issue of why Japanese don't have a rational nor comprehensive view of the war. To explain this, they should learn that, as previously mentioned, the Foreign Ministry has concealed its war responsibility. While the Foreign Ministry, which carried out Japanese diplomacy, had great responsibility for the war, it concealed this fact and placed the blame on the military and militarism. Because of this, it will not, indeed cannot, point out how unfair it is to be confronted by exaggerated criticisms from abroad that are unsupported by the facts. Although other countries criticize Japan for carrying out a war of aggression (which, in general terms, it was), from Japan's perspective this war also involved issues such as *jison jiei* (self-existence and self-defense), and the task of liberating Asia. Why are these two issues never pointed out? It is because they cannot be pointed out. Since the Foreign Ministry has diverted responsibility for the war elsewhere and fabricated history, and has also been subjected to unfair criticism over militarism, it cannot point these things out even if it wanted to. It simply cannot be done.

The Foreign Ministry's inaction about things that should be pointed out, and its passivity towards foreign countries, continues to prevent any proper domestic discussion of the war between Japan and the United States. The people of Japan continue to view things in a distorted way, and remain imprisoned in a "warped linguistic space."

While the start of the war with the United States was clearly a blunder by Japanese diplomacy, this fact is simply not pointed out. Or rather, cannot be pointed out. Nowadays, people simply substitute the issue of militarism. The problem of the "sneak attack" at Pearl Harbor, which caused the war to become more tragic than was ever necessary, is not or cannot be questioned. People like Chiune Sugihara, who saved the lives of 6,000 Jewish refugees, are not or cannot be publicly honored. The accomplishments of Joseph Grew, who went to great lengths to save Japan from being partitioned, are not and cannot be recognized. In other words, this is all because the Foreign Ministry, during the Occupation and postwar period, has consistently covered up its war responsibility, and has not done what it ought to have done. Junior high school students should learn about these things.

Although not directly related to the Foreign Ministry, senior high school students should also learn about an issue relevant to the Occupation and therefore the war between Japan and the United States, namely the Japanese constitution's war-renouncing clause that has confused Japanese education, and befuddled postwar Japan. The Japanese constitution was established by the occupying forces and forced upon Japan. Article 9 is the notorious "war-renouncing" article. Since this article doesn't deny Japan the right to self-defense, Japan today possesses self-defense forces for protection (and therefore accepts the legitimacy of wars in self-defense). As previously stated, the Japan-U. S. Security Treaty allows for American troops to be stationed in Japan, and according to American objectives these troops are free to conduct military activities beyond the defense of Japan. However the "war-renouncing" article prohibits Japanese troops from participating in any such military actions not directly involved with the defense of Japan.

This "war-renouncing" article, however, relates directly to other parts of the Japanese constitution. For instance, the preamble to the constitution states, "We [the Japanese people] have determined to preserve our security and existence, trusting in the justice and faith of the peace-loving peoples of the world." And: "We desire to occupy an honored place in…international society." Nevertheless, Japan does not participate in multinational forces authorized by numerous United Nations resolutions to resolve international disputes, nor in global military activities conducted by United Nations or multinational troops, which in a broad sense are the world's police force. Japan maintains the cunning interpretation that it can renounce war while letting other countries take military action to protect Japan from aggression, even though Japan does not participate in military activities to aid others. This interpretation of the constitution was not forced upon it by the United States, but was voluntarily and perversely acquired by Japan after the war and in particular during the Occupation. This cunning interpretation of the constitution is the result of the overreaction by Japan to a policy the Occupation forced upon it, namely, the psychological disarmament of the Japanese people. At the very least, this should be taught at senior high school.

Paradoxes in Japan's Defeat

Senior high school students should also learn that the complexities of the war between Japan and the United States produced certain paradoxes as a result of Japan's defeat. The teaching of this should be allowed.

In a general sense, until World War I war was the method by which nations resolved their disputes, and it was never necessary to directly tackle the issue of which side was right. Japan too, until the Russo-Japanese War, waged war purely for the good of the nation. However, World War II was waged in the name of justice. It must be made clear to the Japanese people that Japan also had a just cause which forced it to combat the great might of the United States. The American government had to educate its people, who originally favored isolationism, about the importance of the just cause they had to fight for. For Japan, the just causes were namely self-existence and self-defense, and the liberation of Asia. Ironically, Japan heralded the liberation of Asia while it annexed Korea and failed to reach a peaceful compromise with China, resulting in unethical yet unavoidable contradictions. Nevertheless, from Japan's perspective the liberation of the nations of Asia, most of which had been colonized by Europe and the United States, was indeed a just cause. Conversely, why did the American side fight? For the protection of freedom and democracy. These were clearly just causes too.

Therefore, this war was one waged in the name of justice. What does this mean? It means that the just causes fought for by the winning side were recognized by the world as being just. The winning side's justice was promulgated throughout the world as the world's definition of justice. Conversely, what happened to the losing side? The causes it held to be just were not acknowledged as such, and the losing side (Japan) was treated as though it had committed evil. That is, because Japan lost the war it was branded as an evil nation.

But what happened in reality? The Soviet Union, which had only joined the countries allied against Japan a week before Japan's surrender, agreed with the Hitler regime in September 1939 to divide and occupy Poland, thus making the Soviet Union one of the nations whose invasion started World War II. The Soviet Union's entry into the war against Japan was in direct violation of the still-valid Japan-Soviet Neutrality Pact which, incidentally, Japan had observed in mid 1941 when the Soviet Union was in an extremely critical position. Clearly, not all aspects of the Allied war against Japan were just.

What does it mean though if Japan was thought to have committed such "evil" that it merited being attacked in such an unreasonable and illegal manner? Illegal acts committed by the Allied nations are written off as just actions necessary to defeat this "evil." This illegal behavior is rehabilitated, and is considered appropriate action for realizing the greater cause of justice.

In other words, although World War II was fought for just causes and began because Japan was an "evil" country, this "evil" nature was only determined after Japan was defeated. This form of justice was merely a sleight of hand arranged by the victors.

Treating Japan as an evil nation meant, conversely, the United States had to behave like a just one. That is, although the United States won the war, it could not directly benefit in the way winning empires had previously done; this was because, as the just winner, it was restrained by the notion of justice it itself had championed. In a greater sense, the liberation of the colonized peoples of Asia and the foundation of Israel were realized by the justice that restrained the winning nations. Japan paradoxically contributed to the spreading of this justice, even though as a loser nation it was unilaterally branded as evil by the winners who were restrained by this notion of justice. It should also be taught that the idea that human history was advanced because war was now considered a crime, resulted from the fact that Japan fought a war, lost it, and was subsequently treated as a criminal nation. It should be possible for senior high school students, after patient explanation, to understand this paradox.[17]

Treating Historical Science as a Social Science

We have considered above what Japanese education should teach about the war between Japan and the United States. Let me indicate here though to the teachers of Japan the need to be aware that the teaching of modern and contemporary history also involves elements and perspectives from the social sciences.

Historical science is considered to be one of the humanities, which generally examines the working of the human spirit. However, it should be recognized there are also elements and perspectives from the social sciences which inform our understanding of modern and contemporary history, because these are closely related to how society in the future will be run. In other words, modern and contemporary history changes the way society in the future is run, in accordance with how past events in modern and contemporary times are evaluated.

Historical science is something we use to gain a proper understanding of the past, but we must first acknowledge that, strictly speaking, there is no fixed definition for what is meant by "proper" in this context. That is, there is strictly no way of knowing which particular understanding is the "proper" one. Moreover, it must be acknowledged that we may not even be able to understand the times we live through

exactly as they unfold, much less the past where the amount of historical and other materials is limited. Often, contemporary values inform
our perspectives and become entwined in those perspectives. It must be
conceded therefore that it may never be possible to completely understand the past exactly as it happened. Since the understanding of modern
and contemporary history is intimately linked to having a firm grasp of
how society will be run in the future, an understanding of the nature of
the social sciences is essential. In other words, a "proper" understanding
can only be determined, in relative terms, through the fair and open
debate by a society's members. During that process, perspectives which
are false, biased, or distorted can, at the very least, be pointed out and
eliminated. Through this process, we can gradually approach an understanding of the past which, in relative terms, can be considered "proper."

One research method indispensable to the social sciences is "open
debate." Through debate, matters relevant to society can be thoroughly
examined and become more widely known to individual members of
society, and thereby contribute to society. While postwar Japan
obviously is in consensus that it has attained democracy, isn't a truly
democratic society ultimately one where its individual members are
completely free to debate matters concerning the running of that
society? If we accept that modern and contemporary history have
elements and perspectives of the social sciences, we must also recognize
that vigorous debates should be allowed. It is often pointed out that it is
easier to succeed in history lessons dealing with modern and
contemporary history if the "debate" method is incorporated, and this is
because the study of modern and contemporary history has elements of
the social sciences, and is consistent with social science methods.

The following point is also worth considering. Would the Japan-
U. S. war even have occurred if, before the war, the Japanese people had
vigorously debated the issue of war between Japan and the United
States? If there had been a thorough debate, extensive information about
the United States would have been available in Japan, and may even
have permeated down to ordinary people. Japan would therefore have
known earlier how impractical and unproductive the war would be.
Wouldn't serious moves to avoid war with the United States have
emerged in Japan much earlier? With more complete information, and
the ability to foresee the tragic outcome, would the Japanese people ever
have plunged into a war against the United States?

Before the war, there was in fact no freedom of expression in
everyday life in Japan due to strict curbs on speech and thought control
by the government. It is also true that this proved fatal for Japan, and

people's views gradually became even narrower. However the social sciences, which depend on debate to survive, were in reality already declining in strength long before this. After the war, a "U. S. Cultural Science Mission" arrived in Japan in 1948, and published its report the following year. In this context, "cultural science" included both the human and social sciences, but the report pointed out that "Japanese scholars repeatedly have admitted that their country has paid for [the] failure to nourish full grown social sciences."[18] It noted that in prewar Japan, the social sciences (namely, those concerned with the operation of society) were completely underdeveloped. What is essential for the development of these social sciences is obviously vigorous debate.

Perspectives and judgments made in the social sciences, unlike the natural sciences, are not directly derived from experiments and surveys. Strictly speaking, they emerge from human deliberation. The Greek philosopher Aristotle said in the *Eudamonia*: "While we use the things that we observe in our daily lives as evidence and examples, we must strive to obtain certainty through speech [debate]. That is...all people must come to be in clear agreement; but if this is not possible, then at the very least, the best thing is for all people to come to a clear agreement on a certain thing. Because if [through debate] people can be guided step by step, they should be able to reach some agreement."[19] This is exactly right. The process of debate is indispensable for producing more-meaningful perceptions and judgments, and for making these known throughout society. "Debate" for the social sciences is an essential and necessary process. Indeed, it is a fundamental element of the social sciences.

Therefore "debate" can broaden viewpoints and challenge fixed conclusions. This is something the social sciences must be mentally prepared for. A typical example is the notion that war between Japan and the United States may or may not have been avoided depending on how the time frame is defined. Frequently, something which in a certain context appears significant can be denied that significance from an even broader and larger context. This is an unavoidable part of treating history as a social science.

Teaching history on the premise that modern and contemporary history have elements and perspectives from the social sciences, probably allows educators to teach with a much broader vision. Having the proper perspective and understanding of the war, which sacrificed vast numbers of people and brought Japan to the brink of annihilation, is important for later generations, and requires maintaining a perspective steeped in the social sciences.

Chapter 3

Successfully Avoiding the Pacific War: Reexamining the Japan-U. S. Negotiations

Was War between Japan and the U. S. Avoidable?

Whether war between Japan and the United States could have been avoided depends, as discussed in detail in the previous chapter, on how the time frame is defined. Let's examine the negotiations between Japan and the United States that began after Roosevelt's reelection to a third term of office. Regardless of the outcome, the war that began on December 8, 1941 (Japan time), could have been avoided if the Foreign Ministry after receiving the Hull Note had properly assessed the situation and acted appropriately, that is, if it had fulfilled its function as normally expected of a government organ charged with a nation's foreign affairs. In this sense, the Foreign Ministry cannot evade its responsibility for war breaking out at this time.

In an unprecedented act, Roosevelt campaigned hard in the fall of 1940 for reelection to a third term as president. A terrible war in Europe had broken out, which later would be referred to as World War II. Poland had been partitioned by Germany and the Soviet Union, and France had already capitulated to the Germans. The Republican Party put up a strong challenge to stop Roosevelt's reelection, warning that he would embroil the United States in the European war. During all this, Roosevelt swore the following in a speech to the electorate: "I have said this before, but I shall say it again and again and again. Your boys are not going to be sent into any foreign wars."[1] It was an unrealistic compromise to make, given his conviction that the war in Europe simply could not be ignored in this way. However, Roosevelt's ability to make a compromise simply out of expediency was truly terrifying.

In any case Roosevelt was successfully reelected to a third term, but was consequently no longer able to bring about a war on his own initiative. Did Roosevelt actually disengage from the war in Europe though? If we assume he didn't, then he had to arrange to have war declared against the United States since he could no longer take the initiative himself. In fact, Roosevelt was very interested in war, and while not apparent to outside observers, in June 1940 in the latter stages of his second term, he had already taken measures to carry out research on the atomic bomb.[2]

While relations then between Japan and the United States were difficult, the Japanese government clearly should have been analyzing the situation in this manner. However there is no evidence that the government of the day had performed any such analysis. Japan's military, and the Foreign Ministry which was in charge of diplomacy, must bear a grave responsibility. Their inability to perceive the strategic maneuver implicit in the Hull Note when it was thrust upon Japan, was a consequence of their failure to carry out this analysis beforehand.

After Roosevelt secured his third term, Japan took steps to make peace with the U. S. by appointing an old acquaintance of Roosevelt's, Admiral Kichisaburō Nomura, as ambassador to the United States. Nomura arrived in Washington on February 11, 1941. Roosevelt gave every appearance of warmly welcoming his arrival, and gave the impression that Nomura's appointment had succeeded.

However, at the same time then-Foreign Minister Yōsuke Matsuoka made moves that bewildered the United States. On March 12 he left on a tour of Europe, and attempted to persuade the Soviet Union to join Japan, Germany and Italy, the members of the Tripartite Alliance, in a "quadripartite alliance." It was at a time when Hitler had already started Operation Barbarossa to crush the Soviet Union; and Roosevelt knew that Germany had begun preparations against the Soviet Union.[3] Roosevelt must have found the possibility of war between Germany and the Soviet Union, and their subsequent hostility toward each other, cause for celebration. What would have happened if Matsuoka's visit had successfully brokered peace between Germany and the Soviet Union, and the "quadripartite alliance" had been achieved? Roosevelt, and British Prime Minister Churchill, whose country's existence was gravely threatened by Germany, would certainly have felt anxious.

Matsuoka arrived in Berlin on March 26, and energetically held talks with Chancellor Hitler and Foreign Minister Ribbentrop on March 29. He stopped off midway in Rome to meet with the Italian leader Mussolini. On April 3 while in Rome, Matsuoka received a message from Roy Howard through Ambassador Nomura in Washington, inviting him to visit the United States and see President Roosevelt on his return from Europe. Howard was president of the Scripps Howard news service, which was influential in the media world, and Matsuoka had written to him before leaving for Europe.[4] This visit never came about however because Matsuoka planned to stop over in the Soviet Union; Matsuoka then returned to Germany to complete his tour there, and during his stay in Moscow, he received Churchill's secret memo advising him how Japan's continued association with Germany was unprofitable.[5] This was how anxious Roosevelt and Churchill felt about Matsuoka's movements.

To make peace with Japan, Roosevelt then presented a "Japan-U. S. draft understanding" on April 16, 1941 (referred to hereafter as "draft understanding"). As will be discussed in the next chapter, it may be an overstatement to say "presented," but it is true that this "draft understanding" was carefully examined by the U. S. State Department and became the "basis" for continued negotiations with Japan. Although devised outside official embassy channels, Nomura observed in his memoirs that he was duly consulted even as it was being formulated by this unofficial route. Secretary of State Hull agreed it would be acceptable to go on with negotiations on the basis of this "draft understanding." Roosevelt at first disliked this unofficial route,[6] and said that he wanted to conduct the negotiations only through official channels, that is through Nomura; but the fact that he was persuaded by Hull to agree to use this "draft understanding" as a tentative plan for further negotiations, shows that Roosevelt too was sincere in his wish for peace with Japan.[7]

From Matsuoka's personal experience, he believed it was necessary to maintain "a resolute attitude" and work from a "position of strength" to elicit a compromise from the United States. This was primarily his intention also for promoting the policy of alliance with Germany. Matsuoka himself observed that if he had arrived on the diplomatic scene a bit sooner, the Tripartite Alliance may not even have been necessary.[8] Matsuoka meant by this that his late arrival made it necessary to develop a "position of strength" through the Tripartite Alliance, and thereby bring about peace by trying to force the United States to make a move. Had he been involved sooner, Matsuoka would not have been drawn to Nazi Germany, nor directly influenced by Fifth Column activities.[9]

In July 1940, Chiune Sugihara requested permission to issue visas to Jews who were fleeing persecution, but this was denied by Matsuoka who had just been appointed foreign minister. However, when Matsuoka was president of the South Manchurian Railway he had already assisted Jewish refugees.[10] Moreover, Matsuoka in effect made it possible for Jewish refugees, who arrived in Japan with visas issued by Sugihara, to reach their destinations without trouble.[11] Furthermore, Matsuoka did not pursue the matter of disciplining Sugihara for disobeying orders.

Relations between Japan and Germany became close in 1933, at about the time when Japan left the League of Nations and deepened its international isolation; but relations began more formally when Germany cooperated with Japan over its problems in China. At the outbreak of the China Incident in 1937, Germany had many rights and interests in China, and had sent numerous military advisors and made large arms loans to China to recover areas it had lost after World War I; when the China Incident occurred, Germany heeded Japan's request to withdraw its military advisors and suspend military materials supplies, even though it was considered the largest provider of material aid to Chiang Kai-shek.[12]

Matsuoka thus intended the alliance with Germany to inhibit, rather than promote, war with the United States. Matsuoka's visit to Europe was therefore a moment of great triumph, because it prompted Churchill's secret appeal to Matsuoka over how Japan's continued association with Germany was unprofitable, and Roosevelt's agreement, through Hull, to use the April 16 "draft understanding" as a basis for negotiations between Japan and the United States. It was also a moment of success for Ambassador Nomura regarding the peace talks, and therefore for Matsuoka because he had appointed Nomura as ambassador.

However, Matsuoka failed to exploit this "moment of success," and it simply slipped away. On April 22, when Matsuoka returned to Japan and learned about the "draft understanding," he refused to accept it because it had been devised without his prior knowledge or approval.

Indeed, Matsuoka refused to link this "draft understanding" to his own framework, simply because it had been drawn up without his knowledge. However, what were the diplomatic repercussions of ignoring something that had already passed through official channels? Secretary Hull agreed to use the April 16 "draft understanding" as a basis for further negotiations, but cautioned that "if these talks were to be dashed by Tokyo after some progress, it would put the United States government in a difficult position."[13]

The "draft understanding" was devised by Hideo Iwakuro, chief of the Military Affairs Bureau in the Ministry of War, and special aide to Ambassador Nomura; and Tadao Ikawa, a civilian who followed the line of Prime Minister Fumimaro Konoe. It must therefore be conceded that the "draft" deviated somewhat from Matsuoka's framework, which then was premised on the Tripartite Alliance. However, as mentioned above, what about the diplomatic repercussions of ignoring something that had come through official diplomatic channels, and of wasting precious time?

The irrepressible Iwakuro, to evade wiretaps, left Washington for New York and spoke directly with Matsuoka by phone on April 29. Iwakuro recorded this conversation in his memoirs.

Iwakuro: Congratulations on your success in Europe. Regarding the fish we sent you from here, I'm afraid it will spoil if not cooked soon. Everyone at the embassy, from Ambassador Nomura down, is waiting impatiently to learn how you find the taste.
Matsuoka: Oh, I see. Tell Nomura not to try too hard.
Iwakuro: This is no time for complacency. The fish will surely rot if you're not more careful. And in that case, you'll have to bear all the responsibility for it.
Matsuoka: I see, I see.[14]

The conversation lasted roughly seven minutes. After hanging up, Iwakuro, who had channeled all his energies into the call, collapsed from the stress for ten minutes.

Around the same time, Nomura frequently called Matsuoka at the Foreign Ministry. When Matsuoka wasn't available to take these calls, his secretary Toshikazu Kase answered for him. Kase was also told by Nomura that if the "draft understanding" wasn't quickly accepted, "like a fish, it will spoil."[15]

However, Matsuoka still did not respond to these requests, and to the contrary answered in a high-handed manner when he finally did respond. On May 3 he ordered Nomura to suggest, as if it were Nomura's own idea, a proposal for a Japan-U. S. neutrality pact; he also ordered Nomura to present an "oral statement" which the Americans were bound to find ridiculous. In it, he claimed, "The German and Italian leaders are determined never to have peace by negotiation, they demand capitulation. They seem to regard that the war is as good as won even at the present stage...."[16] However since this "oral statement" was conceived with apparently little heed to the actual situation, Nomura did not carry out these instructions as ordered by Matsuoka.[17]

On May 22, Matsuoka ordered Nomura to propose the first "draft response to the United States." However, even though war between Germany and the Soviet Union was becoming more certain with each passing day, Matsuoka's "draft response" clung tenaciously to the Tripartite Alliance, and the United States was simply unable to accept it. The United States toughened its position.[18]

There was nothing the Japanese people could do now; and in a brief moment, pride and a concern for prestige and face rendered calm, rational judgment impossible. Organizations valued their reputations more than the nation, and individuals valued their reputations more than their organizations. In a sense, almost everyone in Japan at the time seemed to be suffering from some form of temporary insanity. Since the Meiji period, Japan had miraculously enjoyed one success after another, and reputations were at stake; anyone who felt their reputation had been denigrated would become enraged and no longer be capable of rational judgment. The Foreign Ministry, which was in charge of foreign policy, can in no way justify how it wasted and ruined this important opportunity. Matsuoka's personal responsibility for this grave error is enormous, but since Kase himself boasts that at the time "[i]t was said that all you needed at the Foreign Ministry were Matsuoka and Kase,"[19] Kase cannot evade this responsibility either.

Another Key Opportunity Lost to Settle Japan-U. S. Differences

Thus, an important chance provided by the "draft understanding" to bring peace between Japan and the United States was lost, but another opportunity emerged. This opportunity was the actual outbreak of war between Germany and the Soviet Union. Despite Matsuoka's private hopes, war between Germany and the Soviet Union became a reality. With the outbreak of this war, Roosevelt and Churchill again concluded that they needed peace between Japan and the United States. Japan enjoyed a military alliance with Germany, and also a neutrality pact with the Soviet Union. From a tactical point of view, what would have happened if Japan had attacked the Soviet Union when the war between Germany and the Soviet Union broke out? Wouldn't the Soviet Union have been caught in a squeeze between Germany and Japan, and have faced possible defeat? That being the case, German power would have become so vast as to be unbeatable.

However, Japan did not realize then that it could have played the diplomatic card of hinting at an attack on the Soviet Union. It couldn't play this card because it didn't realize it had this option. Various sources of information about the war between Germany and the Soviet Union had already reached Japan. On May 9, 1941, from Königsberg in East Prussia, Chiune Sugihara, the principal subject of this book, reported in detail about the German military's preparations to invade the Soviet Union. Philosophy students will recall that Königsberg was where Kant was born and raised; this German enclave in northern Poland shared a border to its north with Lithuania. Japan established a consulate there, and Sugihara took up his appointment as consul in March 1941 and worked on intelligence activities. On May 9, he cabled the Foreign Ministry extremely detailed information regarding invasion preparations by the German military, and this could only mean that Germany was about to attack the Soviet Union.[20]

On June 4, Hiroshi Ōshima, Japan's ambassador to Germany, was advised officially by the German side of their plans to invade the Soviet Union; and on June 5 he also reported to the Foreign Ministry that the German military was without doubt about to invade the Soviet Union. There was no longer any room for wishful thinking. Matsuoka's framework for a "quadripartite alliance" was practically completely shattered at this moment.

The military then argued it was time to advance South because the threat of attack from the Soviet Union had been reduced. Matsuoka was vehemently opposed to this Southern campaign. When the war between Germany and the Soviet Union had already broken out, Matsuoka adroitly voiced his opposition by claiming: "I have never made a mistake in predicting what would happen in the next few years. [However,] I predict that if we get involved in the South, it will be a serious matter."[21]

Matsuoka argued instead for launching an attack upon the Soviet Union. This was no diplomatic card, but an actual call for an immediate attack. However, it was unlikely that Emperor Hirohito would agree to this, nor Prime Minister Konoe either.

Even worse, to hold back the Northern campaign against the Soviet Union, Konoe approved the Southern advance that had always been left pending in the past. Unfortunately, as Matsuoka had predicted, relations with the United States indeed became "a serious matter."

On June 22 war between Germany and the Soviet Union broke out, but the Japanese government had not devised a strategy, nor had any government official even considered playing the diplomatic card of attacking the Soviet Union (even though such an attack was unlikely in practice to be launched). The military, which exerted strong authority over the government, must also share in the blame; but the Foreign Ministry, which did not, or could not, work out a diplomatic strategy, has enormous responsibility for the extraordinary blunder of not preparing, or even trying to prepare, a new strategy to deal with the new situation.

When the outbreak of war between Germany and the Soviet Union was confirmed, the Japanese military imagined from intelligence it received from Germany that the conflict would be resolved in the short term; this would mean the collapse of their old enemy the Soviet Union, and they were overjoyed at their incredible fortune. Research by Shūhei Domon confirms that there is no evidence of rational analysis by the military either on this issue.[22]

Therefore, the decisions and actions of the military too can certainly not be excused. However, direct responsibility for anything beyond that surely belongs to the Foreign Ministry. The framework for any "quadripartite alliance" was premised on cooperation between Germany and the Soviet Union. This premise had disappeared. Despite this though, no new alternative strategy was devised.

It is well known that when Matsuoka visited Germany, the German side repeatedly hinted that it would attack the Soviet Union. Perversely though, Matsuoka imagined this to mean that no attack on the Soviet Union was possible. This was why he signed a neutrality pact with the Soviet Union; but a cable from Hiroshi Ōshima, the Japanese ambassador to Germany, regarding Germany's plans to attack the Soviet Union, had already arrived when Matsuoka returned to Japan. War between Germany and the Soviet Union became more certain by the day. The Foreign Ministry, which had proceeded with Japan's diplomacy based on the premise of the "quadripartite alliance," obviously should have been responsible for preparing an alternative after the chance of a "quadripartite alliance" disintegrated.

The German decision to attack the Soviet Union meant, even in a formal sense, an enormous betrayal of Japan by Germany. The premise upon which Japan's diplomacy had been overwhelmingly based had crumbled.

Formally, the relationship between Japan and Nazi Germany started in 1936 with the Anti-Comintern Pact to counter the threat of the Soviet Union. Yet, in August 1939, without Japan's knowledge, Germany suddenly signed a non-aggression pact with the Soviet Union. The cabinet of then-Prime Minister Kiichirō Hiranuma was forced to resign, and he confessed that Europe was "complicated and difficult to fathom" (*fukuzatsu kaiki*). This was Germany's first serious betrayal of Japan. Then, based on this non-aggression pact, the Tripartite Alliance between Japan, Germany and Italy was signed in September 1940, and later the Japan-Soviet Neutrality Pact was signed. Despite all this, Germany launched its attack on the Soviet Union, again without consultation. This was Germany's second serious betrayal of Japan.

Therefore, if careful preparations had been made at this time by the Foreign Ministry, it should have been able to persuade the military and change the direction of Japan's foreign policy. Indeed, foreign policy should have been changed.

However, during this important period the Foreign Ministry had not prepared any strategies at all. It had not even tried to prepare any contingency plans. The framework for the "quadripartite alliance" rested solely on cooperation between Germany and the Soviet Union. However when war between Germany and the Soviet Union broke out, thereby destroying this premise, the Foreign Ministry did not subsequently devise any alternative preparations or strategies.

Germany's betrayal caused the military to lose much face with the public. Therefore there was a time, a brief moment, when the military hesitated. However because the Foreign Ministry had not prepared any alternative strategies, it was unable to take advantage of that window of opportunity. Soon, reports of Germany's jolting assault upon the Soviet Union, and other successes, arrived one after another. The military seized upon these successes, and by extending the Tripartite Alliance with Germany, took over governing the country.

One might be more sympathetic if the Foreign Ministry had worked out a strategy to dissuade the military, and the military had not listened. The Ministry however had not even devised a plan, and was therefore impotent. Its failure even to work out a plan to accommodate changes of such magnitude was clearly a blunder by the Foreign Ministry, which administered Japan's diplomacy, and exceeded the blunders made by the military.

Not only did Japan at this time not aggressively exploit the diplomatic card of attacking the Soviet Union. It should come as no surprise that, to the contrary, this card was actually used against Japan. On July 5, in a cable to Prime Minister Konoe through the American ambassador in Japan Joseph Grew, Roosevelt hoped "the reports of Japan's decision to enter upon hostilities against the Soviet Union are not based upon fact, and an assurance to that effect from His Excellency the Prime Minister of Japan would be deeply appreciated...." Konoe delivered a message through Matsuoka on July 8 clarifying that, "The Japanese Government wish[es] to state...that [it has] not so far considered the possibility of joining the hostilities against the Soviet Union."[23] Even though the main arena for negotiations between Japan and the United States was supposed to be Washington and to revolve around Nomura, Roosevelt for this matter alone chose Tokyo and used Grew because he didn't want to make use of it as a diplomatic card in the peace negotiations with Japan. Japan could now only conduct an invasion of the Soviet Union if this statement by the prime minister was reversed.

Subsequently, on July 28 Japan began its occupation of Southern French Indo-China. In response, Roosevelt took measures to embargo oil exports to Japan. On this issue, Matsuoka's predictions had hit the bull's-eye. Japan then imported almost all its oil from the United States; if those oil imports were to dry up, Japan's planes and ships would soon grind to a halt, and this would amount to Japan totally losing its military capability. The oil embargo, which meant virtual starvation to Japan's military, was in essence a military action. Roosevelt took advantage of Japan's blunder, and was able to get the American public's support to implement this quasi-military measure.

The United States Had Broken Japan's Diplomatic Codes

While the Foreign Ministry was treating the precious April 16 "draft understanding" like just so much trash, it perpetrated another blunder of horrific proportions.

On May 3, 1941, a secret cable arrived at the Foreign Ministry from Japan's ambassador to Berlin, Hiroshi Ōshima. Although the original cable was apparently incinerated, it was intercepted by the American side and decoded.[24]

> Stahmer called on me this day...and stating that this request was to be kept strictly secret, he said that Germany maintains a fairly reliable intelligence organization abroad..., and according to information obtained from the above-mentioned organization it is quite...reliably established that the U. S. government is reading Ambassador Nomura's code messages, and then asked that drastic steps should be taken regarding this matter. [25]

Foreign Ministry officials, their faces drained of color, transmitted these suspicions to the Washington embassy to ascertain whether they had any validity.

According to a fairly reliable source of information it appears almost certain that the United States government is reading your code messages.

Please let me know whether you have any suspicion of the above. [26]

Nomura promptly responded to this inquiry the same day.

For our part, the most stringent precautions are taken by all custodians of codes and ciphers, as well as of other documents.

On this particular matter I have nothing in mind, but pending investigation please wire back any concrete instances or details which may turn up. [27]

There were further exchanges of messages on this matter, but how did it finally end up? Ultimately, the Foreign Ministry implemented no special measures, except instructions to increase security over codes. It directed that all cables relating to the matter be incinerated, and treated the matter as though nothing untoward had occurred. Although we are familiar with the expression "to cover one's ears while stealing a bell," this situation was akin to covering one's eyes while pretending to ignore something one had just seen. The Foreign Ministry continued to use these compromised codes until Japan was defeated, and the American side continued their decoding. The damaging effects of this inaction also reached Germany. For instance, in June 1944 during the Allied campaign for the Normandy landing, the American side was able to get a firm grasp of the German military's situation from reports Ōshima had cabled to the Foreign Ministry.

Incidentally, let's examine the circumstances surrounding Germany's suspicions that the United States was decoding Japan's diplomatic cables. On April 16, just after Foreign Minister Matsuoka had signed the Japan-Soviet Neutrality Pact in Moscow, Ambassador Ōshima sent detailed coded reports to the Foreign Ministry regarding Germany's intention to invade the Soviet Union. The United States intercepted and decoded them, along with other cables. The United States government, which was trying to persuade the Soviet Union to send troops to the German front, transmitted the information to the Soviet representative in Washington. When the Soviet Union received this report, it passed it on to the German ambassador in Moscow since it was not yet in an adversarial relationship with Germany. The German government then communicated this as a warning to Ambassador Ōshima.[28]

Although there was a risk the United States was decoding Japan's diplomatic codes, and despite being warned by Germany, the Foreign

Ministry took no special measures, and continued until Japan's defeat to use its compromised diplomatic codes while these cables continued to be decoded. This is a blunder that will endure in the annals of world diplomatic history. Ōshima's coded cables, just after the signing of the Japan-Soviet Neutrality Pact, also revealed Germany's intent to invade the Soviet Union, so the blunder of ignoring sound intelligence is closely mirrored by the sloppy handling of the April 16 "draft understanding."

There is another frightening and alarming incident related to the blunder of using diplomatic codes suspected of having been broken by the American side.

While of some importance, this matter is not very well known: Japan was also decoding American diplomatic cables at the time. This fine achievement was something for which the Foreign Ministry ought to have been praised, but someone deliberately alerted the American authorities to this fact. Roosevelt's well-known comment ("It saves time; I don't mind if it gets picked up") indicating that his personal message to Emperor Hirohito just before the outbreak of war could be sent in gray code, was a direct result of that warning.

However this leak was not due to any mistake made by a Foreign Ministry official. In August 1941, Prime Minister Konoe approached Roosevelt enthusiastically about a Japan-U. S. summit meeting. On August 6, Tomohiko Ushiba, Konoe's private secretary, informed John Emmerson, a member of Ambassador Joseph Grew's staff, that Japanese authorities were decoding cables sent by the embassy to the State Department in Washington.[29]

Why did Ushiba leak such an important fact? It is probably worthwhile taking a short detour to examine this.

Konoe was gambling on a Japan-U. S. summit meeting to bring about peace between Japan and the United States. If such a summit meeting had materialized, he was prepared to submit a daring compromise plan. He revealed a portion of it to Grew, but Konoe refused to let Grew transmit it to Washington. If Grew had done this, certain bodies in Japan would have decoded his cable, and it would have become widely known on the Japanese side. If that had happened, opposition within Japan would have ensured the summit meeting would never be realized.[30] Ushiba's warning might have been necessary to convince the Americans of Konoe's strong reluctance to allow this plan to be transmitted to Washington by conventional means. On the other hand, it may have been the preferred method to demonstrate how sincere Konoe's expectations were for the Japan-U. S. summit conference.

Also, because Ushiba remains silent on this issue, we will never know whether his actions at the time had Konoe's approval or were done on his own initiative. We don't know if the Foreign Ministry ever received a report on this matter afterwards. Most likely it wouldn't have acknowledged such a report.

Consequently, all later cables sent by the U. S. State Department to Ambassador Grew in Tokyo were in theory decoded by the Japanese side, and were sent with the understanding that the Japanese side was decoding them. Even though the Japanese side thought it was secretly reading them, they were deliberately being allowed to read them.

This incident had a profound influence on Japan at a decisive moment. When the Hull Note was forced upon Japan, the Japanese side was allowed to read a cable sent to Grew containing a detailed and carefully-considered companion *modus vivendi* that it had been decided would not be presented to Japan. By reading this, Japan assumed that even after further negotiations, nothing more than the Hull Note would be forthcoming. It meant that any subsequent negotiations were pointless. If Japan knew that no further results were possible through continued talks, this cable, which Japan had been allowed to read, clearly would have had a devastating influence at a pressing time when war, if it was considered inevitable, had to begin as soon as possible.[31]

In any case, apart from breaches of security by Allied spies, this is also an incredible blunder by Japanese diplomacy that will endure in the annals of world diplomatic history.

Japan-U. S. Summit Meeting Toyed With

Thus relations between Japan and the United States became extremely tense, and a pallid Prime Minister Konoe proposed holding a summit meeting. Although the idea for a summit meeting had already been broached in the April 16 "draft understanding," the meeting with Roosevelt was the final trump card for Konoe, who had blundered along thus far and was being inexorably cornered.

Roosevelt arrived back in Washington on August 17 after his Atlantic meeting with Churchill, and, despite it being a Sunday, invited Nomura to meet him that day. Roosevelt told Nomura that he, along with "the secretary of state and you the ambassador, sir, we all very strongly aspire to maintain the peace in the Pacific Ocean." He then said he would happily accept Konoe's proposal for a summit.[32] This was even though he had promised Churchill he would provoke Japan. On August 28, Roosevelt read a document prepared by Konoe outlining the position of Japan's government and admired it, saying it was "wonderful."[33]

It seemed the summit conference was on track. However, on September 3 Roosevelt demurred by saying, "In both countries there is public opinion to be taken into account. Even if I made a compromise with Japan, in America there would be repeated demands on me to make no changes in our previous policies."[34] Indeed, an official memo delivered on October 2 dashed all hope for a summit meeting.

In other words, despite the fact there had been no intention from the start to accept a summit meeting, he acted all along as though he might accept one.[35]

While it was unlikely Roosevelt would have accepted a summit meeting, his every gesture made it appear that he might accept one; this is easy to understand by examining certain circumstances at the time.

One factor was the attempt to stop Japan from attacking the Soviet Union. If it had been made explicit at this time that peace between Japan and the United States was impossible, Japan would quite likely have shifted policy to an invasion of the Soviet Union. However the U. S. could not allow an attack on the Soviet Union to occur at this time. It was expedient to dangle the possibility of a summit meeting before the Japanese. Shortly afterwards, during the battle for Moscow between Germany and the Soviet Union, the Soviet Union transferred troops stationed on the border with Manchuria to the Western front, and this ensured their eventual victory.[36]

Second, even if Roosevelt goaded the Japanese as he had promised Churchill, American military defenses in the Philippines were still incomplete. It was necessary to play for time to strengthen these defenses. American troops in the Philippines were later reinforced, right until the Imperial Japanese Navy's attack on Pearl Harbor.[37]

The third factor to consider was Roosevelt's domestic policies. Roosevelt was serving a third term as president after promising the American public not to take the United States into any war, and he had just returned from a secret meeting with British Prime Minister Churchill, the leader of one of the protagonists in the European war. It was therefore not surprising some suspected Roosevelt may have returned with a secret pledge to somehow get the United States involved in the war. To dispel these suspicions, he had to actively pursue a peace offensive at this time. Japan's proposal for a summit meeting provided a unique opportunity.

Thus, after his framework for a summit had been completely toyed with, Konoe had no choice but to dissolve his cabinet on October 16.

On June 25, three days after the war between Germany and the Soviet Union had broken out, Walter Adams, assistant chief of the State Department's division of Far Eastern affairs, suggested a number of approaches the United States could take to immobilize Japan from advancing either north or south: "Moves or gestures by the United States which would render Japan uncertain in regard to the intentions of the United States in the South Pacific would operate in the direction of preventing Japan from becoming involved in Siberia....The immediate freezing of Japanese assets in this country...and increased restrictions upon the export of petroleum products" would "tend to discourage military action by Japan against Russia."[38] Clearly Roosevelt's later negotiations with Japan were deeply influenced by Adams's proposal and drove Japan into a tight corner.

Tōjō Cabinet Also Toyed With

Thus it was that the military-dominated Tōjō cabinet was born. However, like its predecessor, it wasn't set up to wage war with the United States. Rather, it was formed to rein in the military and realize peace with the United States. The Tōjō cabinet was of course mindful that the oil embargo was weakening Japan's military capacity with each passing day, and that if peace wasn't reached with the United States there would be no choice but to launch a war against that country as soon as possible. However, war with the United States was ultimately not its main purpose, and it held negotiations with the United States in good faith to bring about peace.

Shigenori Tōgō, the new foreign minister, devised some break-through draft propositions for peace with the United States, the so-called Proposals A and B, and offered them to the United States government. In response, the American side also prepared drafts to present to the Japanese government. The American proposal consisted of two parts: the first was a draft for a *modus vivendi* covering a period of three months; the other, a draft for a more permanent agreement.

These moves by the American side made it appear the United States was also moving towards peace with Japan. However a closer look at Roosevelt and Hull's behavior at this time clearly shows that these actions were mere camouflage to leave an improved record for the American history books.[39]

Without going into too much detail, the so-called Hull Note, delivered to Japan on November 26, was clearly problematic. The Hull Note was the draft for the more permanent agreement previously referred to, and as such its conditions were tough. Although Roosevelt and Hull obviously realized that Japan would be unable to accept this draft proposition, they presented it anyway.

Interest has recently focused on Harry White, a U. S. Treasury official who released intelligence to the Soviet Union, and his draft for the Hull Note; it would be wrong however to overestimate the importance of the Soviet Union's role in forcing the Hull Note on Japan, even though there may indeed be some foundation to this. Ultimately, White's draft should be seen as little more than reference material for the fundamental structure of Roosevelt's two-part proposal consisting of *modus vivendi* plus permanent agreement.[40]

Hull turned the document based on the White draft, that is, the permanent agreement prepared by the State Department, into an even harsher one. Until November 22, the words "excluded Manchuria" were explicitly specified when it came to the withdrawal of Japanese troops from China. The April 16 "draft understanding" had also been explicit on this point. On November 25 though, just before it was handed to the Japanese, the words "excluded Manchuria" had mysteriously disappeared from the permanent agreement draft, and had been replaced by expressions that could have been misinterpreted by Japan as calling for the immediate withdrawal of troops from Manchuria.[41]

This author may have been the first to point out that, after the Hull Note was forced upon Japan, the State Department advised Ambassador Grew in Tokyo that the *modus vivendi* would not be presented to the Japanese side. This may have been done with the knowledge that Japan was decoding the United States's diplomatic cables, as mentioned above, to deliberately but indirectly notify the Japanese side and dash their hopes for peace with the United States. This is precisely the impression the Japanese side held after decoding and reading Hull's cable to Grew.[42]

As we conclude this chapter, let me examine how Japan could have reacted when the Hull Note was forced upon it. It might be argued that Japan could indeed have accepted it. Since the Hull Note in reality challenged Japan and tried to provoke a war, the United States would have been stalemated if Japan had accepted it. Shortly after the Hull Note was forced on Japan, by chance Roosevelt's war plans were leaked to the press, leaving Roosevelt in a tight spot with the American public. If we consider that Roosevelt would have been compelled to highlight his peace talks with Japan in order to persuade the American public there was no truth to these war plans, it is then possible to conclude from these facts that war between Japan and the United States was avoidable. It would have soon become clear that Germany was losing its war against the Soviet Union and would end up retreating. For Japan, war against the United States would have appeared more and more forbidding.

However, we must also consider the circumstances Japan found itself in at the time. Oil imports had stopped, and if a compromise with the United States couldn't be reached, war had to be launched as soon as possible. December 8 (Japan time) was chosen as the starting date for the war to exploit the dry period before the monsoons, a consideration vital to the Southern campaign; no further delays could be accepted, and the United States was continuing to reinforce its troops on the Philippines. Any further postponements would mean Japan would lose its chance for victory.[43] For that reason, the war had to be launched without regard to the progress of the German-Soviet war, even though it was known behind the scenes that Germany's war was not proceeding according to earlier plans.[44] Curiously, on December 6 (U. S. time), one day before the Pearl Harbor attack, Admiral Kimmel who was charged with securing Pearl Harbor explained to newspaper reporters that, because Germany was failing in its war against the Soviet Union, Japan was unlikely to attack.[45]

One obstacle to the negotiations between Japan and the United States was the rigid ban on discussions about the start of the war: the Imperial Japanese Navy planned the surprise attack on Pearl Harbor and the large-scale plans for its launch in strict secrecy. Isoroku Yamamoto, who planned the surprise attack on Pearl Harbor, must bear much of the responsibility for this. Yamamoto apparently believed that Japan should avoid war with the United States; but if that was indeed the case, he should have helped to establish an atmosphere or set of circumstances in the Imperial Japanese Navy so that people would realize that war against the United States was unfeasible.[46]

At the same time, Japan's response when the Hull Note was forced upon it would probably have been quite different if it had realized the Note's implicit challenge. There were strict limits at the time on the number of people involved in the negotiations with the United States; but if even one person had noticed this challenge, Japan's response may have been different. This book is concerned primarily with examining concrete historical evidence, and hypothetical scenarios have largely been eschewed, but let me indulge in some speculation here: how decisive should the Foreign Ministry have been; and how important was Matsuoka's reputation in understanding the man himself.

If Matsuoka had continued as foreign minister until the Hull Note was forced upon Japan, it is possible he would have perceived the strategic maneuver implicit in the Note. He was extremely resourceful, intuitive, and could also be quite persuasive. Above all, he knew enough to be apprehensive about going to war with the United States. By this time, he would have realized the miscalculation in wasting the April 16 "draft understanding"; and with his uncanny flair he would have seen through the American side's scheme. Once he had come to this awareness, he would have used all his powers to develop arguments to persuade and dissuade the military; as a result, war with the United States might have been successfully avoided. Matsuoka resigned as foreign minister after he had signed the Tripartite Alliance, wasted the chance to compromise with the United States provided by the April 16 "draft understanding," and completely ruined the path towards peace with the United States; so it must be noted that he was a source of grief to the Japanese people. His original hope, however, had been to avoid a war with the United States, so it is possible he may have seen through the strategies on the American side during the final stages of the negotiations, and might have used his powers of persuasion to prevent the outbreak of war. In fact, Matsuoka probably would not have been allowed to continue as foreign minister because he seemed to represent a cancerous growth on any peace with the United States; but for argument's sake, had he continued as foreign minister his efforts, to the contrary, may have enabled Japan to overcome this difficult crisis.

While we are discussing hypothetical situations, what would have happened if Teijirō Toyoda, who replaced Matsuoka in Konoe's third cabinet, had continued as foreign minister in the Tōjō cabinet and had received the Hull Note? Toyoda teamed up with Eiji Amō who became vice foreign minister at Toyoda's invitation. The third Konoe cabinet, forced to step down because talks for the summit meeting were toyed with, was unable to produce any results. However, it could be argued that Toyoda and Amō would have had more strategic sense than their counterparts in the Tōjō cabinet, Shigenori Tōgō and his secretary Toshikazu Kase. If Toyoda and Amō with their superior sense of strategy had received the Hull Note, while they might not have seen through its implicit strategy, it is likely they would have reacted in a very different way.

On October 8, 1941, Foreign Minister Toyoda cabled Ōshima, his ambassador in Berlin, and explained that "the conflict between Germany and the Soviet Union, contrary to Berlin's calculations, has reached a deadlock. Now the Soviet Union is going over to the Anglo-Saxon camp and we must make ready to cope with this situation." He continued: "Prospects for the war between Germany and the Soviet

Union, which was started by Germany, are completely contrary to expectations due to sudden changes in the situation, and only Japan's relationship with the United States remains resolvable." On October 13, days before the resignation of the third Konoe cabinet, Toyoda delivered the document "The Empire's external policies for coping with the present international situation" [*Genka kokusai jōsei ni shosuru Teikoku taigai hōshin*] to the prime minister, in which he argued,

> Rather than sit back and face annihilation, or stake everything on a way out of this dead-end, even through modest debate it would be revealed there are no materials to be gained by heading north, because sources of such materials have always been scarce in the North; and while the South has abundant materials, proceeding with force will only bring about the destruction of the facilities to develop these materials....
>
> At this time, the Empire's most urgent task is to persistently preserve our national strength, and make all the necessary arrangements where it can most effectively use it without fear of embarrassment in a national emergency at a later date.[47]

Putting conjecture aside, it should probably be conceded that discerning the challenge implicit in the U. S. government's intentions, at the time Tōgō and Kase received the Hull Note, was rather difficult. Even Hull's secret cable, advising Grew of the decision not to deliver the *modus vivendi* to Japan, was a very clever ploy to provoke Japan by the Roosevelt-dominated government, which had at its disposal an overflowing abundance of intelligence reports.[48] If for instance we exclude the fanaticism and narrow vision shared by responsible individuals on the Japanese side at the time, we can still argue that, among the range of skills normally expected of diplomats, the ability to discern the underlying intentions of Roosevelt and the others should have been paramount. Clearly, in this pressing situation it was no simple matter to see through the ploy. This is not the only example in history where something which in hindsight appears rather obvious is in fact quite difficult to see at the time.

Nevertheless, by looking exclusively at these negotiations which lasted less than a year, this author can only reach the overall conclusion that war with the United States might have been avoided, at this stage at least, if the Foreign Ministry had possessed the skills and performed with the abilities usually expected of a country's foreign service. My conclusions would be the same regarding the hypothetical situations concerning Matsuoka. Clearly, because the Foreign Ministry did not possess these abilities, the war with the United States was unavoidable. The people of Japan must come to a common understanding of the Foreign Ministry's shortcomings, and how they contributed to the outbreak of war with the United States.

Chapter 4

Toshikazu Kase's Research on the 1941 Japan-U. S. Negotiations

The Facts Europeans and Americans First Learned about Japan's Plunge Into War

This chapter deals with the issue of Toshikazu Kase's research on the history of the negotiations between Japan and the United States.

On September 2, 1945, Kase attended the ceremony for the signing of surrender documents aboard the U. S. S. *Missouri*. As discussed in chapter 1, Kase was then the Cabinet Information Bureau's third department chief responsible for foreign affairs. However, when the Bureau was abolished at the end of 1945, Kase lost this position. He returned to the Foreign Ministry because he was concurrently chief of the Ministry's public relations section; but just as he thought he could continue in that position, the closure of the information bureau left him without work. This apparently came as quite a shock to Kase, and he made some radical changes in his life: he decided to make a name for himself as a writer.[1]

Six months later Shigeru Yoshida, who was serving concurrently as prime minister and foreign minister, reinstated Kase to the Foreign Ministry in June 1946 at the rank of embassy counselor. However, this was at a time when Japan had no embassies or consulates abroad, so there was no actual work for Kase to do. Kase assisted Prime Minister

Yoshida by drafting texts in English, and independently wrote articles for private-sector newspapers and magazines.

Using this free time, Kase wrote his first earnest piece of work *Journey to the Missouri* in English. This book was published in 1949 by Yale University Press. It was strictly prohibited to take manuscripts out of Japan at the time, so it was no easy matter to arrange to send the manuscript to the United States and have it published there. It was under these difficult circumstances that the book appeared.

As the title suggests, the book describes the various stages of how Japan entered the war, was defeated, surrendered, and then signed the instrument of surrender aboard the *Missouri*, while at the same time tracing the strands of Kase's life.

We examined in chapter 2 a statement by Gordon T. Bowles, the U. S. State Department's representative in the first education mission to Japan. Bowles claimed he "had no idea why Japan went to war, nor why Japan thought it could win."[2] Even ordinary people from Allied countries couldn't understand why Japan started such an incredibly irrational war, only to be defeated. Ordinary soldiers and private citizens in the Allied countries were puzzled why Japan would challenge the United States, even though it had absolutely no chance of victory.

It is reasonably well understood why Nazi Germany took the actions it did. Even regarding the German-Soviet war, it is understood why Germany attacked the Soviet Union and why it felt compelled to do so; it is also accepted that Germany began the war because it thought it had a chance of winning, even though ultimately it was a miscalculation. However, why did a small Asian nation like Japan, not considered to have progressed in the modern sciences to any degree, take on a war with the United States, then surely the world's strongest power? It was quite a mystery, despite disgust over the "sneak attack" at Pearl Harbor. Starting with these sorts of questions, Kase's *Journey to the Missouri* explained Japan's circumstances to people in Europe and the United States. For the first time they learned the sequence of events behind Japan's slide into the sudden outbreak of war, even though deep down it had tried to avoid war with the United States.

People in Europe and the United States also discovered that the steps taken towards bringing about Japan's surrender surpassed even the best mystery novel; they learned that, like walking across thin ice, surrender was only realized after successfully clearing numerous crises.

In the foreword to Kase's book, David Nelson Rowe from Yale University made the following observation about Roosevelt's diplomacy at Yalta where the U. S. president concluded a secret agreement with the Soviet Union. "[T]he diplomacy of Yalta can be explained only as based upon a monumental failure of American political and military intelligence on wartime Japan. It is either that or a serious failure to make use of, and to interpret for policy actions, the information that was available."[3]

People became aware that, at this late stage of the war, it had become unnecessary to punish Japan to such an extent. It also became known that Japan had its own rationale for being forced to fight. Therefore, it must be conceded that the publication of Kase's book was significant, even if only because Rowe, an American, had made skeptical comments like these.

Although somewhat lengthy, let me again quote from Rowe's foreword:

> The price paid at Yalta was the re-establishment, with our support, of the early twentieth-century Russian imperialist position on Chinese soil. It is surely one of the most bitter truths of recent history that this involved nothing less than the sacrifice of that traditional American policy toward China, the support of which led us into war with Japan in the first place. Mr. Kase's book does much to convince us that this was unnecessary in view of conditions in Japan in February, 1945. In addition, his discussion of the basic elements in Far Eastern international relations may convince even doubters that this expedient should have been avoided even if the cost had been heavy. [4]

In China in 1950, Chiang Kai-shek had already been driven from the mainland, and the Cold War between the United States and the Soviet Union was firmly established. The United States was perplexed by the outcome of its war with Japan. It was under these circumstances that it first learned about the way in which Japan had undertaken the war and subsequently capitulated, so the impression Kase's book left was extremely vivid. It greatly helped bring about a reappraisal of Japan, and feelings of familiarity. It must be said that, in this sense, Kase's book made a great contribution to Japan.

The text was also poignantly written. Kase movingly recalled how former prime minister Fumimaro Konoe, who had participated in efforts to end the war, took his own life by ingesting poison the day before he was due to be arrested. An open copy of Oscar Wilde's *De Profundis*, borrowed from Kase, lay near his death bed. Kase warned that, when it came to his personal assessment of Konoe, he had to confess to some bias because he had witnessed Konoe's final state of tranquillity, like a candle about to flicker out.[5] He also explained that, "none of them

[Japan's elder statesmen], I believe, surpassed Konoye in zeal for the welfare of the country."[6]

Problematic Aspects of Historical Portrayal

However, problems arise when examining this book as a piece of historical research on the process of the Japan-U. S. negotiations, whereby Japan launched the war against the United States.

This book cannot be treated as a piece of historical research because it was originally written with the intentions outlined in the previous section. However, these intentions must above all be seen as aspects of the historical portrayal of the Japan-U. S. negotiations, and in their own right they played their role in broadening historical interpretations. It may be acceptable to view this book with a historical researcher's critical eye, but doing so brings with it serious problems.

For instance, after the war people made statements like those by David Nelson Rowe cited above, but strictly speaking, it would have been better if they had been saying and thinking those things before the war started. The United States should have been comprehensively informed of the prewar circumstances that drove Japan into a corner. Furthermore, Japan had already made diplomatic mistakes throughout the prewar period, not least of which was the blunder at the Washington embassy that led to the "sneak attack" at Pearl Harbor. However, these matters were already long past by the time Kase wrote this book, and recounting them would have seemed as redundant as calculating a dead child's age. Therefore, the issue will not be pursued here, but Kase's book is nevertheless guilty of serious crimes of omission.

One of the inexcusable and perhaps "criminal" problems with the book is that it completely avoids questioning the Foreign Ministry's war responsibility. It pushes the entire blame for Japan's war responsibility during the Japan-U. S. war upon the military, and completely absolves the Foreign Ministry of any guilt.

Japan was under Allied occupation when the book was published, and although Japan's military had been dismantled, the Foreign Ministry continued to exist. Not only did it continue to exist, the Foreign Ministry also undeniably played an active role in the Occupation. According to Kase, at the start of the Occupation the occupying forces urged that the Foreign Ministry also be abolished. By definition, "occupation" means primarily stripping a country of its diplomatic authority, and in that sense nothing could have been done if the Foreign Ministry had been abolished. However, since Japan's occupation followed its acceptance of the Potsdam Proclamation, Japan was not to lose its national sovereignty entirely. Only "restraints" would be placed on this sovereignty. Under the just notion of keeping these "restraints" to a minimum, the Foreign Ministry's ongoing existence had to be permitted, even during the Occupation. The Foreign Ministry came to be seen as sovereign Japan's negotiating window with the occupying forces. Certainly, even the occupying forces could see the merit of using the Foreign Ministry, with the Ministry's complicity, to ensure their smooth administration of the Occupation. In any case, understandings of this sort were reached, and the Foreign Ministry escaped abolition. Kase also strove to ensure the Ministry escaped abolition.[7] It was thus inevitable that he avoided making observations which would "bring harm" to a Foreign Ministry that was fighting for its existence. Conceivably, keeping quiet about the Ministry's responsibility was unavoidable during the Occupation.

If we make allowances for these extenuating circumstances, then it is perhaps understandable how this book failed to consider the Foreign Ministry's war responsibility regarding the war between Japan and the United States.

However, although the occupying forces at the start of the Occupation considered the Foreign Ministry a proponent of militarism, they tacitly and intentionally agreed to overlook the Foreign Ministry's evasion of its war responsibility. They shared the Foreign Ministry's view of pushing all war responsibility onto the military. As firm evidence, Kase makes comments to that effect throughout his book.

The Foreign Ministry's crusade to avoid abolition meant, as mentioned above, minimizing "restraints" upon Japan's sovereignty. However, once the Ministry's continued existence was guaranteed by the occupying forces, it cooperated with those forces, and as a result, came to exert pressure on the Japanese people. The Foreign Ministry no longer represented the Japanese people nor told the occupying forces things that needed telling; instead, it became an agent of the occupying forces and transmitted and forced the wishes of those forces onto the Japanese people.

To reward the Foreign Ministry's cooperation, the occupying forces overlooked the Ministry's pushing and transferal of its own responsibility for the war with the United States, and for other wars Japan had been involved in before that, onto the military. Although the occupying forces obviously knew the Ministry was evading and transferring its responsibility for Japan's wars, including the Japan-U. S. conflict and others before it, they had to turn a blind eye because the Ministry gave them its complete cooperation, and did nothing to provoke them.

Moreover, the Japanese people then lacked any freedom of expression because of the Occupation's severe censorship system. It was impossible for the Japanese people to criticize the way the Foreign Ministry was behaving. Not only were they deprived of any freedom of speech on general subjects, it was ultimately also impossible for them to criticize the Foreign Ministry which cooperated with and was protected by the occupying forces, because this would have been seen as an indirect criticism of those forces. Under the Occupation's absolutist system, the Japanese people couldn't observe what the Foreign Ministry was doing to conceal its war responsibility, and could not criticize the Ministry even if for instance they had observed it.

Kase's book is therefore important because it was the first to introduce people in Europe and the United States to the course of events by which Japan launched, and concluded, the war. Nevertheless, for Japan this book must be taken as good indirect evidence of the Foreign Ministry's unique relationship with the occupying forces, which then preserved the Ministry, and of the presence of the unique linguistic space that prevailed during the Occupation.

After the Occupation was lifted, this book took on another life that unfolded in an untoward direction. Thanks to the publication of this book, after the Occupation Kase became the foremost researcher on the history of the negotiations between Japan and the United States, negotiations he himself had participated in; and afterwards, this book formed, and was presented as, the basic paradigm for the history of those negotiations. This basic paradigm, which totally absolved the Foreign Ministry of any war guilt, was accepted as legitimate research on the history of those negotiations. From this perspective, even if Kase had not intended it when he wrote the book, later developments demonstrate that its actual role has been criminal.

Transferring War Responsibility Onto "Militarism"

Let's examine some specific claims *Journey to the Missouri* makes that the Foreign Ministry had no responsibility for the war, and that this responsibility lay wholly with the military. Kase stated,

> The fighting services, the Army in particular, took care to discredit the Foreign Office in the eyes of the public. Other branches of government customarily deferred to the armed forces. The Foreign Office alone had the courage to challenge the military and to oppose their aim of aggression and aggrandizement.[8]

He also claimed the following.

> Again, when negotiations between Tokyo and Washington entered the crucial stages in the winter of 1941 we in the Foreign Office were totally unaware of the extent to which the fighting services had completed preparations for war. We had no way of knowing, therefore, that the breaking off of the parley would probably mean an immediate opening of hostilities—hostilities which we were trying our best to avert. The Army and Navy confided nothing to the Foreign Office, which continued negotiations without any knowledge of their true intentions, not to speak of their strategic plans. Our efforts were thus completely pointless. As a matter of fact the American government was far better informed than we of the secret designs of our military. Hence success in the negotiations was difficult to achieve.
>
> In short, those normally responsible for diplomacy had hardly any control of it during the decade preceding the war, despite sincere efforts to the contrary. Our endeavors for peace were doomed to be futile. The truth is that although we possessed diplomats we did not have diplomacy. This was largely because our diplomats had no roots in the soil of their own country.[9]

Clearly, it is possible to cite any number of examples of actions taken by the military that domestically were high-handed, and that abroad would inevitably be considered acts of aggression. We can certainly understand that these military actions caused Foreign Ministry officials to feel increasing unease. However, for anyone with even a slight knowledge of the Foreign Ministry's history, Kase's comments that "[o]ther branches of government customarily deferred to the armed forces," and that "[t]he Foreign Office alone had the courage to challenge the military and to oppose their aim of aggression and aggrandizement," were excuses shameless enough to prompt speculation about whom Kase thought he was kidding!

Let's examine Kase's comments more closely. Why were five former Foreign Ministry officials (Kōki Hirota, Toshio Shiratori, Shigenori Tōgō, Mamoru Shigemitsu and Yōsuke Matsuoka) among the 28 defendants arraigned as class A war criminals at the Tokyo Trial? Or six if the ambassador to Germany, the former Army officer Hiroshi Ōshima, is included. Why were so many individuals connected with the Foreign Ministry arraigned at the Tokyo Trial?

Kase's comments, cited above, were originally published in English in the United States, and were first made, admittedly, during the warped linguistic space unique to Japan's occupation.

While the arrival of the Shōwa period did indeed see Japan's military move recklessly into China, didn't the Foreign Ministry instead, at a time when Japan ought to have been most supportive of a new China founded in 1915, force its Twenty-One Demands on the Chinese, incite anti-Japanese sentiment, and fundamentally shatter Sino-Japanese relations? Didn't diplomatic measures to force the Twenty-One Demands on China actually precede military action, and didn't the Foreign Ministry actually take a leading role in the rise of militarism? While it is true the military provided a pretext in 1933, wasn't the Foreign Ministry responsible for Japan's withdrawal from the League of Nations? During the conflict between Japan and China in 1938, Prime Minister Konoe made a careless and irreversible statement to China to "cease from henceforward to deal with the Nationalist Government"; but wasn't the Foreign Ministry directly responsible for this because it drafted the statement to restrain a military that had guarded hopes for China? Even though the military was directly involved in the signing of the 1936 Anti-Comintern Pact between Japan and Germany, didn't the Foreign Ministry actively conclude the Tripartite Alliance in 1940? Surely no-one could claim that the conclusion of this Alliance was forced by the military? It is obvious that the Foreign Ministry was very much involved with militarism.

Although in April 1941 the military actively supported the so-called "draft understanding" between Japan and the United States as an excellent opportunity to reconcile bilateral relations, didn't the Foreign Ministry, during the period when Toshikazu Kase was in a responsible position, shelve the "draft" and fail to exploit it to bring about that reconciliation? Furthermore, is it entirely the military's fault that Japan stayed on the Axis side in June when war between Germany and the Soviet Union broke out? Surely the Foreign Ministry, charged with Japan's foreign policy, should bear much more responsibility than the military for failing, or being unable, to devise a policy that accommodated the new situation arising from the outbreak of the German-Soviet war. A foreign observer claimed that the Foreign Ministry had then fallen heavily under the influence of the Nazi "Fifth Column," but even so, was it simply the case that the Ministry was being intimidated by the military?[10]

Furthermore, during the final stages of the negotiations between Japan and the United States, no responsible officials within the Japanese government, including the military, were able to see through the maneuver implicit in the Hull Note when it was forced upon Japan.

Shouldn't the Foreign Ministry ultimately bear the main responsibility for that ignorance? Even though it might have been difficult to see through this maneuver at the precise moment the Hull Note was thrust upon Japan, as the organ of foreign policy shouldn't the Foreign Ministry have properly studied and examined the U. S. government's Japan policy since Roosevelt's reelection to a third term of office the previous year? Moreover, isn't the Foreign Ministry to blame that the prewar American public were unaware of Japan's position, so much so that after the war Americans would wonder why Japan challenged the United States at all?

Isn't the Foreign Ministry also responsible for the blunder in delaying the delivery of the "declaration of war" which led to the "sneak attack" at Pearl Harbor? Even if the military did indeed withhold all military intelligence from the Ministry during the final stages of the negotiations between Japan and the United States as Kase states above, does this in any way excuse the Ministry's unprecedented blunder?

And what about the Ministry's blunder of using compromised diplomatic codes, until the end of the war, which the American side continued to decode?

In other words, it would be more accurate to say that the Foreign Ministry sometimes clearly played an active part in militarism. At other times, when the military acted recklessly, the Foreign Ministry was unable to restrain the military because it neither possessed adequate information regarding the world situation nor analyzed the information at its disposal to draw sound conclusions; moreover, it had no effective powers of persuasion which embraced a vision for the future, and ultimately it simply followed the military's lead. In the area of diplomacy, which was supposedly its exclusive province, didn't the Ministry consistently commit one mistake after another at critical moments? As a result, didn't Japan's prewar Foreign Ministry in fact bring disaster upon the Japanese people, incredible though that may seem? Kase's book completely avoids and feigns ignorance of the Foreign Ministry's war responsibility.

Under normal conditions, that is, if after defeat there had been no occupation and the Japanese people had enjoyed freedom of speech, the Foreign Ministry would most certainly have come under intense public criticism. Criticism would have focused on its clumsy handling of the negotiations with the United States that resulted in the outbreak of war; but the trigger for that criticism would ultimately have been the Washington embassy's blunder in delaying the delivery of the "declaration of war," which led to the "sneak attack" at Pearl Harbor at the outbreak of the Japan-U. S. war, and which so infuriated the American public and the United States military. This blunder was absolutely inexcusable. Starting with this case of ineptitude, the Ministry would also certainly have been criticized for its incredible incompetence regarding the April 1941 "draft understanding." Moreover, criticism might have extended to the Ministry's error in continuing to allow its diplomatic cables to be decoded by the American side, right until Japan's defeat.

If the Japanese people had been free to express themselves after Japan's defeat, these blunders and ineptitude would never have escaped criticism. Before long, criticism of the "sneak attack" at Pearl Harbor would also have focused on the production of the clean copy of the "final notice" in English and why career diplomats unable to type English properly, such as the embassy counselor and secretaries, were posted to the United States where English was used;[11] questions would also have spread to the selection and training systems for diplomats. The reputation of the Foreign Ministry would then have totally disintegrated, and domestic calls for the dismantling of the Foreign Ministry might even have emerged from the Japanese people themselves. If the Japanese had been free to express themselves shortly after Japan's defeat, the Foreign Ministry would never have escaped criticism by the Japanese people after they learned of circumstances on the American side regarding the outbreak of the Japan-U. S. war.

As we saw in chapter 1, however, under Shigeru Yoshida's direction and with Toshikazu Kase's involvement, the blunder which led to the "sneak attack" at Pearl Harbor was concealed immediately after Japan's defeat. With this critical flaw, the Foreign Ministry was allowed to survive under the Occupation; and although it should have represented the Japanese people and conveyed Japan's views to the occupying forces, it collaborated with those forces and became their proxy organ when dealing with the Japanese people. Thus the Foreign Ministry, backed by the full prestige of the occupying forces, escaped public criticism, and completely evaded all public censure for its war responsibility. Around the time the Occupation was lifted, the two diplomats directly responsible for the blunder which led to the "sneak attack" at Pearl Harbor were even brazenly promoted to vice foreign ministers.

The United States government under Roosevelt's leadership also had considerable responsibility for starting the war between Japan and the United States; certain parts of the American public and the occupying forces came to understand this, and came to feel subconsciously a certain sympathy for Japan. However, this concern about domestic criticism is precisely why the occupying forces could never allow the Japanese people to freely debate matters concerning who had started the war. As a result, any concrete pursuit of Japan's war responsibility was transformed by the occupying forces into an abstract criticism of "militarism" without a clearly defined target. Amid feelings of shame at having excessively punished Japan, the occupying forces may have realized deep down that they needed to bring about a psychological reconciliation with the Japanese. This was because, psychologically, the whole of Japan could no longer be viewed as the enemy.

Policy failures toward Germany after World War I brought the valuable lesson that occupation programs which harbored grudges were entirely imprudent. Therefore, after war with Japan broke out, the United States carefully conducted ongoing studies of occupation policies for Japan; nevertheless, the desire at the start of the Occupation to punish Japan was impossible to avoid. For example, the first objective of the "United States Initial Post-Surrender Policy Relating to Japan" issued by the U. S. government on September 22, 1945, was "to insure that Japan will not again become a menace to the United States or to the peace and security of the world." Clearly though, this included an element of wanting to punish Japan. Legally, by accepting the Potsdam Proclamation, Japan's capitulation was obviously a conditional surrender. However, once Japan had surrendered, the United States modified its interpretation to one of unconditional surrender; and forcing this upon Japan can only be interpreted as part of a wish to punish Japan.

However, after the Occupation began, sympathy for Japan emerged when people developed a more detailed understanding of the American government which at the start of war had been under Roosevelt's leadership, and of circumstances on the Japanese side regarding the start of the Japan-U. S. war. Why was it imperative that Japan be occupied? The whole of Japan could no longer be viewed as the enemy. If responsibility for the war could be blamed on a vaguely defined "militarism," then it would be unnecessary to regard Japan itself or the entire Japanese people as the enemy, and it would also be possible to bring about a psychological reconciliation with them.

The occupying forces thus came to adopt a liberal stance towards the Foreign Ministry which had offered its complete cooperation. Although the occupying forces had some idea of the nature of the prewar Foreign Ministry (as can be seen by the number of its diplomats arraigned at the Tokyo Trial), they did not want to cause any particular problems for a postwar Ministry that presumably would not disobey them, despite any discomfort they might have felt over how the Ministry had shifted its war responsibility onto "militarism." Theoretically, any criticism of the Foreign Ministry was a problem for Japan and the Japanese people themselves.

The Foreign Ministry benefited enormously under the Occupation's absolutist system, which permitted this expediency by the occupying forces. In the unique linguistic space thus formed during the Occupation, the Foreign Ministry—which had pursued a bumbling prewar diplomacy and brought disaster upon the Japanese people—never uttered a single apology for its war responsibility. It shifted its war responsibility entirely onto the military and militarism, and minimized and distorted a war responsibility which it, along with Japan and the Japanese people, should have borne.

Although the following will be discussed in detail in chapters 5 and 6, the postwar Foreign Ministry formed around a core group of individuals from the sections most responsible for the prewar diplomacy that brought about the worst possible outcome: the outbreak of war with the United States. These sections were the first division of the American affairs bureau, the Japanese embassy in Washington, and finally, the Japanese embassy in Berlin. In the interest of concealing the Foreign Ministry's war responsibility, the postwar Ministry formed around this group of officials who by rights should have shouldered the most responsibility. In the quote above, Kase claims that "our diplomats had no roots in the soil of their own country." Although contrary to what Kase intended, this comment reveals that, during the Occupation, these diplomats did not share the life or feelings of the Japanese people, did not have a domestic base, and were from a different world. Examining their bumbling prewar diplomacy forces us to conclude that the selection process for diplomats, in operation since the Meiji period and which produced this sort of diplomat, was against the people's interest.

The book by Kase introduced here is best seen as evidence of how the Foreign Ministry under the Occupation avoided its war responsibility, and of the presence of a unique linguistic space. In 1951, a Japanese translation of *Journey to the Missouri* was published, and it can only be read while taking these other issues into account.

Problems with *Nichi-Bei kōshō*, Kase's Official History

In 1970, with the appearance years after the Occupation of his *Nichi-Bei kōshō* [Negotiations between Japan and the United States], Kase Toshikazu became recognized as an official researcher on the history of the negotiations between Japan and the United States. Let us examine this official history, along with Kase's memoirs published in 1986.[12]

Kase's analysis of the April 16, 1941 "draft understanding" is as follows: Japan's ambassador to the United States Kichisaburō Nomura, and his group, who sent the "draft understanding" to Japan, promised the United States it could widen its interpretation of the right to self defense, in exchange for not forcing Japan to abandon the Tripartite Alliance; Nomura and the others thereby violated the original intentions of the Tripartite Alliance.[13] Hideo Iwakuro, who was directly involved in the preparation of the "draft understanding," had strictly upheld the spirit of the Tripartite Alliance during those preparations,[14] so his thinking on this particular point coincided precisely with that of Foreign Minister Yōsuke Matsuoka. Part of Matsuoka's intention for the Tripartite Alliance was to dissuade the United States from joining the war in Europe, and Matsuoka's conclusion that the "draft understanding" opposed the Tripartite Alliance was not entirely inaccurate. Matsuoka showed the "draft understanding" to Kase, who reported, not inaccurately, that "the 'draft understanding' has too many unclear points, and might be incompatible with the Tripartite Alliance."[15]

Originally, however, wasn't the overriding concern of the negotiations between Japan and the U. S. to avoid a confrontation between the two countries? The American side naturally concentrated on splitting Japan from the Tripartite Alliance; and because the United States knew Japan would not readily accept this, it obviously strove to prevent Japan from fulfilling its obligation to enter the war under the Axis Pact's third article. However, wasn't the "draft understanding" precisely the key to reconciling relations between Japan and the United States?

Therefore, the negotiations under Ambassador Nomura, who was originally sent to the United States to reconcile relations, had so far come together quite well. It must be conceded that Nomura, along with Tadao Ikawa and Hideo Iwakuro who were also involved in the preparation of this "draft understanding," did well to bring the negotiations this far, considering they had no knowledge of Germany's plans to attack the Soviet Union, and had to work with the Roosevelt administration that was attempting to win Japan over to the American side in anticipation of the German-Soviet war. Although this "draft understanding" was not an official proposal from the U. S. government, it is true that the American side recognized it as a basis for further negotiations between Japan and the United States.

On the other hand, what about Matsuoka? Just before his tour of Europe, the German government frequently advised Matsuoka of its intention to wage war against the Soviet Union. However, Matsuoka interpreted this to mean that Germany was intentionally leaking this information to contain the Soviet Union. He was then convinced that war between Germany and the Soviet Union would never break out, so it is perhaps inevitable that, based on this premise, he would assume the "draft understanding" was contrary to the Tripartite Alliance.

However, as discussed in chapter 3, by the time Matsuoka and Kase set eyes on the "draft understanding," they had already received an official report from Japan's ambassador to Germany, Hiroshi Ōshima, that war between Germany and the Soviet Union was extremely likely. It was precisely because of these circumstances that Matsuoka received, during his tour of Europe and through the American Roy Howard, an invitation to visit the United States. Also, while Matsuoka was in the Soviet Union, he received a memorandum from British Prime Minister Churchill advising the disadvantages of associating with Germany. Matsuoka and Kase were then in a much better position than Nomura, Ikawa, or Iwakuro to appreciate the United States's intentions.

The notion of a "quadripartite alliance," by adding the Soviet Union to the Tripartite Alliance, also contradicted the aims of the "draft understanding." Therefore, news of a German-Soviet war, which would have destroyed all German-Soviet cooperation and thus the basic premise for any "quadripartite alliance," should have stung like a red-hot poker. Above all, intelligence about the German-Soviet war should first have been checked for its veracity. However, neither Matsuoka nor Kase gave the matter any thought.

In his official history, Kase deliberately cites a number of reasons to find fault with Nomura and the others. For instance, when Hull agreed it would be acceptable to use this "draft understanding" as a basis for negotiations, Kase compared the Japanese translation of the "draft" with the original English text, in search of mistranslations and distortions. Kase complained that Nomura failed to advise Matsuoka at home office of the four basic principles that the United States had communicated: (1) respect for the territorial integrity and sovereignty of all nations; (2) non-interference in the domestic affairs of other countries; (3) the principle of equality of opportunity; and (4) non-disturbance of the status quo in the Pacific, except by peaceful means. Kase also criticized Nomura for reporting this "draft understanding" to Matsuoka as though it had been an official proposal from the American government. Kase called Iwakuro a schemer, perhaps recalling Iwakuro's activities during the conclusion of the Tripartite Alliance; he also denounced Ikawa for being a person of infamous notoriety.[16]

However, even if the points he raised were indeed correct, they weren't central to the "draft understanding." Even if the "draft" had problems, wasn't it more important to exploit the opportunity it presented, and build momentum to bring about reconciliation between Japan and the United States?

The notion of a "quadripartite alliance" was then the main thrust of Japan's diplomatic policy, so how would Japan react when the premise for this notion was shattered by the German-Soviet war? This must have been the question that most perplexed the United States. The United States thus made all sorts of attempts to win Japan over to the American side.

Therefore, doesn't this explain why the United States government accorded the "draft understanding" some significance, albeit unofficial? Rather than taking issue with the content of the "draft understanding," wasn't it more pressing, in response to the collapse of the "quadripartite alliance," to use it as an opportunity to increase momentum for the negotiations between Japan and the United States? The crux of the problem lies not in any shortcomings in the "draft understanding" itself, but rather in the wasted opportunity to reconcile bilateral relations that this "draft understanding" presented.

On April 29, Iwakuro telephoned Matsuoka from New York, and struggled to point out directly to the foreign minister his concern that the "fish" (that is, the "draft understanding") would spoil if it wasn't cooked promptly. Nomura also told Kase (who was answering for Matsuoka) that if the "draft understanding" was not accepted, it would spoil like a fish. On both occasions, Matsuoka and Kase were better placed than Iwakuro to know what this "spoiling" entailed. Although difficult for Nomura and Iwakuro in Washington to infer, the chance of war between Germany and the Soviet Union was mounting; but as mentioned in chapter 3, news of this gradually began arriving at home office to Matsuoka and Kase, through reports such as those sent by Consul Chiune Sugihara in Königsberg. Nevertheless the Foreign Ministry, under Matsuoka's direction, failed to devise any new strategy to respond to this critical change in its basic foreign-policy premise. They didn't even attempt to devise one.

During his return from his tour of Europe, Matsuoka stopped in Moscow and met with the U. S. ambassador to the Soviet Union, Laurence Steinhardt, and passed on the idea of a Matsuoka-Roosevelt-Chiang meeting. After Matsuoka had already boarded the train out of Moscow on his journey back to Japan, he received a cable from Steinhardt claiming that the "talk with Roosevelt went well."[17] It is generally believed that Matsuoka, for a brief moment, thought the "draft understanding" was a response to his summit idea; however, he was infuriated to learn that this was not the case, but rather that it was the product of an unofficial channel in which he had no direct involvement. This general belief is probably accurate. The Matsuoka-Roosevelt meeting he had envisaged had turned into a Konoe-Roosevelt summit, and it may well have annoyed him that someone else would get the glory.[18]

Kase also seemed at this time to be extremely dissatisfied with the "draft understanding," mainly because of anger over the amateurish diplomacy conducted in the Washington embassy. However, this does not justify tearing up the "draft understanding" and killing any chance of reconciling relations between Japan and the United States, or not fulfilling his proper diplomatic function.

War between Germany and the Soviet Union broke out on June 22, 1941. Before that, Prime Minister Konoe recorded the following in his diary on June 13.

> There was clearly an antagonistic conflict between American Affairs Bureau Chief [Tarō] Terasaki who tried somehow to organize the negotiations between Japan and the United States; and a group (Foreign Minister Matsuoka's group) that opposed them, which included Vice Minister [Chūichi] Ōhashi, Europe-Asia Bureau Chief [Mizuo] Sakamoto, South Seas Bureau Chief [Ototsugu] Saitō, and Secretary [Toshikazu] Kase. [19]

Even as late as June 13, we can see that Kase still firmly supported the Tripartite Alliance. The aforementioned influence of the Nazi Fifth Column and Kase's pride as a "diplomat" worked together to destroy the greatest chance to reconcile relations between Japan and the United States. At the end of 1945, it is conceivable that Kase was ousted from the Foreign Ministry because of questions concerning his sympathies at this time. The reaction by the Foreign Ministry, under Foreign Minister Shigenori Tōgō's leadership, to the so-called Hull Note in November 1941 may also have been problematic; however, Kase's reaction to this "draft understanding" was no simple error in judgment, and he deserves to be criticized for an obvious dereliction of duty. In his memoirs, Kase wrote that he "played a key role as secretary to a succession of foreign ministers, and knew that some were envious of this."[20] But upon examining all the facts, one cannot help concluding that Kase's ousting was not simply due to envy.

Japan's Diplomatic Codes Broken by the United States

From the above discussion, Toshikazu Kase clearly committed some serious mistakes as a diplomat during this period.

However, Kase was involved in another blunder by the Foreign Ministry at this time. As discussed in detail in chapter 3, the Foreign Ministry home office, during internal confusion over the "draft understanding," received a report speculating that the United States may have broken Japan's diplomatic codes. This was a cable from Japan's ambassador to Germany Hiroshi Ōshima, dated May 16, 1941. Even though the Ministry was thus alerted, it failed to implement a thorough investigation; moreover, cables to and from Tokyo regarding this investigation were later destroyed, and the Ministry carried on as though nothing was amiss.[21]

In fact, in 1929 Kase had a peculiar experience regarding the breaking of Japan's diplomatic codes. Kase was then posted to the Japanese embassy in Washington. An American visitor to the embassy told him that "all Japan's codes have been broken." This American was none other than Herbert O. Yardley, head of the United States government's code-breaking unit. It is now widely known that, during the 1921 Arms Limitation Talks in Washington, Japan's diplomatic codes were broken thanks to Yardley's efforts. Yardley leaked this information to Japan, perhaps out of spite, in an attempt to sell his code-breaking skills after losing his job with the arrival of the Hoover administration. Kase was the person directly responsible for the negotiations with Yardley. Shortly thereafter, Yardley disappeared and the talks came to nothing, but through unimpeachable evidence Kase was able to confirm the facts Yardley had revealed about the code breaking.[22] Given this experience, it is difficult to understand why, in 1941 when he was alerted to the possibility that Japan's diplomatic codes may have been broken, the same Kase treated the matter so insensitively.

In the latter half of his life, Kase has been the foremost expert on the history of the negotiations between Japan and the United States, but he has never once mentioned the facts concerning the report that Japan's diplomatic codes may have been compromised in 1941. As far as this author is aware, Kase refers only once to this intelligence war in his memoirs, with the observation that the Japanese side was decoding the cables Ambassador Grew in Japan was receiving from the United States.[23]

Efforts Too Late to Prevent Japan-U. S. War

With Yōsuke Matsuoka's expulsion from the cabinet on July 18, 1941, Kase was left with little work to do, despite remaining on the Ministry payroll. However when the Tōjō cabinet was formed on October 18, Kase returned to the Ministry as secretary and concurrently as a key department chief under Foreign Minister Shigenori Tōgō. Kase tried to prevent what seemed to be an unavoidable war between Japan and the United States, and apparently worked quite earnestly at this time. He must have then increasingly realized that the greatest chance to reconcile relations between Japan and the United States had come precisely during the period when the Ministry had been thrown into confusion by the April 16, 1941 "draft understanding."

Despite Kase's efforts, the outbreak of war between Japan and the United States was inevitable. The Hull Note was in substance a written challenge, and as discussed in detail in chapter 3, no responsible officials in the Japanese government perceived the strategic maneuver implicit in it. However, if Kase is going to criticize others for amateurish diplomacy and raise the issue of having pride as a diplomat, it should be noted that it was precisely this moment when the Foreign Ministry ought to have grasped its opponent's intentions during the diplomatic negotiations, avoided a confrontation, and devised a course of diplomatic action in Japan's favor. Adopting an adversarial position doesn't always mean resorting to war.

While time was indeed short, there is no indication that any effort was made to determine the American side's underlying motives. The strategic foresight of the Tōgō/Kase team, who received the Hull Note, was undoubtedly inferior to that of their predecessors Foreign Minister Teijirō Toyoda and Vice Foreign Minister Eiji Amō.[24]

In any case, Kase undoubtedly felt then that war between Japan and the United States had to be avoided, and to be fair he probably fought in earnest to that end. Although there has been criticism that the wording of the "final note" may have disqualified it as a declaration of war, recent evidence clearly shows that the Foreign Ministry consulted Tokyo Imperial University professor Kisaburō Yokota, an authority at the time on international law, to verify that it met all the conditions necessary for a war declaration.[25] Such was the attention to detail paid by the Ministry.

This "final notice" was not written by Toshikazu Kase, but by his supervisor American Affairs Bureau Chief Kumaichi Yamamoto. However, even today, it vividly captures the mentality of the Japanese people at the time, and is a good example of the wording for a "declaration of war." It revealed that, even though the Japanese side had struggled solemnly and sincerely to reconcile relations, the United States had made little attempt to respond, and instead of rational diplomacy had committed infuriating acts of deception. The Japanese side felt it had to express its dissatisfaction here, and even though this brought deep regret, it calmly selected the right words to concisely voice that disappointment. When Japan clearly communicated this mass of evidence that attested to the American side's lack of sincerity during the bilateral negotiations, the United States government, namely Roosevelt and Hull, must have felt astonished and disappointed. From this perspective, the wording of the "final notice" was indeed well drafted.

However, even this "notice" was lightly brushed aside by Secretary of State Hull. Although the American side in substance failed to show sincerity during the negotiations, the United States government, under the leadership of Roosevelt and Hull, overwhelmingly won the diplomatic war by stressing the procedural question of who declared war first, that is, who made the first move to start the war. Japan's diplomacy suffered a total defeat because it didn't realize beforehand that, for the American people, the procedural issue of who had made the first move was more important than the question of who had acted in good faith during the negotiations.

When he received the "declaration of war," Hull made the following statement regarding its delivery after the designated time, that is, after the attack on Pearl Harbor had already begun.

> In all my fifty years of public service I have never seen a document that was more crowded with infamous falsehoods and distortions— infamous falsehoods and distortions on a scale so huge that I never imagined until today that any Government on this planet was capable of uttering them.[26]

These comments could not have been spontaneous, and probably came from a pre-prepared statement. This statement may have been readied beforehand in the expectation the Japanese side would deliver its "note" at the designated time; and even though the attack on Pearl Harbor had occurred first, perhaps Hull decided there was no need to make changes to his statement, or to make only minor changes in some parts. Then right on cue, Hull immediately called his stenographer into his office, dictated the statement, and made it part of the historical record. He gave the American people the impression that the United States was right, and that what the Japanese side had to say was not even worth considering; it was a calculated statement (or measure) whose purpose was to incite the American people to war. Here too, Roosevelt and Hull scored another crushing diplomatic victory.

Failure to Deliver Note at Designated Time

Kase regards the bungled delivery of the "final notice" as a serious miscalculation. The Japanese embassy in Washington failed to deliver this "final notice" at the designated time. Kase is not alone in feeling incredulous that there was no sense of urgency then at the embassy. Orders had been given to destroy two of the embassy's three coding machines, and these had already been disposed of. The day before the attack on Pearl Harbor, a cable had been sent advising the embassy that a memorandum would soon follow.

> Concerning the time of presenting this memorandum to the United States, I will wire you in a separate message. However, I want you in the meantime to put it in nicely drafted form and make every preparation to present it to the Americans just as soon as you receive instructions.[27]

No-one could have imagined though the disgraceful events that were to unfold. Further orders were given that typists were absolutely not to be used. Even after all these clues, it did not occur to the Washington embassy that the outbreak of war was imminent. Even if the intention to start a war did not occur to them, no atmosphere was established to "make every preparation."

Kase sent the order instructing when the "final notice" was to be delivered: "Will the Ambassador please submit to the United States government (if possible to the Secretary of State) our reply to the United States at 1:00 p.m. on the 7th, your time."[28] Then, with enormous relief that everything had been completed, he sent a cable offering his "deepest thanks to both you ambassadors for your endeavors and hard work, as well as for what all the members of the Embassy have done."[29] However, although Kase had composed these cables with the utmost earnestness, the meaning behind his words completely failed to register and came across as little more than the clatter of code numbers. One is again struck by the cold-heartedness of Clio, History's muse.

How inferior were the abilities of Japan's diplomats then, compared with those from other countries? Although Kase was undoubtedly quite capable when it came to exercising discretion, Hideo Iwakuro reported an episode that exposes the incompetence of officials in the Washington embassy. When war was about to break out between Germany and the

Soviet Union on June 22, 1941, Nomura called his key staff together and canvassed their opinions on the likelihood that a German-Soviet war would occur. Iwakuro offered the view that war was inevitable, but most of the embassy staff either believed there would be no war, or that it was impossible to predict. In particular, Secretary Hidenari Terasaki, the embassy's intelligence chief, argued that Germany and the Soviet Union would not go to war. However, when the meeting broke up and he dropped into the teletype room, the radio was apparently broadcasting the news that war had just broken out between Germany and the Soviet Union![30]

It is not my intention here to take issue with the overall abilities of Japan's diplomats. The more important question is how Kase, in his own research on the history of the negotiations between Japan and the United States, treats the blunder of failing to deliver the "final notice" at the designated time. In Kase's *Journey to the Missouri*, mentioned at the beginning of this chapter, he does not touch on this issue at all. Conceivably, it was perhaps omitted because of publishing circumstances and other reasons when *Journey to the Missouri* was published. (On the other hand, it should also be conceded that these very circumstances and reasons made it vital then to forcefully demonstrate, to defend Japan's reputation, that the Pearl Harbor "sneak attack" had actually been caused by an administrative error.)

In any case, it is inexcusable that Kase, as a researcher, omitted this issue. In the preface to *Journey to the Missouri*, David Nelson Rowe stated that "this [expediency at Yalta] should have been avoided."[31] However from a researcher's point of view, Kase should have clarified the issue of the "sneak attack" at Pearl Harbor which caused American misunderstandings. No account of the events is complete without a discussion of what the effects of the Pearl Harbor "sneak attack" were, an attack that contradicted the Japanese government's intentions, and in which Kase was involved.

Recently, Kase uncharacteristically expressed dissatisfaction about the delayed delivery. However, in *Nichi-Bei kōshō*, his official history published in 1970, he only touches briefly on the matter.

> Although there was plenty of time to spare, and moreover a cable with a strict warning had arrived, for some reason there was a breach of orders which delayed the decoding and preparing of the clean copy. Regardless of the situation, it is extremely regrettable that the notice ending the negotiations was delivered after war had begun. Because of this, Japan has been stigmatized by the infamy of launching a sneak attack during diplomatic negotiations.[32]

He criticizes, to a certain extent, the delayed delivery of the "final notice" that led to the "sneak attack" at Pearl Harbor; but while he was well aware of the reasons for the delay, he was pressured by the Foreign Ministry not to discuss this issue publicly, and indeed, not one word is mentioned. Kase's comments are in complete harmony with the Foreign Ministry's position on the issue at that time.

Moreover, there is absolutely no indication that Kase, as a researcher, has ever criticized or examined the fact that, around the time the Occupation was lifted, the two officials directly responsible for this blunder were promoted to vice foreign ministers. To the contrary, Kase published *The Last Words of Shigeru Yoshida* in 1967 when the former prime minister died, and praised Yoshida who had promoted these two culprits.[33] Even if Kase had been taken into Yoshida's confidence and was indebted to him, it was probably inappropriate for Kase as a researcher to praise Yoshida, who promoted the officials responsible for the Pearl Harbor "sneak attack" and thereby hid the blunder from the Japanese people. Or is Kase ever prepared to admit that he was an accomplice and actively took part in this cover-up of responsibility? Here lies the inherent contradiction for Kase the researcher.

Yoshida Hid Foreign Ministry's War Responsibility

To sum up, Kase's research into the history of Japanese diplomacy has ultimately been an effort to hide the Foreign Ministry's war responsibility. And behind him stood Shigeru Yoshida, Kase's postwar patron. Let's now examine how far during the Occupation the Foreign Ministry, under Yoshida, acted against the Japanese people's interest. Let's then look at how it handled the issue of Chiune Sugihara, the main subject of this book.

As discussed in chapter 1, on September 27, 1945, Shigeru Yoshida, with Toshikazu Kase's involvement, supplied a false report to the emperor that Hideki Tōjō had arranged the "sneak attack" at Pearl Harbor. Yoshida also suppressed an internal Foreign Ministry investigation, conducted in June 1946, into the blunder at the Washington embassy over the delay in delivering the "final notice" that led to the "sneak attack." In compliance with Yoshida's wishes at the time, Director General Katsuo Okazaki terminated the investigation.

Moreover, as was also described in detail in chapter 1, the emperor was given a false report when he met with MacArthur on September 27, 1945, to the effect that Hideki Tōjō had arranged the "sneak attack" at Pearl Harbor. However, it was unlikely that this was the general understanding within the Foreign Ministry, which from the start would have known the circumstances of the delay on the Japanese side. It was then thought within the Foreign Ministry that the delay was caused by the cable staff's slow work. Straight after the war Katsuzō Okumura, the person directly responsible for the blunder, interpreted at the meeting between Emperor Hirohito and MacArthur; however, the Washington embassy's cable section chief had then yet to arrive back in Japan, and the blunder was therefore blamed on him. In March 1946, this cable section chief returned to Japan and was furious when he found out about it; this triggered an investigation into the truth, and is the reason an investigatory committee of sorts was set up. Examining the issues that were scheduled to be investigated reveals the Ministry initially intended to do a proper investigation to uncover everything. However just as this investigation was being launched, it was called off personally by Okazaki who was in charge.[34]

It should be pointed out that Okazaki also participated in some questionable activities at the Tokyo Trial. During the Nanking Incident of 1937, Okazaki was working in Nanking as an unattached consul general, and he submitted an affidavit to the prosecutor's section on June 20, 1946, shortly after the Tokyo Trial was convened. Regarding the Nanking Incident, he testified that "the army was totally out of control," and that General Iwane Matsui "made no apologies at all."[35] This affidavit was not presented to the court, but through it we can see that Okazaki sided with those who were making the indictment against the Nanking Incident, and that he stood idly by while the Army came under attack.

Furthermore, it is worth noting the following about the Nanking Incident. It is well known that the Japanese side rigorously defended this matter at the Tokyo Trial. On May 5, 1947, the defense section entered the rebuttal stage and offered opposing evidence and arguments. Shinrokurō Hidaka appeared at court that day to give detailed testimony, but spoke out in defense of the Japanese side. Although Hidaka had by then left the Ministry, at the time of the Nanking Incident he had been in Shanghai and was accredited as counselor to Japan's Nanking embassy.[36] Conversely, Okazaki behaved in precisely the opposite way.

On February 4, 1947, Okazaki became vice foreign minister. In June 1947, the same time Hidaka was giving his testimony, Okazaki sacked Chiune Sugihara, saying that, "It is because of that incident in Lithuania. We can no longer take you under our wing."[37] It will be recalled that Sugihara, just before war broke out, disobeyed Ministry orders and issued visas to save 6,000 Jewish refugees in Lithuania.

As was just mentioned, Japan had entered the defense phase over the Nanking Incident at the Tokyo Trial, and it then faced an extremely difficult fight. Officials at the vice foreign minister level would have been aware of this.

Indeed, the efforts of Japanese like Sugihara in saving Jews fleeing from Hitler was already known in the United States during the war, and Jewish-American scientists pleaded with the United States government not to drop the atomic bomb on Japan.[38] Hainry Rubenstein, a Jewish financial mediator from the U. S. east coast, requested that the Japanese government appoint Sugihara as ambassador to the United States if a peace treaty was to be concluded during the Shidehara or Yoshida cabinets.[39] Under the prevailing circumstances of the day, it was inconceivable that a request from such a prominent American would have failed to reach the Foreign Ministry. Which means Okazaki must have been quite aware of Sugihara's usefulness.

To understand Okazaki's mysterious behavior concerning Sugihara, let's look at the circumstances at the end of July 1940 when Sugihara disobeyed Ministry orders. Yōsuke Matsuoka, foreign minister before the outbreak of war between Japan and the United States, was a pariah within the Foreign Ministry in 1947, the year Sugihara was dismissed from the Ministry. Sugihara had broken the rules by disobeying Matsuoka's orders. It could have been argued therefore that Sugihara should have been treated favorably within the Ministry in 1947. Moreover, Sugihara had not been punished in 1940 because he had disobeyed orders for humanitarian reasons, and the matter had been dropped. When Sugihara disobeyed orders, Japan was finalizing the Tripartite Alliance, and had to strengthen its Axis association. Even at this time though, Sugihara was not punished and the matter was dropped, probably because his transgressions were humanitarian acts.

The organized slaughter of the Jews called for in a secret Nazi decision of January 21, 1942, namely the Holocaust, could not necessarily have been foreseen when Sugihara issued the visas in 1940, even though Jewish refugees were then facing fierce persecution all over Europe. Sugihara disobeyed orders to issue visas at this time, but his rule breaking did not bring serious consequences, and was simply ignored. He was not punished at the time.

However, when Sugihara was in effect punished in June 1947 for disobeying orders, his visa-issuing activities were becoming more widely known, activities that resulted in saving the lives of thousands of people whose exact number is still unknown. In 1947, during worldwide condemnation of Nazi Germany's slaughter of the Jews, it is highly unlikely that anyone could have been ignorant of the significance of Sugihara's achievement.

The spread of Jewish persecution throughout Europe, including the Soviet Union, began after World War I. As Yukiko Sugihara, Chiune's widow, observed, there was a sign banning Jews (*Juden nicht zuganglich*) at the entrance of the park near the Japanese consulate in Lithuania where Sugihara issued his visas to Jewish refugees,[40] and this confirms that persecution against the Jews had spread all over Europe. In Poland too, even before Nazi Germany's invasion in September 1939, it was Poland itself and not German troops that persecuted Jews. The number of Jewish refugees started to increase dramatically when Nazi Germany began to aggressively persecute the Jews. The only escape route then available to Jewish refugees in Poland was to transit through Japan. If they were issued transit visas through Japan, they could escape via the Soviet Union.

When Israel's President Chaim Herzog visited Japan in February 1989 to attend Emperor Hirohito's funeral, he said, "During World War II, when many countries of the world closed their doors, Japan and territories under its control offered a place of refuge to tens of thousands of Jews. We will never forget this action by the people of Japan. Japan's attitude towards the Jews was completely opposite that found then in Europe, and was magnificent."[41] This is an example of the kind of praise Japanese humanitarian actions have garnered in this context.

With all this in mind, it is highly unlikely that, in June 1947 when Sugihara was dismissed, Vice Foreign Minister Katsuo Okazaki was unaware of the significance of Sugihara's visas. Even though Sugihara disobeyed Matsuoka, he escaped punishment because he had committed a humanitarian act; and it is clear this humanitarian act saved the lives of thousands of Jews whose exact number is still unknown. Moreover, Okazaki dismissed Sugihara at a time when Japan faced one difficult struggle after another at the Tokyo Trial over the Nanking Incident.

There is another issue worth mentioning. To date, no-one has ever connected the issues of the Tokyo Trial, the Jewish question, and the Nanking Incident. The relationship among these three issues is indeed difficult to see on the surface, but there are complex reasons for this. Namely, basic policy about the Jewish question had been decided in Japan well before Sugihara disobeyed orders and issued large numbers of visas to Jewish people. While Japan's partnership with Nazi Germany was deepening, a Five Ministers Conference, attended by the ministers for foreign and home affairs, finance, and the two military services, was held on December 6, 1938. Although it didn't actively support the

Jews, it approved "Summary of Jewish Measures" [*Yudayajin taisaku yōkō*], a policy directive to treat them fairly and, in principle, in the same way as other foreigners.

When the League of Nations was established after World War I, Japan supported the abolition of racial discrimination. However, even when Japan felt it had to strengthen its partnership with Nazi Germany, it chose a humanitarian policy that meant, in principle, treating Jews fairly, and which was based on a policy Japan had advocated for many years, namely that of abolishing racial discrimination. Although Foreign Minister Yōsuke Matsuoka imposed severe restrictions when Sugihara asked permission from the Ministry to issue visas to Jewish refugees, the reason he didn't deny permission altogether was presumably the policy found in this "Summary."[42]

One other thing about this issue is worth mentioning. The person who proposed this "Summary" was Seishirō Itagaki, then Japan's army minister, who instigated the Manchurian Incident (1931) and was later sentenced to death at the Tokyo Trial. As a main proponent of Japanese militarism, he was one of the principal defendants at the Tokyo Trial.[43]

Itagaki was not directly involved in the Nanking Incident; nevertheless, Japan was faced with a difficult struggle when the defense section, as previously mentioned, entered the rebuttal stage on May 5, 1947, and offered opposing evidence and arguments. Okazaki sided with those making the indictment against the Nanking Incident; and his June 22, 1946 affidavit, in which he testified that "the army was totally out of control," was based on a series of protest letters about specific, individual episodes. These letters had been sent during the Incident by the International Committee for the Nanking Safety Zone. Although referred to as an "Incident," numerically these letters can only prove an extremely small number of deaths, perhaps a few dozen. The Nanking Incident was blown out of all proportion at the Tokyo Trial, and Okazaki's version, that is, the protest letters Okazaki based his testimony on, clearly evolved from fanciful accusations. According to the "Summary Report on the Investigations of Japanese War Crimes Committed in Nanking" issued by the Chinese side on August 29, 1946, 340,000 people were either killed or injured, of whom over two hundred thousand people were massacred. During the proceedings of the Tokyo Trial, this was inflated into an absurdly massive incident.[44]

What would have happened if Chiune Sugihara's achievements had then been revealed to foreign reporters and duly recognized in Japanese society? Policies contained in "Summary of Jewish Measures" would have become widely known, and it would have been demonstrated that

Seishirō Itagaki, a defendant at the Tokyo Trial, had been instrumental in the drawing up of that "Summary." It would have been proven that, unlike Nazi Germany, Japan had devised an admirable policy that eschewed racial discrimination. Hatred towards the Japanese by people around the world would have been toned down. It would also have greatly helped the Japanese side as counter evidence during the largely unsubstantiated attack on the Nanking Incident at the Tokyo Trial. This was the moment that the Foreign Ministry chose to dismiss Chiune Sugihara who would have had such a positive influence.

When Japan was faced with a difficult struggle and the defense section entered the rebuttal stage and offered opposing evidence and arguments, the Japanese public learned practically nothing about the court proceedings because of the strict censorship system imposed by the Occupation. Chiune Sugihara, incarcerated abroad after the war for a lengthy period, returned to Japan at the start of April 1947; he knew nothing about the Tokyo Trial's handling of the Nanking Incident because he had just returned to Japan. Sugihara had no clear idea then about the visas he himself had issued in Kaunas, nor whether Jewish refugees were able with those visas to escape safely to places of refuge.

However, Katsuo Okazaki's position as vice foreign minister would have given him a ringside view of developments at the Tokyo Trial, and he would have been able to observe the events as closely as if they had taken place before his own eyes. We don't know whether he was aware of the relationship between Seishirō Itagaki and the "Summary of Jewish Measures." However, one glance at the huge collection of prewar and wartime materials in the Ministry's files on race issues, in particular those related to the Jewish question,[45] means it is unlikely Okazaki, then a vice foreign minister, would not have known that prewar Japan (including the military) had accomplished the real achievement of a laudable and humanitarian policy towards the Jews. As vice foreign minister, Okazaki must have realized what might have happened if he had then revealed Japan's prewar policy towards the Jews, of which ample evidence had survived as historical materials in the Ministry's archives, or if he had then publicized and recognized Sugihara's achievements as a testament to this policy.

If we carefully examine the course of events and the prevailing circumstances, at least from this lateral perspective, Sugihara's dismissal by Okazaki cannot simply be dismissed as a random occurrence. They were not ignorant of the significance of Sugihara's achievements, and we can categorically rule out that he was a target of the staff cutbacks the Foreign Ministry was then under pressure to make. Which means the only conclusion we can draw is that Sugihara was dismissed in the full awareness of his usefulness.

Whether Okazaki and his immediate boss Yoshida really intentionally went this far is probably unimaginable nowadays, and it is difficult to rashly accept. However, it would be instructive to recall that, around the time the Occupation was lifted, Yoshida and Okazaki recalled to the Ministry the two officials directly responsible for the Pearl Harbor "sneak attack," and promoted them to vice foreign ministers, the highest positions within the ministry. Okazaki was a favorite of Yoshida's, and worked as foreign minister on three occasions from April 30, 1950, through December 10, 1954, the day Mamoru Shigemitsu took over his position. At this time, the aforementioned two officials directly responsible for the blunder at the Washington embassy that led to the "sneak attack," namely Sadao Iguchi and Katsuzō Okumura, were brazenly promoted to vice foreign ministers. Everyone accepted the promotion of these two officials as a commonplace event, but the issue of Chiune Sugihara's dismissal escaped notice and left no trace, like a single drop of rain in a scattered shower.

As mentioned in chapter 2, although the war between Japan and the United States was a tragic one, it would be unacceptable to assume its tragic character was unavoidable because that is simply the nature of war. There are also wars that end as abruptly as they start, and others that end after a ritualized battle. At the very least, there are many wars where, to minimize the number of tragic casualties, the side that has obviously lost surrenders in a timely manner. On the other hand, the confrontation between Japan and the United States was a tragic war that remains difficult to comperehend. It continued beyond the moment victory or defeat became apparent, until Japan was almost "destroyed." And in a perverse twist of history, the selection and promotion to vice foreign ministers of the two officials directly responsible for the "sneak attack" at Pearl Harbor, and who provided the direct cause for why the war became so tragic, were lauded, while issues such as Chiune Sugihara's dismissal were hardly noticed.

The worst outcome that the blunder of the "sneak attack" might have caused was Japan's potential "destruction" or partition. Moreover, this blunder had clearly violated explicit orders "to put [the final notice] in nicely drafted form and make every preparation to present it to the Americans just as soon as you receive instructions." Nevertheless, the fact that these two culpable officials were promoted to vice foreign ministers means that things such as Chiune Sugihara's sacking were entirely possible.

Incidentally, it is now becoming clear from various sources that Shigeru Yoshida was unhelpful when it came to defending Japan's reputation at the Tokyo Trial. Even though the Japanese side should have proved to the United States that the "sneak attack" at Pearl Harbor was caused by an administrative blunder at the Washington embassy, historical materials related to the Pearl Harbor issue that were only declassified on November 22, 1994, unambiguously exposed Yoshida's clear intention to hush the blunder up and consign it to oblivion.[46] At the Tokyo Trial, Yoshida went to great lengths to draw as little attention as possible to the Foreign Ministry's blunder, and did not lift a finger to help restore Japan's reputation. In Yoshida's memoirs, published between 1957 and 1958, true to character he did not utter a single word of substance regarding the Tokyo Trial. This is preposterous for the memoirs of the prime minister who led the nation during the Occupation. It was probably Yoshida's intention to disregard the devastating fury of the Tokyo Trial.

It would probably be stating the obvious to say that the Foreign Ministry, under Yoshida and Okazaki during the Occupation, clearly betrayed the people's interests.

Participants in Diplomacy Shouldn't Be Researchers

Let us return now to Toshikazu Kase, who at the very least should not have become a researcher on the negotiations between Japan and the United States.

Kase originally had a virtual monopoly on the materials and information for researching the extremely delicate diplomatic issue of the Japan-U. S. negotiations; and by pursuing that research, without realizing it he steered the study of that history in a certain direction. Various materials and information were unavailable then to other researchers. With this preferential access, he steered research in a certain direction, and presented only those materials and information that were favorable to his version of the events; only after a fundamental research paradigm was established did he present voluminous amounts of material and information, but failed to put these in their correct context. Or in other words, Kase fabricated his own version of history.

The Japanese translation of Kase's 1951 *Journey to the Missouri* was superseded by his aforementioned 1970 official history *Nichi-Bei kōshō*, and essentially forms the fundamental paradigm for today's research into the history of the negotiations between Japan and the United States.

This point is worth considering. Why is the hidden significance of the Potsdam Proclamation still not understood in Japan? Although Japan was in danger of being partitioned, why has it forgotten the achievements of Joseph C. Grew, the American ambassador to Japan at the start of the war, who took great pains within the State Department to try to prevent Japan's partitioning? Why isn't it more widely known among the Japanese people that the Foreign Ministry took no appropriate measures after it had been alerted to the possibility that Japan's diplomatic cables were being decoded by the United States? Although Japan was also decoding the American side's diplomatic cables, why is it virtually unknown what influence this may have had on Japanese policy making? Why does the general public know practically nothing about the fact that Japan was decoding the American side's diplomatic cables, even after it was revealed in 1948 in the Japanese translation of Joseph Grew's memoirs *Ten Years in Japan*, that someone had informed the American side of this during the negotiations?[47] Why is it that, even today, the Japanese people have never once denounced the Foreign Ministry's serious policy vacuum around the time war broke out between Germany and the Soviet Union? And why are we no longer aware of the influence of the Nazi Fifth Column?[48] The answer to these questions is because Kase, a participant in these events, and despite being aware of such issues, has not touched upon them in his research. For Kase, these issues are too inconvenient.

In other words, Kase's research on the history of the Japan-U. S. negotiations entirely overlooks the Foreign Ministry's responsibility for the talks, while putting Kase himself in a favorable light. He completely glosses over the Foreign Ministry's responsibility for allowing those talks to end with the outbreak of war between Japan and the United States, and for plunging the Japanese people into an unprecedented tragedy.

A Japanese proverb says that "a defeated general should not talk of battles," but this author takes issue with this way of thinking. A defeated general must also talk. Without revealing why a battle was lost, a valuable lesson can never be handed down to later generations. Therefore, anyone who made mistakes during the Japan-U. S. negotiations must be given a margin of freedom to talk about those negotiations, and indeed should be encouraged to do so. However, such people should not engage in research. This is because research must be pursued while maintaining as much objectivity as possible. Participants in historical events should refrain from presenting their research as "objective" conclusions. In other words, for posterity's sake, it is perfectly acceptable for such participants to write memoirs about the course of history and discuss the prevailing circumstances, how they felt, or what they did. However, the memoirs of such participants don't always reflect the way things really were. Despite the best intentions to remain impartial, a writer faces certain obstacles, such as memory lapses or unconscious justifications, because they are describing things after the event. Nevertheless, they can still make an enormous contribution to historical research.

Ultimately, the history of the Japan-U. S. negotiations that is now commonly accepted completely glosses over the Foreign Ministry's responsibility, and was pushed in that direction by Kase. We, the Japanese people, have embraced a flawed historical perspective on the history of the negotiations between Japan and the United States.

In 1997, Kase published *Nihon gaikō wo shikaru* [Reproving Japanese diplomacy].[49] The first chapter is titled "Drifting Diplomacy Ruins The Nation." A cursory survey reveals section headings such as "Drifting Diplomacy which Loses Its Bearing Ruins The Nation"; "Display Courage, Cast Off Subordination to the United States"; "Bias In The Media"; "Promptly Establish Rearmament, Japan-U. S. Security Treaty, and Policy on China"; "Discard Illusory Pacifism; Constitutional Revision Without Delay"; and "Drastic Reforms to Postwar Education is *The* Urgent Task." Finally, in the ninth chapter we find "Put the Tokyo Trial of Fifty Years Ago On Trial!" This author would like to believe this is where Kase's true feelings and principles lie.

However, the flawed understanding about World War II, and particularly the war between Japan and the United States, has greatly influenced what today's Japan has become, a Japan that disappoints even someone like Kase. Why did such a flawed understanding of the war arise? Wasn't this largely caused by Kase's erroneous portrayal of history? Isn't Japan's continued pursuit of a diplomacy that acts against the people's interest, and its lack of regret for the prewar period, precisely because of historical accounts by the Foreign Ministry that completely omit any regret? Despite his criticism of the Tokyo Trial, isn't Kase's own research on the history of the Japan-U. S. negotiations largely to blame for why the judgment of the Tokyo Trial, in substance, still prevails; and didn't it produce the social framework where the "historical perspective of the Tokyo Trial" freely circulates?

As discussed in chapter 1, it would be highly desirable if Kase made any important historical materials in his possession, and/or including his diaries, available to the public. This would greatly assist in a reappraisal of what that war really represented. Kase would then behave, perhaps for the first time, in a manner truly consistent with the feelings and principles discussed above.

Japan's Diplomacy In Future

Incidentally, Kase, a veteran diplomat who served as Japan's first ambassador to the United Nations, severely criticizes the current state of Japanese diplomacy in his *Nihon gaikō wo shikaru*, mentioned above. This author concurs with much of the content of that book; however, let us examine here a few points that are difficult to agree with.

Kase contrasts Japan's prewar diplomacy with that practiced today.

> Prewar foreign ministers, ambassadors and ministers had great insight, and were provided with broad authority. Also, communication methods were not advanced at the time, so envoys abroad had a wide margin of freedom to act on their own discretion because asking the home government for instructions was not timely. Nowadays, there are a great variety of methods to transmit information, such as cable, phone, internet and e-mail, so asking for instructions is quite simple. On the other hand, however, growing accustomed to asking for instructions weakens one's sense of responsibility, and dulls the spirit. [50]

To a certain degree, this author can agree with the point Kase is making. As he claims, the nature of diplomacy has completely changed with the diversification and acceleration of methods to transmit information. Therefore, it can also be said there was a tendency in the prewar period for diplomats of great stature to emerge. However, after examining the makeup of the Japanese embassy in Washington at the outbreak of the Japan-U. S. war, it should be pointed out that many diplomats there were not competent at diplomatic office work, and the diplomatic selection and training system no longer suited the circumstances of the times. Although diplomatic exams conducted by the Foreign Ministry will be abolished from 2001, the current diplomatic selection system, in a broad sense, needs serious reexamination.

In *Journey to the Missouri*, Kase states that "our diplomats had no roots in the soil of their own country,"[51] however what this really means, conversely, is that before becoming a diplomat, one must be thoroughly familiar with some other kind of work in Japanese society, that is, outside the Foreign Ministry. Being familiar with some other kind of work in society means one can develop skills of organization, planning, responsibility, and sociability, and above all put down roots among the people. Although these are qualities diplomats in particular should have, in practice being a diplomat, perversely, makes it difficult to develop them.

Occasionally, diplomats give illuminating interviews like the one in the February 1999 issue of *Bungei Shunjū* by the former ambassador to the United Nations Hisashi Owada, titled "Finishing Up as U. N. Ambassador: My Suggestions for Japanese Diplomacy."[52] This author generally agrees with the suggestions Owada makes regarding diplomats. However, he doesn't mention that, in training diplomats and developing the proper qualities, trainees first need the experience of being familiar with some other kind of work in another ministry or in the greater society. Unlike bureaucrats from the education, health and welfare, or construction ministries, diplomats have little contact with members of the general public. Since working abroad gives them special authority because of their diplomatic privileges, diplomats especially need the right qualities when pursuing interpersonal relationships and duties; but being a diplomat seems to make it very hard to develop these qualities. The training system for diplomats must be completely overhauled. Furthermore, while the diplomat to an influential country serves as a broad portal for bilateral relations, it would be better to appoint learned individuals, including members of the public from outside the Foreign Ministry, rather than professional diplomats. Japan can then adopt and absorb the vitality of a new diplomacy that is firmly rooted in the people, through the diplomatic skills of ambassadors who are not diplomats by profession. The professional diplomats could then use their professional skills to assist the ambassador, and the highest-ranking among them could receive other designations, for instance, "embassy administrative director."

Next, let's examine a heading from Kase's book, that "The Key to Diplomacy is Sincerity." This is a paraphrase of a quote by the early-twentieth century French diplomat Jules Cambon: "The best method to resolve international disputes, in general, is the sincerity of diplomats."[53] Generally, this way of thinking is quite reasonable. However, it did not necessarily apply during the arbitrary negotiations between Japan and the United States in 1941. The sincerity during those negotiations of Kichisaburō Nomura, Saburō Kurusu, and Shigenori Tōgō, was unimpeachable. However, it could be argued that Roosevelt and Hull abused this sincerity to promote their policies, and plunged Japan into an abyss. If Kase insists that diplomats demonstrate sincerity, then they should first demonstrate sincerity towards the people of their own nation. When a diplomatic official's own nation is imperiled, they must not cloud their rational judgment to save face. Although dealings with negotiators from other countries should generally be premised on sincerity, shouldn't they also be premised on the notion that the other side might betray that sincerity; and isn't the diplomat's basic mission at least to try not to damage their own nation's interests?

This author takes stronger issue with Kase's claim that "the maxim 'diplomacy shouldn't fan a spark into a conflagration' is as true now as it was in the past,"[54] which he makes under the heading "The Leadership Expected of Politicians."

This viewpoint is clearly unsound. During periods when wars could result from a single diplomatic error, it may have had some relevance. This maxim could indeed be applied to the prewar negotiations between Japan and the United States. In April 1941, a "fire" had started, but it was still only a "spark" compared to the "conflagration" of a full-scale war. This is because, conceivably, if every effort had been made at this time to extinguish the "spark," the "conflagration" of war between Japan and the United States may not have occurred.

However, this maxim can no longer be a rule of conduct for Japanese diplomacy today. Take for instance the incident regarding mistaken media reports over school textbooks in 1982. The Foreign Ministry extinguished this "spark" by settling matters with an apology, even though it acknowledged false media reports had been made. Perhaps it followed this maxim, and felt it worthwhile to extinguish this "spark." However, what was the result? Didn't this deliver control over Japanese education into the hands of foreign nations?

This point is worth considering. With the end of hostilities between Japan and the United States, Japan was forced to bear the entire responsibility for the war, and the postwar international order was determined on that basis. The world community compelled Japan to be "reborn."

Therefore, because of this confrontation, Japan renounced (or was forced to renounce) war, and came to rely on the military strength of the United States for its defense, through the Japan-U. S. Security Treaty. Depending on one's perspective, Japan's security now came to be safeguarded by far more power than it ever had before the war, when Japan had guaranteed its own security. For Japan, the chances of war had declined dramatically.

In which case, what should postwar Japanese diplomacy have focused on, and what might it have achieved? Japan should have clearly pursued a diplomacy that was just and virtuous, lawful and decent, and stuck to the principle of being fair and just by not flinching before the strong, and being unassuming before the weak. Wouldn't this sort of diplomacy have placed postwar Japan in a world class of its own?

When diplomacy fails to point out that an incident was caused by false media reports and simply carries out "damage control," or concedes on matters that Japan should not give in to and harms the nation's identity, it no longer deserves to be called diplomacy.

We should also note it is extremely unlikely nowadays that any war will ever reach "conflagration" proportions, as occurred in the past. In earlier times, when cities had mostly wooden houses and few fire fighting facilities, for instance fire hydrants, a single lighted cigarette could spark a huge fire. Therefore, putting out small fires was extremely important then. Today, however, cities generally have comprehensive fire fighting facilities and individual buildings are fully fire-proofed, so a lighted cigarette will rarely damage more than its immediate surroundings. Even when a fire does break out, in most instances only a single room might burn down before the fire is put out. A conflagration engulfing an entire city is now inconceivable. To prevent a war during the era when wars started easily, a falsehood could sometimes end any trouble on the spot. In such times, diplomacy indeed followed the maxim: "Don't fan a spark into a conflagration." However nowadays, when wars are less likely to occur, this maxim is no longer so relevant. Instead, diplomacy today must be legally correct. The pursuit of a legally correct diplomacy overwhelms small incidents with a series of just actions, and these incidents come to an end naturally. For instance, it means that even an incident caused by a diplomatic administrative error rarely escalates into a big affair, and it becomes crucial to handle situations honestly. The viewpoint contained in Kase's maxim is quite problematic.

This final section has examined Kase's book *Nihon gaikō wo shikaru*, but the only conclusion that can be drawn is that Kase himself, during the postwar period, has still not properly atoned for what ultimately was the greatest failure in Japanese history, namely the diplomacy that led to the war between Japan and the United States.

Chapter 5

A Portrait of Chiune Sugihara, and His Motive for Issuing Visas to Jewish Refugees

No Greater Motive Than Compassion

One objective of this book is to examine the Foreign Ministry's unjust postwar treatment of Chiune Sugihara, who saved the lives of approximately 6,000 Jewish refugees. Since the story of the visas he issued in Kaunas is already relatively well known and has been told many times before, there is no need to go over the details again here. In 1993, Sugihara's widow, Yukiko, published *Rokusen-nin no inochi no biza* [Visas for 6,000 lives] (Taishō Shuppan). It has subsequently been translated and published in the United States, France, Brazil and Portugal, and has been read around the world.

However, as Chiune Sugihara's actions have become more widely known, various books have appeared providing interpretations of those actions from different perspectives. In 1998, a Japanese translation of Hillel Levine's *In Search of Sugihara*[1] was published under the title *Chiune: Ichiman-nin no inochi wo sukutta gaikōkan Sugihara Chiune no nazo* [Chiune: The enigma of Chiune Sugihara, the diplomat who saved 10,000 lives].

In Search of Sugihara is an impressive work, even though it contains some minor errors and to a certain extent lacks the care one might expect from a serious piece of research. The biggest problem with its content seems to be Levine's claim that Sugihara's motive for issuing those visas is still a mystery. However, from a Japanese perspective, Levine seems to be dwelling on the point unnecessarily. Under the apparent influence of Levine's book, writer Masahiko Shimada presented his interpretation in *Biza no hakkyū no dōki, izen nazo no mama* [Motive for issuing visas remains a mystery].[2]

Levine makes the following observation. "Sugihara was concerned about the Jews, whose lives, he knew, were in danger. He analyzed the situation in terms of the little he might do to help and the risks that he and his family would face. Sugihara was not one to act on whims."[3]

Kindness alone could not have inspired his actions. The situation was a matter of life or death; and kindness, uncoordinated and impulsive, would be ineffective, and at times even harmful. Sugihara, as a Japanese diplomat, could not afford to be careless. Even if Sugihara had an innate sense of kindness, he needed mental resolve and attention to detail to bring it into play.

At the time, Sugihara could not have foreseen that the persecution of the Jews would reach the massive scale of the slaughter during the Holocaust; however, in view of Japan's relations with Nazi Germany, which advocated the persecution of the Jews, he was aware that issuing visas to Jews would ultimately bring misfortune to himself and his family. Sugihara definitely did not let his wife Yukiko assist in issuing these visas, and this was most certainly a precaution against bringing harm to his family.[4] Perhaps what was needed was indeed a "conspiracy" that paid attention to detail, namely the "conspiracy of goodness" which Levine frequently mentions.

Between 1919 when he was sent by the Foreign Ministry to study in Harbin, Manchuria, and 1933 when he was employed by the Manchurian Government Foreign Ministry, Chiune Sugihara had ample opportunity to have contact with Jews who had gathered in Manchuria after World War I, and to become acquainted with the Jewish question.[5] Moreover, he already had an accurate grasp of the issue regarding the persecution of Jews by Nazi Germany. In July 1940, when great numbers of Jewish refugees fleeing Poland flocked to his consulate in Kaunas, Sugihara had a precise understanding of the situation these refugees found themselves in.

At the same time, he also had to take into account that Lithuania was about to be annexed by the Soviet Union, and his consulate was soon to close. That is, the consulate was to shut down on August 25, and Sugihara knew there was little time left for what he could achieve.

If Sugihara issued transit visas through Japan to the refugees, they could reach Japan by crossing the Soviet Union, and then escape elsewhere. He could at least enable them to leave Lithuania where they would soon probably be in danger.

Foreign Ministry regulations required prior home office approval before entry visas to enter and stay in Japan could be issued, but consuls themselves could decide whether to issue transit visas allowing passage through Japan. Sugihara made use of this procedural leeway and set out to issue a large number of transit visas.

Consuls had broad discretionary powers over issuing transit visas. For instance, even in situations where applicants met all the conditions for issuing a visa, such visas could in effect be delayed by saying that it would impede consulate operations. Sugihara as a rule issued transit visas readily, contrary to the consulates of other countries in Lithuania. When news of Nazi Germany's persecution of the Jews became known, the United States consulate in Lithuania severely restricted the issuing of visas and cited limits imposed by American immigration law. Britain too applied rigid quotas on entry permits for Palestine, then under British rule.[6]

In contrast, Sugihara stretched his discretionary authority to the limit, issued visas to Jewish refugees who were at risk of persecution, and let as many as possible leave Lithuania, a place that would soon become very dangerous for them. Sugihara was surely referring to this situation when honored in 1969 during his first visit to Israel, when he claimed, "I decided to help the refugees, provided my own actions were not illegal."[7]

Sugihara's kindness was seamlessly complemented by the cooperation of Jan Zwartendijk, then honorary consul of the Dutch consulate in Kaunas. Zwartendijk had issued certificates, indistinguishable from entry visas, which stated, "The Dutch consulate confirms that no entry visa to Curaçao, Surinam, or other Dutch territories in South America, is required."[8]

Although this did not explicitly approve entry to Dutch-ruled Curaçao, there was nothing untrue in the statement either. The certificate could have been interpreted as an entry visa, but strictly speaking, it wasn't an entry visa at all. Nevertheless, it didn't make any false claims.[9] Sugihara could have rejected such applications because they didn't satisfy an important condition for issuing transit visas through Japan, namely, clearly establishing a final destination. In fact, a consul would normally have been required to reject such applications. However, Sugihara deliberately looked favorably on these certificates and interpreted them as broadly as possible. Moreover, Sugihara first ascertained whether the Soviet Union would allow passage across Siberia if Japan issued such transit visas; he only posed questions that the refugees could readily answer; and he gladly applied the rules as broadly as he could. Furthermore, within the limited time before the consulate had to be shut down, he endeavored to let as many refugees as possible escape Lithuania and its dangers.

Of course, Sugihara was clearly violating orders. On July 23, Foreign Minister Yōsuke Matsuoka cabled the Japanese embassy in Berlin and ordered that transit visas through Japan only be issued to persons who had completed their entry visa procedures to final destinations beyond Japan.[10] While Sugihara had not been totally prohibited from issuing the transit visas, on August 16 the Foreign Ministry ordered they be strictly limited. "Please ensure that persons regarded as refugees not be issued transit visas unless they possess entry visas to their final destinations, travel funds, and sufficient money for the duration of their stay in Japan."[11] Therefore, Sugihara clearly must have known that he risked dismissal when he violated these orders. He must have been aware that, even if he wasn't dismissed, he would at least have to give up any hope for further career advancement.

Levine makes the following observation.

> Surely, Sugihara's act can be compared to Oishi's strategizing in the story of the forty-seven *ronin*. The vice consul acted just as boldly, behind his own scrim of false leads, calculated risks, and crucial loyalties. In preparing to stretch the rules, even to break some, what appears to be the uncharacteristic behavior of an obedient Japanese civil servant is actually, more historically and profoundly, quintessentially Japanese. In the end, Sugihara acted in the name of a great tradition. So much so, he even keeps up the game until the end of his life![12]

He follows up on this view of Sugihara's actions by remarking that,

> In 1967, at age sixty-seven, he continues to project the careful falsehood of himself as groveling, asking for permission that he would not receive, and ultimately defying and suffering the consequences. He portrays himself as that "tragic hero" deep within the coordinates of his own culture. He never touches on his own astute powers of strategy, subterfuge, and heart....[13]

As Mencius said, "The sense of compassion is the start of benevolence." Suppose we came across a child who was about to fall into a well. What would we most likely do? Even if, for instance, we were hurrying elsewhere, we would probably rush to the well and rescue the child as it was falling. This illustration demonstrates that people are born inherently good, as Mencius postulated. Indeed, if someone's life was in danger and a passerby was the only one around who could save that person, that passerby would probably help, even if they themselves had nothing to gain.

The only rational action at this time would be to save the child. It would be pointless to preach to people nearby that covers be put on wells or that all those not in use be filled in, even if these suggestions are indeed relevant to a basic solution to the problem. Preaching about the overall problem would not be the immediate action needed.

What Sugihara had to do at this time was neither protest that Nazi Germany stop its persecution, nor propose to his government that the Foreign Ministry caution the German government against persecuting Jewish refugees. Nor was it to suggest Japan should not align itself with a country like Nazi Germany that persecuted Jews. Within his authority as acting consul, and within the limited time available before the consulate was to close, Sugihara had to devise (indeed, had no choice but to devise) some way in this pressing situation for as many Jewish refugees as possible to escape, because the only way they could do so was via Japan.

First, Sugihara had to evacuate Jewish refugees with no exit routes to safe areas outside Lithuania, which was soon to become a dangerous place for them.[14] On September 1, 1940, Sugihara cabled the Foreign Ministry, and requested that only those who had met all visa requirements be allowed to board ships at Vladivostok bound for Japan, while those who hadn't could be denied boarding.[15] This would still mean, however, that the latter could also escape Lithuania. In a sense, Sugihara's actions were quite "creative."[16]

In other words, Chiune Sugihara disobeyed orders while exercising his authority as consul broadly, and helped Jewish refugees, whom one day might be killed by Nazi Germany, escape Lithuania in any way they could. Sugihara indeed had no other ulterior motives. Sugihara wrote in his memoirs: "In any case, due to the pandering of thoughtless, irresponsible and reckless professional military groups to pro-Nazi cooperation, many would always bear the Jewish people a grudge, believing that they are a clandestine force throughout the world; but how could I refuse to issue them visas on the pretext that their travel papers were not in order, or that they were a threat to public security? Did this really further the national interest?"[17] This too only strengthened his resolve to save the Jewish refugees. At the time, no-one could have predicted with certainty the mass slaughter of the Holocaust. However, when Jewish refugees came thronging to the consulate, fleeing from persecution that at some time and for some reason might cost them their lives, how could anyone claim that Sugihara had any other motive except to save those refugees?

Levine also claims in the passage quoted above that Sugihara portrayed himself as "groveling, asking for permission that he would not receive." However, it was not inevitable that Sugihara's request would be denied. As we will soon see, Japan's basic policies to that time clearly did not favor any other peoples over the Jews; and since it was unthinkable Japan would side with Nazi Germany and join its brutal persecution of the Jews, it wasn't out of the ordinary for Sugihara to request such permission. One more thing which needs to be pointed out is that Sugihara's postwar behavior clearly demonstrates that he was not (as Levine claims) a "tragic hero." Not once did Sugihara ever try to promote himself or his actions.

Journalist Kinue Tokudome published a short but remarkable article titled, "Are we correctly carrying on the legacy of Chiune Sugihara?" In it, she relates what Rabbi Harold Schulweis was told by people who had helped the Jews. Schulweis met with several hundred people who had saved Jewish lives, and asked them why they risked personal danger to rescue Jews. Most people claimed, "Actually, there was nothing else we could do."[18] That is, they had no ulterior motives.

Nazi Germany's persecution of the Jews was then already widely known. However, as noted above, the United States did not readily accept Jewish refugees, and the United States and European nations, including the Soviet Union, were generally unresponsive towards their plight. Those Jewish refugees who made it to the Japanese consulate in Kaunas, where Chiune Sugihara was vice consul, had no other way to escape except to travel on transit visas to Japan.

Chiune Sugihara, A Gentle and Capable Individual

Jadvyga Ulvydaite, a Lithuanian who lived on the third floor of the building where Chiune Sugihara set up the Japanese consulate, is still alive and well today. When visited by Katsumoto Saotome, she told him that Sugihara was a kind person.[19] Ulvydaite, who praised Sugihara's character, made apple juice for Sugihara on a number of occasions when she saw him with bloodshot eyes caused by lack of sleep from his work issuing visas.[20]

Solly Ganor, a Jewish refugee, had the most unusual fate of being interned in a Nazi concentration camp for Jews despite receiving a visa from Sugihara, yet was liberated in the final stages of the war by the 522nd Regiment of the U. S. Army, a unit comprising Japanese-Americans. Ganor was only a young boy when he met Sugihara in December 1939, around the time of the Jewish Hanukah festival. He was depressed because he had no pocket money after donating all his savings to the Jewish Refugee Fund, and could no longer go to the cinema and watch the latest movies. After Ganor's aunt introduced the boy to him and Sugihara heard this story, he told the boy to "think of me as your uncle," and gave him some money.[21]

In 1995, staff from the city desk of the *Chūnichi Shimbun*, a Japanese newspaper, visited people who had been saved by Sugihara's visas, and asked them about their memories of Sugihara. These recollections were later published in book form, under the title *Jiyū e no tōsō: Sugihara biza to Yudayajin* [Flight to freedom: Sugihara's visas and the Jews].[22] These recollections reveal unmistakably that Sugihara was a person with a gentle disposition.

However my portrait of Sugihara would be incomplete if I didn't point out his other qualities, namely, his competence as a diplomat.

Sugihara's extraordinary talent for languages is borne out by the following anecdote. In 1919, when sent by the Foreign Ministry to study Russian in Harbin, he had acquired enough of the language within four months to carry on a passable conversation in everyday Russian.[23]

We also know that, apart from his knack for languages, he was very capable in other professional skills. In 1926, he prepared a report based on personal observations called "Sobieto Renpō kokumin keizai taikan" [General survey of the national economy of the Soviet Union], which was "recognized as a very worthwhile work reference" and issued as a 608-page publication by the Foreign Ministry's European and American affairs bureau. This was how outstanding the report was.[24]

In 1935, Japan acquired the Northern Manchuria Railroad from the Soviet Union. The talks reportedly almost broke down then over the transfer price, but Sugihara carefully recalculated the property evaluation and helped enormously to bring about a compromise.[25]

We have discussed in detail in chapter 4 how contrived Chiune Sugihara's 1947 dismissal from the Foreign Ministry was, but his dismissal seems even more unusual if we take into account how outstanding his Russian ability and other professional skills were. A person with such outstanding talents would have been extremely useful to the Foreign Ministry.

Although it is true Sugihara was engaged in espionage, there are those who would criticize him for the "dubious" nature of this work. It would be wrong though, as is customarily done, to disparage this intelligence work. There are times when a country fights a war that could mean life or death. Obtaining accurate intelligence can be vital to the fate of the nation. Occasionally, certain methods used to attain that objective cannot be recounted openly for the historical record because of their "dark" nature, but the objective itself is one that is solemnly undertaken.

Quite frankly, it must be said that Sugihara's intelligence activities produced some outstanding results. On March 6, 1941, before war between Germany and the Soviet Union broke out, Sugihara was appointed consul of the Japanese consulate in Königsberg. Despite careful scrutiny by the Germans who considered him a spy, Sugihara gathered extremely valuable intelligence for Japan. He collected vital information by persistently asking about matters such as troop movements and the evacuation of children.[26]

From intelligence he collected, he sent a cable to the Japanese Foreign Ministry, dated May 9, 1941.

ITEMS FOR YOUR REFERENCE ON INFERENCES REGARDING GERMAN-SOVIET RELATIONS FROM INFORMATION RECEIVED THIS PAST WEEK

1. According to sources familiar with circumstances in Berlin, ten trains per day for military purposes continue to move north, and carriages are mostly from the French railroad.

2. Local military sources say that at present in East Prussia, a large force second to none is amassing in the direction of Lublin, and it appears that some decision will be made in June about German-Soviet relations.

3. Many field officers have been ordered to familiarize themselves by the end of May with enough Russian to read maps, and at present local Baltic Germans and White Russians are in demand as teachers.

4. In Pillau harbor, one 30,000-ton vessel and approximately ten other steamships have already been moored for a month.

5. For several days now, German tanks have moved out along all main roads towards the borders with Lithuania, and in response the Russian side has similarly moved forward to hold its ground.

6. The Ukrainian leader in Berlin Colonel Dyatchenko, who has investigated the military and bureaucratic experiences of refugees from Berlin and Lithuania, as well as their knowledge of roads east of Kaunas and Vilnius, has been sent in secret to Lvov.

7. The Russian side is expanding the no-man's land on the Prussian border; on April 15 it completed evacuation of residents from within

three to five kilometers of the border, and set up a network of closely-positioned observation posts as far as the front.

8. Train crews on the Lithuanian railroad which crosses the German border have all been replaced with new staff from the interior.

9. Since April, additional troops have continued to be drafted in the Smolensk and Oryol regions.

10. Although Soviet grain shipments through Eydtkuhnen have been disrupted since March 23, an extremely large quantity of grain from Minsk suddenly arrived at that station on the 8th.

Relay to Berlin, Moscow.[27]

As early as May 9, 1941, Sugihara had come to the conclusion that war between Germany and the Soviet Union was inevitable, and he sent this critical intelligence back to home office. In a sense, this cable ranks in significance with the well-known cable sent by the Japanese military attaché in Stockholm Makoto Onodera just before the outbreak of war between Japan and the United States, that mistakenly claimed, "A Japan-U. S. war is impossible."[28]

What did the home office do at this time? In turmoil over the issue of the so-called April 16 "draft understanding," the Foreign Ministry had temporarily lost its usual capacity to make decisions. As a result, no heed was paid to Sugihara's extremely accurate and competent analysis that war between Germany and the Soviet Union seemed inevitable.

It is tempting to think of espionage as an activity with a "dark" nature which cannot be recounted openly and is easily erased from the historical record. But as I mentioned previously, this is a misconception; one should be proud of activities to obtain accurate information about a war that could determine a nation's survivial. The nature of such actions might be somewhat ambiguous, and they are therefore sometimes omitted from official histories, but the objective for undertaking them is a solemn one. In Sugihara's case, he was able to collect vital intelligence based on his sources of information and personal observations, and sent this back to the home office.

At this time, Foreign Minister Yōsuke Matsuoka, Vice Foreign Minister Chūichi Ōhashi, and Secretary Toshikazu Kase, all overlooked Sugihara's methodical intelligence analysis. They must bear great responsibility for not paying attention to such valuable and accurate intelligence. (As a minor digression, I would like to point out how much the training system to produce elite diplomats, devised and handed down since the Meiji period, is against the people's interest.)

It is therefore unfair and absolutely unforgivable to consider the valuable intelligence sent diligently by Sugihara as "dubious" simply because it was obtained through espionage. Although Sugihara performed indispensable intelligence work and sent such valuable information, his presence after the war must have been embarrassing for the elite bureaucrats who failed to make use of his information but plunged recklessly without a clear policy into war with the United States. For Sugihara, this embarrassment was later to have unfortunate consequences.

It is clear Sugihara represented an awkward presence for the Foreign Ministry, an organization that entered the postwar era centered on people with great responsibility for Japan's prewar diplomacy leading to the outbreak of war, including Sadao Iguchi, Katsuzō Okumura, and Toshikazu Kase. Sugihara, who had sent such valuable information, was deprived of his livelihood by those who ignored his intelligence and brought tragic disaster upon the Japanese people.

Japanese Culture and Policy towards The Jews

The above issues must also be considered with regard to Japanese culture, and Japan's policy then towards Jewish people.

As previously discussed in chapter 4, a Five Ministers Conference (attended by the ministers for foreign and home affairs, finance, and the two military services) was held on December 26, 1938, when the government's "Summary of Jewish Measures" was decided. Japan would treat the Jews basically like other foreign nationals. We also mentioned that it was Seishirō Itagaki, instigator of the Manchurian Incident, who proposed it. Teruhisa Shino, writer of a biography of Chiune Sugihara for children (*Yakusoku no kuni e no nagai tabi* [Long journey to the promised land]), described Itagaki's act as curious,[29] but it was nothing of the sort. While Itagaki clearly was a militarist, his act only seems curious because of excessive prejudice against anyone thought to be a "militarist."

Sometimes a "nation" is forced to go to war. Or at least, the countries of the world before World War II conducted themselves with this view of nationhood. It could be argued that the phenomenon of "militarism" appears during the threat of war and escalates that threat; but it should be recognized in Japan's case that militarism arose not only due to the military's despotism and arrogance, but also because of Japan's ideals and sense of mission. As the middle of the twentieth century approached, the problem for Japan of *jison jiei* (self-existence and self-defense) became closely identified with the issue of liberation and independence for the weary nations of Asia who had been colonized by the European and American powers; it also became tied up with Japan's own ideals and sense of mission. No-one could fault Japan after World War I (when conditions seemed ripe for the emergence of an Asian century) for being keenly aware of this historical dilemma, one that deeply influenced Japan's ideals and sense of mission.

For those who had become militarists and were psychologically constrained by Japan's ideals and sense of mission, it was intellectually impossible to diverge from these constraints when the nation's official policies were being drafted. Obviously, the national interest was a concrete objective for members of the military who were instrumental in directly pursuing Japan's goals, and they understood perfectly well that these practical interests could be pursued in a Machiavellian manner. The military would not tolerate the pursuit of ideals that were not firmly grounded in reality.

At the same time though, cleaving to options that focused on concrete interests—precisely the bold acquisitive style of a Machiavelli—led to the pursuit of a national interest that coincided with practical military objectives; however, publicly manifesting this as a national goal only tainted the nation's reputation, which in turn undermined the spiritual basis for militarism. The highest policies of the nation had to measure up to the ideals and sense of mission of militarists. Militarism in Imperial Japan was embraced by these militarists with the utmost reverence.

"Summary of Jewish Measures" reveals the psychology of the militarists of the time. "In principle we should certainly avoid actively tolerating Jews in our Empire whom our allies so vehemently reject. But adopting the stance of shunning them to the extreme, as the Germans do, does not accord with the spirit of racial equality that our Empire has insisted on for many years."

On March 11, 1942, after war with the United States had begun, the Imperial Headquarters Liaison Conference (*Daihon'ei renraku kaigi*) replaced "Summary of Jewish Measures" with "Jewish Measures in view of the Present Situation" [*Jikyoku ni tomonau Yudayajin taisaku*]. The fair attitude towards the Jews was somewhat reversed to strengthen ties with Germany, but even so, Japan never directly persecuted them.[30]

Japanese militarism never produced a formidable dictator like Hitler, and despite tragic atrocities that occurred due to the senselessness of war, the psychological mindset of Japan's militarists ensured that until the end of the war no policy was implemented to unilaterally slaughter and persecute another race like Nazi Germany did the Jews.

However, writing noble ideals into public documents can sometimes backfire, and degenerate into a situation where it is assumed these fine sentiments are applied to conceal a darker Machiavellian intent.

Let's examine this issue as it relates to the militarist slogan "For the Emperor" [*Tennō no tame ni*] which was used in Imperial Japan. Those of us born in later generations must realize that this slogan was subsequently distorted, and used to either narrow the vision of the Japanese people, or direct the outbreak and expansion of the war in certain directions. It must also be recognized that this slogan could not have come into existence without Japan's ideals and sense of mission. This slogan first came into being when these ideals and sense of mission were widely believed. In other words, the slogan "For the Emperor" came into being in the midst of these broad historical trends.

To reiterate, if the slogan "For the Emperor" had merely been an expression to conceal some evil purpose, it would have been impossible to create a broad-based militarism involving ordinary people. While militarism obviously has elements of arrogance and narrow-mindedness, it came about clearly because of the issue of self-existence and self-defense that all nations would accept, and because of certain historical ideals and a sense of mission. Otherwise, it would have been impossible to carry out, let alone explain, the attacks by people willing to sacrifice themselves, such as Japan's special *kamikaze* squads. Japan did not fight for no reason at all. If we don't recognize there was a reason for Japan's fighting, then even criticizing the slogan "For the Emperor" does not constitute a proper criticism of militarism.

Incidentally, the book published by the above-mentioned research team at the *Chūnichi Shimbun* contained interviews with people whose lives were saved by Sugihara's visas, and they discuss their first impressions on arriving in Japan.

When refugees disembarked in the port of Tsuruga, a bashful youth of 16 or so approached them with a basket of apples and tangerines. He hadn't come to sell them, but to give them to the refugees to eat.[31] While returning from a shop in Kobe to buy some eggs, a Jewish refugee was called over and stopped on the road by a policeman. He was asked how much he had paid for the eggs. Although unaware of what was going on, he told the policeman, in broken Japanese, the price he had paid. Whereupon, the policeman escorted the Jewish refugee back to the shopkeeper who had sold him the eggs. The policeman said something to the shopkeeper, struck him, then grabbed some change from the till and handed it to the stunned refugee. In other words, the policeman questioned the Jewish refugee because he suspected the shopkeeper had sold the eggs at a highly inflated price to take advantage of the man's difficult situation; when the policeman found this was true, he went to the shop and returned the amount the man had been overcharged.[32]

The latter anecdote demonstrates that not all Japanese were kind and honest, because some unscrupulous shopkeepers overcharged Jewish refugees and took advantage of their difficulties. Clearly though, not everyone behaved this way. Japanese at the time were generally kind and honest. It is obvious that Japanese then were much poorer than people are today. However, they were also much kinder and more honest than people are now. Those *kamikaze* squads were made up of Japanese who typified this kind and honest group of people. They realized they were fighting for an ideal, and went to war and gave up their lives. Japan's war can generally be called a war of aggression, but if no proper explanation is given for why these special squads, and their particular form of attack, emerged from the Japanese military, then there can be no proper criticism of this war of aggression or militarism.

Masanori Miyazawa, a researcher on the Jewish issue in Japan, has pointed out that, unlike the irresponsible tone taken by many newspapers of the day to expel the Jews, the prewar Japanese government maintained a coherent policy towards Jewish refugees, a policy that it had nothing to be ashamed about. Under the national policy of "universal brotherhood" (*hakkō ichiu*), Japan consistently maintained a policy of not discriminating against the Jews.[33]

Those of us from later generations must recognize that the prewar Japanese militaristic notion of "universal brotherhood" was not spurious, and that this was how the emperor system in effect purified government policy. Any criticism of militarism without a firm understanding of this point cannot be a proper criticism of militarism.

When viewed in this light, we can see that today's critique of militarism, which brought about the dismantling of Japan's military and the portrayal of militarism as the incarnation of evil, has become extremely warped. Japanese militarism was indeed arrogant and narrow-minded, and any number of examples for violent acts of craven despotism within Japan and invasion outside Japan can be given. There can be no disagreement over the general conclusion that militarism nearly destroyed Japan. But the discussion cannot end there.

It would be a great misconception to think that the Japanese military was a brutal force, or that the Japanese were a brutal people. They had ideals and a sense of mission; pitifully, one horrific battle unfolded after another because they refused to be defeated in the war. However, these horrific battles weren't a matter of choice. The United States, which dropped the atomic bomb on Japan, would similarly deny that the bomb was dropped on Japan because it took pleasure in acts of brutality.

A brief survey of Japan's history clearly demonstrates that Japan is not a brutal nation, and the Japanese are not a brutal people. Glancing at its history, we can see that Japan with its emperor system has generally been a peaceful nation and has fought few wars. We can also understand it is a country that has developed with a high degree of order.

Although it should not (and cannot) be hastily concluded that China is a brutal nation and the Chinese are a brutal people, it is undeniable that China has experienced a brutal history. The Chinese people have always lived with the fear of violent or wrongful death. The development of Chinese history has been brutal because it unfolded while those deaths steadily accumulated.

Sugihara's widow Yukiko describes an interesting anecdote in *Visas for Life* that she overheard during a stopover in Potsdam before the war. This is where the world-renowned palace of King Friedrich is located; the king, who hated the loud noise made by a nearby windmill, issued an order for it to cease operation. But the old man who ran the windmill said, "To grind is my job; that is how I make my living. If I cannot use my windmill, I cannot live." He sued the king in court, and won.[34] This story has been handed down in Potsdam with great alacrity, and tells of the absurdity of a commoner suing a king. However, at the same time, it also reveals that people in Europe have lived closely with the idea that they too could sue the monarch.

However, the situation in China and Japan was very different. Commoners could never sue an emperor, not even in their dreams. Chu Yüan-chang, who overthrew the Yüan dynasty to found the Ming in 1368, was suspicious of his accomplished prime minister Hu Wei-yung, and executed 15,000 people related to Hu. He then became suspicious of General Lan Yü, and killed him and his entire clan. Together with the other 15,000, Chu was said to have put to death over 50,000 people connected with these two individuals. In China, people have always lived with the fear of violent or wrongful death.

The Warring States period in sixteenth-century Japan was a time of brutality, but compared to China the rest of Japanese history developed very peacefully. Oda Nobunaga was probably the most violent general during the period, but he had little option since nothing except brute force was then recognized. He had no choice but to be ruthless.

Perhaps, however, it would be more accurate to say that Oda Nobunaga's times were typical of what would be considered normative in Chinese history. As argued above, while China's history has been brutal, the Chinese people cannot therefore immediately be assumed to be brutal. In Nobunaga's defense, careful inspection reveals that his brutal acts all had precedents in China. There was also a case in China where the skull of a general who betrayed and fought his lord was used as a cup for drinking wine. Nobunaga was a keen student of Chinese history, and we can see he must have taken his lead from there. Presumably, Nobunaga in particular studied Genghis Khan, founder of the Yüan dynasty, because the Mongol leader was the most brutal of China's dynastic founders. Nobunaga's military strategies not only treated war as a struggle on the battlefield but also incorporated economic warfare (which until then had been quite unusual in Japan), and undoubtedly resembled the war strategies of Genghis Khan.

What I hope to demonstrate by raising these examples is that Japan's history developed at a moderate pace. If we consider China a country of "revolution," one in which great upheavals occurred periodically every few decades or centuries, and where "justice" could be temporarily suspended, then Japan is a country of the "emperor system." More precisely, it wasn't that the "emperor system" made it possible for Japan's history to develop at a moderate pace with peace, order, and a notion of justice; rather, the development of this peaceful and orderly history gradually converged with the "emperor system."

In any case, Japan evolved a peaceful and orderly history, even more peaceful and orderly than the nations of Europe and America, while in proximity to China which developed a turbulent history. Thus the notions of justice, fairness, and order flourished in Japan, as they did in the nations of Europe and America. It could even be said the sense of justice amongst Japanese during the militarist period was even more acute than that of their counterparts in Europe and America. Acts of brutality, of which any nation's military is capable, surely occurred during Japan's wars with China and the U. S.; but it is unlikely that a military whose nation is steeped in the notions of peace, justice, fairness, and order, would perpetrate extremely undisciplined acts of brutality.

Without dwelling on the point, let us consider why the Japanese military came up with such dauntless battle tactics, like the special *kamikaze* squads who sacrificed their own lives to attack the enemy. Suicide squads would not be sanctioned in conventional war strategies, nor are they being recommended here, but why did men who were prepared to make the ultimate sacrifice step forward from the Japanese military and the Japanese people? Upon reflection, it is unlikely they would have emerged if they hadn't had a sense of mission. Imbued with this sense of mission, these brave fighters probably stepped forward because they felt they had something to protect, something to accomplish.

Hence one should clearly explain these things before accusing the Japanese military of being brutal. As described in chapter 4, proper criticism of militarism is impossible and has become distorted, because such criticism has become entangled in the Foreign Ministry's evasion of its war responsibility. This is why the Foreign Ministry cannot properly explain to the outside world why Japan waged war, nor for what reasons Japan fought. Thus, Japan and its people are unable to explain matters to the outside world. Militarism rightly deserves to be criticized, but this criticism ought to be conducted properly, and not in a distorted manner.

More on the Issue of Rescuing Jewish Refugees

Let us return now specifically to the issue of the Jews. Historically Japan, unlike Europe and America, never had any particular enmity towards the Jews. Even when aligned with Nazi Germany for pragmatic reasons, the Japanese government could not stipulate the persecution of the Jews as actual policy.

Strictly speaking, for Japan the abolition of racial discrimination was a national policy, and the persecution of the Jews violated the spirit of this policy. Although Japan was careful not to upset Nazi Germany with whom it wanted a stronger alliance, it had an absolute policy against specific discrimination, or endorsing specific discrimination.

"Summary of Jewish Measures" gives a practical reason for not persecuting Jews. "From the perspective that we must avoid further deterioration of relations with the United States, we should consider the great likelihood that damaging consequences may result." However this didn't explain why the Jews were not persecuted; rather, what was emphasized was the act of not discriminating on the basis of race.

Although difficult to substantiate, Chiune Sugihara probably acknowledged this basic policy of the Five Ministers Conference when he issued his visas. At the very least, he was confident Japan would never adopt a policy like Nazi Germany's which called for broad persecution of the Jews. Conceivably, Sugihara stretched his authority as vice consul to the limit, based on this fundamental policy or his confidence in it, and took shortcuts to allow these refugees to leave Lithuania, which for them would soon become a dangerous place.

Also, when Levine asserts that Sugihara's motives for issuing the visas are unclear, this raises a problem with Levine's understanding of Japanese culture and its notions of law. Japan and Western countries interpret the concept of law in different ways. As previously stated, Japan had strong notions of fairness and justice, as did Europe and America; however before the Edo period (1603–1868), legal terms such as legal benefits and legal compulsion did not exist for individuals as "freedoms," "rights," or "duties" as they did in Europe and America; so it could be argued that there was no clarity over the legal notions regarding these terms. Therefore, it could be said that considerable differences existed between Japanese on the one hand and Europeans and Americans on the other regarding these legal concepts. As mentioned in chapter 4 with regard to Japan's "declaration of war" against the United States, there was a conflict between Japan's legal notion of giving precedence to substantive issues, namely, who in real terms had made unreasonable demands; and America's legal notion of giving precedence to procedural issues, namely, who had resorted to the act of starting the war. However, to manifest justice, the notion of procedure is paramount in the Western legal system, which is fundamentally grounded in notions of "rights" and "freedoms."

To manifest justice in the West, it is important that issues of procedure are dealt with firmly, and this alone strongly guarantees that justice is done; however, it is also possible to legally conceal a crime or commit an evil act by making sure that procedures are clearly completed beforehand. Therefore, the manifestation of justice can paradoxically be ambiguous. However, justice can be given greater clarity by not just considering procedural issues alone, but by focusing instead on the legal notion of manifesting justice, because after all it is this we should be concerned with. It can be argued that the Japanese, who developed a firm sense of justice in their highly ordered society—in proximity to China with its brutal history—brought greater clarity to certain legal notions than either Europe or America.

In Japan, the expression *Ōoka sabaki* [The judgment of Ōoka] means sometimes there is value in deception if it exposes the truth. Legal justice is then perfectly served by imposing a punishment which accurately fits the truth that has been exposed. Punishment for crimes that are similar but have different degrees of turpitude should hopefully accommodate those differences in turpitude.

An incident from the *Chūshingura* appears in the text above quoted from Levine. Asano Takuminokami, seeking revenge, brings about the stabbing incident in the Corridor of Pines, and commits ritual suicide without an inquiry being held. In Europe or America, there would have been a great procedural dilemma if someone was made to kill themselves without an investigation. In Japan, however, this was not necessarily the case. Even though Asano was expelled from the feudal clan, he was more furious and indignant about the injustice of Kira Kōzukenosuke not being reprimanded at all, rather than the procedural problem of someone being made to kill themselves without any investigation. Asano broke into his lord's house to kill Kira and redress this injustice.

Thus for Japanese people, procedural problems over Sugihara's visas would not have been important in view of his worthy objectives. Levine's dwelling upon "shrewd strategy and tricks," that is, issues of procedure and expedience, is pointless. The sincerity needed to accomplish his goal obviously had to include some shrewdness. Sugihara knew he could not rescue those Jewish refugees if he didn't use his authority as vice consul. This was something that Sugihara as an individual was prepared to do. As Sugihara later said, acting strictly within legal boundaries was obviously not only vital for the refugees, but also for himself. Levine's "conspiracy of kindness" was a necessary condition for Sugihara's sincerity. As stated, since his actions were clearly not taken on an emotional sympathetic whim, the "shrewd strategy and tricks" referred to by Levine were obviously needed if he was going to show compassion. Otherwise, both the Jewish refugees and Sugihara would have been ruined.[35]

Sugihara sent a cable to the Foreign Ministry home office suggesting that those arriving in Vladivostok without entry permits to third countries be refused permission to board vessels. Sugihara was determined to stay within the bounds of legal behavior here also, but nevertheless he achieved definite results because even these Jewish refugees escaped elsewhere, and were able to leave Lithuania which for them was about to become a dangerous place. Sugihara only took action after accurately interpreting the situation.

Saburō Nei was the Japanese consul in Vladivostok. Sugihara's junior by two years at the Harbin Gakuin National University, Nei decided not to restrict boarding onto ships by Jewish refugees with Sugihara visas who had made it to Vladivostok. This was despite home office orders severely restricting them, Nei argued, because, "It is unfavorable from the perspective of the prestige of our Empire's embassies and consulates abroad, to refuse approval to those with visas from our Empire's consulates who have made it all the way here, even if their documentation for a third country is only the claim that they are traveling to Central America." What is notable in Nei's cable is the same quality we have seen in Sugihara's case. Nei may have been motivated by respect for Sugihara, who was his senior at university, but more poignantly, all the Jews who received Sugihara visas were in fact rescued because of Nei's claim that it was "unfavorable from the perspective of the prestige of our Empire's embassies and consulates abroad" to refuse them.[36] By emphasizing the "Empire's prestige," all these Jewish refugees were rescued. Nei here exploited the normally mundane expression "unfavorable" (rather than using the term "undesirable") to achieve his intent. This deliberately broadened legal interpretation allowed all these Jewish refugees to be rescued.

It also seems paradoxical that Matsuoka himself issued orders strictly limiting the issue of visas. Although Matsuoka gave orders that only those with entry permits to third countries could have their transit visas through Japan recognized,[37] he nevertheless allowed them to enter. Sugihara's transit visas allowed a ten-day stay in Japan, but this was insufficient time to make preparations to leave the country; when they entered Japan, Matsuoka himself suggested and implemented the expedient step of issuing permits to stay for a month.[38]

Regarding Sugihara's benevolence, Levine also claims Sugihara was an "ordinary person"[39] and seems to imply that he was therefore not a hero.[40] However if Sugihara's compassion is taken into account, then Levine's appraisal is incorrect. If Sugihara was indeed "only" an ordinary Japanese, he would deserve even more recognition. After the war he did not bring any attention to his actions, and endured the humiliation of dismissal from the Foreign Ministry; he lived the rest of his life as though he had forgotten the past, and this is precisely his worth as a Japanese. It is unclear what exactly Levine means by the term "hero," but if Sugihara had done these things to become a "hero," then this motivation alone would have disqualified him.

To the contrary, Sugihara in a sense attracted attention to himself by issuing transit visas to Jewish refugees under the pressing circumstances of the Kaunas consulate's imminent closure. As an "ordinary person," Sugihara deserves even greater honor because he exerted himself to the limit and jeopardized his future prospects, but as a result literally saved the lives of 6,000 Jews.

In other words, Levine's description of Sugihara as an "ordinary person" is important from a Japanese perspective. Japanese should be proud that, when an emergency arose, even an ordinary person was able to carry out such a good deed. Sugihara didn't want to "be a hero" nor did he have any other ambitions, but often ordinary people do charitable deeds to achieve goodness within limitations they set for themselves. This is what makes Sugihara's benevolence significant, and why his good deeds have struck a chord in the hearts of the Japanese people.

Incidentally, there is something that should be noted when a nation honors Sugihara's actions. The issue of honoring Sugihara no longer only involves the question of Chiune Sugihara the individual, nor that of the Sugihara family, including his widow Yukiko. Sugihara himself may not even have wanted to be honored. However, the act of honoring Chiune Sugihara as an individual shows rather that a Japanese national did this, and that someone from Japan was capable of this sort of behavior. The significance of this transcends the intentions of Chiune Sugihara the individual. Therefore we must all respect the privacy of the Sugihara family when we honor Chiune Sugihara.

Chapter 6

Chiune Sugihara and the Postwar Foreign Ministry

Chiune Sugihara's "Voluntary Retirement"

Let us finally discuss the issue of Chiune Sugihara and the Foreign Ministry in the postwar period. This chapter deals with how the Foreign Ministry treated Chiune Sugihara after the war, and will clearly demonstrate how the postwar (and prewar) Foreign Ministry worked against the national interest.

Shortly after returning to Japan from a long period of internment, Chiune Sugihara was summoned to the Foreign Ministry in June 1947, and was told of his dismissal. Formally, Sugihara had voluntarily retired. His wife Yukiko recalled the events of that day.

> With some foreboding, I asked Chiune, "What happened to you?"
> "I was called into the office of Vice Foreign Minister Okazaki," he answered, "and told, 'As we no longer have a post for you, please resign. We can no longer take you under our wing!' " I could only look at my husband in silence—there was nothing I felt I could say in response. I later learned that Vice Foreign Minister Okazaki had actually said, "You are being held responsible for that incident [in Lithuania]. We can no longer take you under our wing."
> Chiune had expected something like this to happen eventually. But he was clearly disappointed to be treated this way after returning to Japan, since he had worked so hard for the Foreign Ministry. This

outcome was inevitable though, once he disobeyed orders from home office and issued visas to save the Jews. But Europe was far from home, and time then seemed to pass by without incident. However, even after Kaunas, my husband dutifully and faithfully served the Foreign Office. And so the postwar period began...[1]

The Foreign Ministry was then in the middle of drastic staff cuts. It was a government organ that suffered a truly tragic fate after Japan's defeat, second only to the Imperial Japanese Army and Navy which were completely dismantled. Its diplomatic powers were suspended, and personnel from embassies and consulates abroad were all recalled. It began an administrative reorganization of its employees, as well as a purge of many of its staff from public service.

After the war, staff numbers (including consular police) were reduced from 6,500 to 2,300 after August 15, 1945, and reduced further to 1,680 in 1947. In fact, over two-thirds of the Foreign Ministry's staff were dismissed.[2]

However, to prepare for the lifting of the Occupation, in March 1946 the Foreign Ministry set up the Diplomatic Staff Training Institute, a facility to develop capable diplomats in readiness for the future. Sugihara was not employed here either as a key member of staff.

As discussed in detail in chapter 4, Sugihara's dismissal was not a result of the waves of inexorable staff cuts. At the time, Japan was embroiled in difficulties over the Nanking Incident due to developments in the Tokyo Trial; consequently, the value of Sugihara's achievement in saving 6,000 Jewish refugees would then have shone at its brightest. The person best placed to recognize that value had in fact dismissed him. Moreover, in no way was Sugihara incompetent. As discussed in chapter 5, Sugihara had an excellent grasp of Russian; and during the Occupation, Sugihara to the contrary would have been a valuable staff member because of the involvement of the forces of the Soviet Union, a late signatory to the Potsdam Proclamation and one of the key nations allied against Japan. His intelligence report from Königsberg dated May 9, 1941, moments before war between Germany and the Soviet Union actually broke out, and which warned that this war was certain, had been a valuable piece of information for the Japanese people.

As discussed in chapter 1, the Foreign Ministry made a false report about the outbreak of war between Japan and the United States to the emperor. This report, used during his first meeting with General MacArthur on September 27, 1945, concealed the blunder at the Washington embassy that had caused the delay in delivering the "declaration of war." Thus, early in the Occupation the Foreign Ministry concealed its own enormous and direct war responsibility. Afterwards, an internal investigation between April and June 1946 into this blunder was suspended, and those who were responsible were let off. Even during these severe staff cuts, not one individual from the Washington embassy at the outbreak of war connected with this blunder was dismissed. To the contrary, Secretary Katsuzō Okumura, who was directly responsible for this blunder because on the eve of hostilities he failed to type up the "declaration of war" and was supposedly at an acquaintance's house playing cards, became vice foreign minister after the Occupation was lifted, and later ambassador to Switzerland; Sadao Iguchi, who allowed Okumura to leave the embassy and failed to put the embassy on the appropriate alert, despite home office orders to "make every preparation to present [the 'declaration of war'] to the Americans just as soon as you receive instructions," also became a vice foreign minister after the Occupation was lifted. Iguchi went on to become ambassador to Canada, and then the United States. Not one member of the Washington embassy staff at the outbreak of war was dismissed, and several were even promoted.[3]

Chiune Sugihara was dismissed under these circumstances, at a time when his honor was at a peak, his moral authority was beyond reproach, and his virtue shone at its brightest.

When Sugihara returned to Japan, he was aware that he might be fired because he had disobeyed orders. However, his pride was obviously hurt when he was dismissed by Okazaki and told that, "You are being held responsible for that incident [in Lithuania]." Sugihara at the time was unaware of developments in the Tokyo Trial. Sugihara himself was scarcely aware of the remarkable nature of his own actions. To the contrary, he had no reliable information about the Jewish refugees who had received his visas and presumably crossed Siberia, nor whether they had successfully escaped or survived. He had no detailed knowledge of the fact that, as a result of the visas he issued, practically all of them escaped and survived by safely transiting through Japan. Later, Sugihara went to the newly opened Israeli embassy in Tokyo to inquire after them, but the embassy had no information to give him at the time because it had just been opened. Thus, for a long period, Sugihara didn't know what had resulted from the visas he had issued. [4]

Taking Money for Issuing Visas

During the Occupation, the Foreign Ministry not only forced Chiune Sugihara to resign, but also treated him in a duplicitous manner.

Rumors circulated within the Ministry at the time, that "Sugihara should have enough money because he took payment from the Jews when he issued those visas."[5]

Clearly, this rumor was totally groundless. Zorach Warhaftig, later to become Israel's minister of religion, was directly involved in Sugihara's visa-issuing work and narrowly escaped death thanks to the visa he himself received; he made an indirect reference to this in his book.[6] He also provided concrete confirmation that this rumor was false in an interview with Katsumasa Watanabe, author of a book about Sugihara published in 1996.[7]

In 1969, before Chiune Sugihara received the "Righteous among the Nations" award, the highest honor that can be bestowed on those who saved Jewish people during the Holocaust, Israel awarded Chiune Sugihara a medal of honor. It wasn't until 1985 that he received the prestigious "Righteous among the Nations" award. Why was there such a delay in presenting him this? It was because the Israeli government believed Sugihara had issued those visas based on orders from the Japanese government. In other words, this time lag tells us indirectly that he only collected nominal processing fees when he issued these visas. According to Yukiko Sugihara, midway he even stopped charging the processing fee.[8]

Chiune Sugihara was an upright and honest individual, and Moshe Zupnik, who assisted with the visa-issuing work, bore witness that Sugihara didn't receive any payment for issuing these visas.

Zupnik escaped to New York thanks to a Sugihara visa, and is now the proprietor of a successful fabric store. During his work issuing visas, Zupnik gave Wolfgang Gudze a packet of cigarettes as a gift to show his appreciation. Gudze, who was of German descent, was Sugihara's secretary and assisted in issuing the visas. (Gudze was in fact a Nazi Gestapo agent.) Zupnik claims that Sugihara saw this, and warned him against such behavior.[9] This was how honest Sugihara's visa-issuing operation was.

Therefore, the rumor that Sugihara received payment for issuing visas, mentioned above, was particularly vicious and unfair.

Invariably, the identity of those who peddle rumors remains obscure, and this is precisely what makes rumors effective. At the time, it was probably uncertain precisely how many Jews had been saved by Sugihara's visas; but within the Foreign Ministry it was definitely known that at least several thousand Jews had been saved, and clearly information about that situation could be easily obtained. Therefore, the dismissal of Chiune Sugihara, whose visas in the end literally saved the lives of several thousand Jews, and even though this result would have been unforeseen when the visas were issued, means there must have been those in the Foreign Ministry who surmised Sugihara had done some good. The rumor that Sugihara received payment for issuing visas was used to erase these positive impressions. In effect, it prevented anyone in the Ministry from sympathizing with Sugihara. Seen in this light, this rumor certainly fulfilled a definite purpose.

However, let me remind the reader that the behavior of then-Vice Foreign Minister Katsuo Okazaki, who told Sugihara he had been fired, cannot be excused on the grounds that he was influenced by this rumor.

One year earlier, between April and June 1946, Okazaki headed a committee to investigate the blunder at the Washington embassy which lead to the "sneak attack" at Pearl Harbor; but he suspended this committee which he himself had set up, and the thorough investigation came to nothing. This investigatory committee had originally been set up to disprove the rumor that the blunder was due to decoding delays by the cable section; but even though he was aware that this rumor had absolutely no foundation (or was it precisely because he did know it), he suspended the committee and the investigation came to nothing. In other words, Okazaki had just been in a situation where subterfuge had been used to substantiate an unfounded rumor. Furthermore, Okazaki knew perfectly well that without such subterfuge, no-one would believe the rumor that Sugihara had received payment for issuing visas. Therefore, it can be maintained that Okazaki didn't dismiss Sugihara due to a casual belief in this rumor. To the contrary, Okazaki may even have been one of those who spread the rumor. In view of Okazaki's other activities around this period, such behavior would not have been entirely out of character.

Furthermore, lets consider this money issue in the following way. Let's imagine for instance that when Sugihara issued the visas, it did indeed appear that he had accepted payments on top of the processing fee. Let's even imagine that he did indeed accept money for issuing visas. Does this still mean that Sugihara's dismissal was justified? After careful consideration of these circumstances, it would still not have been justified. Even if for impure motives Sugihara had issued a large number of visas to make some money, this would still have inadvertently resulted in saving the lives of around 6,000 Jews. It can be demonstrated that, politically, Japan drew a clear distinction between itself and Nazi Germany regarding the persecution of the Jews, and never intentionally persecuted nor discriminated against the Jews. When the world heaped criticism upon Japan during the Occupation, this difference would have had great political value. Therefore it must be conceded that, for his political value also, Sugihara should not have been dismissed.

As a matter of fact, there is someone else from Japan who witnessed, albeit briefly, the circumstances at the consulate when Chiune Sugihara was issuing these visas to Jewish refugees. This was Kin'ya Niizeki, a language trainee who was studying Russian in Latvia at the time, and who after the war became ambassador to the Soviet Union, and later Mongolia. Niizeki visited the Japanese consulate in Kaunas when Sugihara was vice consul. At the exact moment when Jewish refugees were thronging to the consulate, Niizeki had to push his way through the crowd of Jewish refugees to enter the consulate premises, and he stayed a night there.[10] Above all else, Niizeki has a moral duty to testify that there is no truth to this rumor.

Honoring Chiune Sugihara, and an Indictment by Gerhard Dambmann

Even after his dismissal, the Foreign Ministry remained consistently disdainful towards Chiune Sugihara.

In July 1968, an opportunity arose to tell the world about Sugihara's achievements. Yehoshua Nishri, one of the five people delegated to represent the Jewish refugees when Sugihara was issuing the visas, had been posted to Japan as counselor to the Israeli embassy, and he telephoned the Sugihara residence. The two met up again, and their meeting was reported in the August 2 evening edition of the *Asahi Shimbun.*

However, Nishri apparently had considerable trouble locating Sugihara. Before being posted to Japan as the Israeli embassy's counselor, Nishri had visited Japan on business on many occasions, and had looked for Sugihara. However he had never been able to locate him.

As one of the five delegates representing the Jewish refugees, Nishri promised to look up the Japanese consul again, so he asked Sugihara his name when he left Kaunas; Sugihara told him it was "Senpo" Sugihara since this was easier for Jewish people to pronounce than "Chiune." Nishri therefore subsequently inquired at the Foreign Ministry for "Senpo Sugihara" rather than "Chiune Sugihara." However the Foreign Ministry told him there was no-one in the Ministry who could respond to his inquiry.[11]

It might be argued that it was not unreasonable for the Foreign Ministry to respond this way because Sugihara's name had been pronounced incorrectly. However in the mid-1960s, a movie based on the *Diary of Anne Frank* had become a big hit worldwide, and there was widespread public interest in the rescue of Jews during World War II. Even though Nishri had inquired about "Senpo Sugihara, the Japanese consul in Lithuania," it was surely quite contrived for the Ministry to say that no-one could respond to his inquiry, simply because he had mispronounced "Chiune" as "Senpo." It can only be concluded that the Foreign Ministry, which dismissed Sugihara in 1947 in the manner described above, had already decided to keep quiet about Sugihara and ignore him.

In any case, Nishri finally located Sugihara and brought about their reunion. This event was reported in the press, and created an opportunity for the public to learn of it. However, the Foreign Ministry took no action whatsoever, and remained aloof. Undeniably, this is precisely why Sugihara's achievements, for a long time afterwards, were not brought to the public's attention.

It was Gerhard Dambmann, a German journalist, who unambiguously alerted Japan and the Japanese people to the fact that they had ignored Sugihara's achievements in this way. Dambmann had lived and worked in postwar Japan for many years, and when he left Japan in 1981 he published *Koritsu suru Taikoku Nippon* [Japan, The Isolated Power] (TBS Britannica). Surprisingly, it was dedicated to Sugihara. "This book is dedicated to Chiune Sugihara, a Japanese diplomat who suffered the displeasure of his homeland for saving the lives of 4,000 Poles during World War II." The book became a best-seller at the time and was widely read, and through it many Japanese learned for the first time about Sugihara's achievements.

Dambmann writes about Sugihara in his book in the following way.[12] Although rather lengthy, the passage is certainly worth reproducing here.

As for the number of transit visas Sugihara issued, he was unable to coolly disregard the anguish of these people, and didn't keep count because he wasted no time and got on with his work. Conceivably though there were around 4,000 people. He stamped his last visas at the railway station in Kaunas. Since he had been ordered to leave Lithuania, he was unable then to confirm whether all these people held visas for Curaçao. All the refugees obtained new identification papers and were able to reach Japan; they went into hiding until the end of the war, mostly in Kobe. Despite repeated protests from the German embassy in Tokyo, they escaped investigation, and survived.

During the war, Sugihara stayed on in Europe as a Japanese diplomat. With Germany's invasion of the Soviet Union, lines of communication to Asia were cut off. Later, the Allied forces placed him for a few months in a Romanian internment camp for enemy aliens, before he finally returned to his home country in 1947. There, some unexpected and bad news awaited him. His superiors at the Foreign Ministry notified him that there were no positions available within the Ministry for diplomats who had disobeyed orders from home office. He was told to shoulder his responsibility and tender his resignation. Even in 1947, the fact that Sugihara had saved the lives of 4,000 Polish Jews did not impress the Foreign Ministry. Under difficult circumstances, Sugihara had decided on his own to disregard instructions from his superiors who strove to collaborate with Nazi Germany; and this decisively sealed his fate of being driven out of the Foreign Ministry in postwar Japan. Even though Sugihara built a new life for himself after that as a businessman, it was a considerable effort. He certainly did not enjoy a lavish lifestyle. Even in his old age, he tortured himself by asking countless times whether ultimately his actions had not been mistaken.

Furthermore, Sugihara had to sit back and watch his colleagues from the Berlin embassy, who strove to please Nazi Germany, rise to high office in postwar Japan. When Sugihara was invited in later years to visit Israel by a number of Jews whose lives he had saved, including the Israeli government's minister of religion and the deputy governor of Tel Aviv, the Japanese embassy in Israel ignored his stay.

It is difficult to fathom why postwar Japan's Foreign Ministry, during the American Occupation, did not honor a diplomat like Sugihara, but instead drove him out; why his story is not cited as an example in school textbooks; why writers have not adapted his life story for drama programs; or why newspapers and television have not picked up on his life. Clearly, those diplomats who built postwar Japan's democracy were the same group whose orders Sugihara had disobeyed, and who had played a part in Sugihara's ousting in 1947.[13]

There are some slight discrepancies between Dambmann's estimates that 4,000 Jewish refugees were rescued by Sugihara's visas,[14] and present estimates based on facts discovered subsequently. However Dambmann made his charges vigorously in 1981 in an outburst of righteous indignation.

Incidentally, there is a portion of his lengthy indictment that is worthy of particular note. Dambmann argues that "Sugihara had to sit back and watch his colleagues from the Berlin embassy, who strove to please Nazi Germany, rise to high office in postwar Japan." He also claimed, "Clearly, those diplomats who built postwar Japan's democracy were the same group whose orders Sugihara had disobeyed, and who had played a part in Sugihara's ousting in 1947."

Throughout the period when negotiations between Japan and the United States were floundering and ultimately resulted in the outbreak of war, the Japanese embassy in Berlin, headed by Ambassador Hiroshi Ōshima, consistently sent mistaken intelligence reports to Japan. The sections within the Foreign Ministry most responsible for the prewar Japanese diplomacy which resulted in the outbreak of war between Japan and the United States were the first division of the American affairs bureau, the Japanese embassy in Washington, and finally, the Japanese embassy in Berlin. For the people of Japan, it is outrageous that certain individuals from these sections remained at the center of the postwar Foreign Ministry and became its core members of staff.

Although the point has frequently been made, Sadao Iguchi and Katsuzō Okumura, the two Washington embassy officials who directly caused the unprecedented blunder of not delivering the "declaration of war" at the designated time before war between Japan and the United States was about to break out, were promoted to vice foreign ministers around the time the Occupation was lifted. Toshikazu Kase, who was chief of the first division of the American affairs bureau at the time, later became Japan's first ambassador to the United Nations. What about the diplomats at the Berlin embassy when war broke out? According to Dambmann, they also rose to high office in postwar Japan.

This author looked into the matter to see if this was really the case. Indeed, several of those who had been posted to the Berlin embassy when war between Japan and the United States broke out had remained at the core of the Foreign Ministry, and had attained prominence and distinction. The above-mentioned Kin'ya Niizeki, who arrived in Kaunas from Latvia in time to observe Sugihara issuing the visas, was also a diplomat at the Berlin embassy when war broke out. Niizeki was later to become ambassador to the Soviet Union after the war. A number of diplomats from the Berlin embassy, apart from Niizeki, also achieved prominence and pursued active careers in the Foreign Ministry in the postwar period. As a German journalist, Dambmann may have been more attuned to matters relating to the Japanese embassy in Berlin, but upon further scrutiny his observations are undoubtedly correct.

The blunder that led to the delay in delivering the "final notice" was deplorable. However, the same could be said of these sections within the Foreign Ministry: the Japanese embassy in Washington which failed to provide effective analysis reports of the U. S. government's diplomatic policies; the first division of the American affairs bureau, which was extremely lacking in strategic judgment and which had failed to take effective measures; and the Berlin embassy, which was clearly an organ that promoted the Tripartite Alliance, which consistently sent information favoring the German side even after the war between Germany and the Soviet Union began, and which from start to finish continually led Japan in the wrong direction. In the end, the postwar Foreign Ministry formed around people from the sections most responsible for a Japanese diplomacy that resulted in the outbreak of war between Japan and the United States, and furthermore, around those individuals most responsible for that diplomacy. Officials from the sections that brought about the failure of Japanese diplomacy and had the strongest militarist connections pushed the war responsibility that rightfully belonged to the Foreign Ministry upon the now-dismantled military; and while they criticized militarism on the one hand, they actually remained at the heart of the Foreign Ministry.

Chiune Sugihara, who never sympathized with the Tripartite Alliance and faced the dangers of Gestapo surveillance, issued as many visas in Lithuania to Jewish refugees as he could. Ambassador Hiroshi Ōshima cabled the Foreign Ministry on June 5, 1941, advising that war between Germany and the Soviet Union was certain; but as discussed in chapter 5, approximately a month earlier on May 9, and despite close surveillance by Germany, Chiune Sugihara had already cabled the Foreign Ministry, from his consulate in Königsberg, information he had painstakingly gathered which concluded that war between Germany and the Soviet Union was inevitable. Sugihara also sent this cable to the Berlin embassy. One could almost say with certainty that the outcome of negotiations between Japan and the United States would have been different if, at this time, serious attention had been paid to the fact that the prerequisites for forming a "quadripartite alliance" (by adding the Soviet Union to the Tripartite Alliance) no longer existed, and if a serious attempt had been made to put other measures into place. Nevertheless, the Berlin embassy was partly responsible for why no attention was paid to this. Sugihara, who had sent the precious intelligence he so painstakingly collected, was dismissed by those who ignored and failed to exploit his precious intelligence, and who brought about the devastating outbreak of war between Japan and the United States.

Seen in this light, a new perspective comes into view, namely that Sugihara's dismissal in June 1947 was deeply rooted. We must realize anew that his dismissal came about because the Foreign Ministry is an organization that acts against the Japanese people's interest. We can also see that the criticism of militarism by the Foreign Ministry, which entered the postwar period in this shameful manner, is distorted, twisted and completely false.

Foreign Ministry's Reluctance to Honor Sugihara

Dambmann describes above how the Japanese embassy in Israel ignored Sugihara's 1969 visit, when he was invited there for saving the lives of 6,000 Jews. Even when his great achievement was widely being recognized at this time, the Foreign Ministry conversely showed, by maintaining its unyielding attitude, how it was prolonging its bumbled entry into the postwar period. Ultimately, the Ministry was conducting diplomacy, not on behalf of the Japanese people, but for itself.

There is another passage by Dambmann that is certainly worth repeating here. "It is difficult to fathom why...[Sugihara's] story is not cited as an example in school textbooks; why writers have not adapted his life story for drama programs; or why newspapers and television have not picked up on his life." Perhaps in response to this criticism, in 1983 Fuji TV screened a dramatization of Sugihara's story, which has since been rerun several times. Sugihara's story is now also appearing in school textbooks. It would be a mistake to say the people of Japan have coldly failed to express an interest in Sugihara's benevolence.

However, why has there been no widespread movement to publicly honor Sugihara? There are probably quite a few other Japanese people who think this strange. It would only be natural to assume the Foreign Ministry's cool reaction, both publicly and privately, has had an influence, and the following examples clearly demonstrate this. We can see how the Foreign Ministry has conducted diplomacy on its own behalf, and not for the people of Japan.

In January 1985, a reception to welcome Foreign Minister Yitzak Shamir to Japan was held at the Jewish Community Center in Hirō in Tokyo. Chiune Sugihara was accorded the courtesies befitting a recipient of the "Righteous Among the Nations" award. The Israeli side invited Sugihara, whom they considered a savior of the Jewish people, to this reception as an honored guest, and introduced him to Prime Minister Yasuhiro Nakasone and Foreign Minister Shintarō Abe who had also been invited. Both the prime minister and foreign minister were taken aback, and neither seemed to have the slightest idea who Sugihara was.[15] In other words, the Foreign Ministry had failed entirely to brief them about Sugihara, a man who had become quite well known to the Japanese people. This was clearly an example of the Foreign Ministry's attempts to conceal how it has ignored Chiune Sugihara's presence as much as it could.

Chiune Sugihara passed away on July 31, 1986, and the Foreign Ministry was able ultimately to avoid taking any action at all to honor

Sugihara's achievements during his lifetime. Naturally, media around the world criticized the Foreign Ministry at this time.

However the Foreign Ministry made no attempt to change its stance. When Lithuania regained its independence in October 1991, the Ministry decided to open a consulate there. To prepare for a visit to Lithuania, Vice Foreign Minister Muneo Suzuki decided to meet Chiune's widow, Yukiko Sugihara, before leaving Japan. This was only natural because Lithuania had constructed and named a road after Sugihara in recognition of his achievements. However, there was then strong resistance within the Ministry to such a meeting, and Vice Minister Suzuki had to spend three days breaking down this resistance. Only then was he able to meet with Yukiko at the Iikura Government Building.

On March 11, 1992, at the House of Representatives Committee on the Budget, Diet Representative Shōzō Kusakawa brought up the Iikura meeting between Suzuki and Yukiko Sugihara, and called into question the fact that Chiune Sugihara's humanitarian actions had long been neglected and had never been publicly honored. Surprisingly though, Foreign Minister Michio Watanabe hadn't received any report about the Iikura meeting. Even though Kusakawa asked Watanabe on several occasions in the Diet to answer this question, and even specified the minister by name, Nagao Hyōdō (director-general of the Foreign Ministry's European and Oceanic affairs bureau) intervened as the government's spokesperson. He refused to allow Watanabe to take the floor, and instead made the reply himself. This episode illustrates the Ministry's deep-rooted intention not to allow the foreign minister to publicly acknowledge the Sugihara matter.[16]

On September 20, 1994, NHK reported that Chiune Sugihara was dismissed from the Foreign Ministry because he had opposed the policy of the Japanese government at the time. Two days later, the Foreign Ministry issued a statement in response titled, "[Sugihara's] Dismissal from Foreign Ministry Not Due to Question of Responsibility for Issuing Visas." Indeed, it is true that when Sugihara issued the visas (from July through August 1940), no orders had been given completely banning the issue of visas to Jewish refugees. Therefore, his dismissal was not specifically a disciplinary action for disobeying the Foreign Ministry's orders.

However, if that was indeed the case, why didn't the Foreign Ministry actively take the lead in honoring Chiune Sugihara during the mid-1960s, when the movie based on the *Diary of Anne Frank* was being highly acclaimed? Why was it only when the German journalist

Gerhard Dambmann voiced his angry indictment that Japan took action to make its people aware of the facts? When Sugihara was first invited to Israel in 1969 to receive an award, why did the Japanese embassy there apparently ignore his visit?

Above all, it is impossible to fathom why Sugihara was dismissed in 1947, at a time when his achievements and exceptional acts of kindness would have shone most brightly.

It would be instructive to relate here the following incident which occurred only recently. The Foreign Ministry may have been involved to some extent, but in 1998, thanks to the efforts of the Japan-Israel Chamber of Commerce and Industry (JICCI), a relief of Chiune Sugihara was donated to the Simon Wiesenthal Museum of Tolerance.

However, part of the original inscription beneath the portrait was removed, namely, the commonly held belief that "Sugihara disobeyed the orders of his government and continued to issue visas."[17]

This deletion probably reflects the view Nobuo Fujiwara, head of the JICCI, gave in an interview, that "Chiune Sugihara was no anti-government hero." In January 1940, then-Foreign Minister Kichisaburō Nomura cabled Vice Consul Sugihara at the consulate in Kaunas, and ordered him to issue transit visas through Japan to some Polish Jews; taking this as his lead, Fujiwara was trying to say that Sugihara issued the visas based on his government's orders.[18] However, this is an extreme distortion of the facts.

As discussed at length in chapter 5, it is clear Japan had established a basic policy whereby Jewish people were not to be treated differently to other foreigners. Therefore, it is conceivable that Nomura did indeed give the orders mentioned above; it is also conceivable that this basic policy explains why, when Sugihara was issuing such a large number of visas to Jewish refugees, Foreign Minister Yōsuke Matsuoka did not give orders banning these visas outright.

When Sugihara issued those visas, he had not received any orders explicitly approving his actions. It was true Japan had a basic policy of not discriminating between Jews and other people, and it had clearly distanced itself from the persecution of Jews that was occurring in Europe. However, when Sugihara issued those visas, he had strict orders to give them only to those who met certain conditions; by granting visas to Jewish refugees who had not fulfilled any of these key conditions, Sugihara clearly disobeyed orders. He had stretched his authority as vice consul to the limit. However it should be noted that, while correct in a literal sense, documents provided by the Dutch consulate claiming its South American colony Curaçao did not require entry visas were, by themselves, insufficient to prove the bearer had a "firm end visa"; these documents had no legal standing, despite being technically legitimate. Even though these documents were not technically *illegal*, Sugihara interpreted procedures as broadly as possible, and issued the visas. His goal was clearly to save Jewish refugees, and to do this he had to take actions that violated orders.

Above all, if the Ministry in September 1994 did not consider his dismissal as a disciplinary action, why when Sugihara returned to Japan after the war was the fact that he disobeyed orders given as the reason for that dismissal? As discussed above, Director-General Hyōdō acknowledged during the Diet's budget committee that Sugihara's actions had violated orders. Nevertheless, if Hyōdō insists that Sugihara's actions accorded with Japan's long-standing basic policy of non-discrimination against the Jews, then Chiune Sugihara, who was dismissed for disobeying orders, deserves an apology. Why wasn't the fact that Japan had such a benevolent policy towards the Jews clarified when he was dismissed, or indeed made publicly known during the Tokyo Trial's most intense phase to improve world public opinion, no matter how slightly? After it apologizes to the Japanese people, the Ministry should probably also admit that Sugihara's actions broadly conformed to this basic policy.

As journalist Kinue Tokudome quite aptly wrote, "The assertion that 'Consul Sugihara only acted in line with Japan's policy at the time' shows, incidentally, that perhaps we haven't truly carried on the legacy of Chiune Sugihara."[19]

Foreign Ministry Inherently Opposes National Interest

As noted in the passage by Gerhard Dambmann above, it was difficult to understand why schools, writers, and media such as the press and television hadn't tried to honor Sugihara's achievements publicly; but the matter does now appear in school textbooks, and since 1992 the theater group *Dōra* has publicly performed a piece called "Senpo Sugihara." The Ministry of Posts and Telecommunications boldly decided to issue stamps in 2000 to commemorate Sugihara. Ultimately though, the Foreign Ministry must share some blame for the delay in Sugihara's public recognition because, both publicly and behind the scenes, it obstructed all attempts to appraise Chiune Sugihara more highly.

As discussed in chapter 1, and as this author examined in greater detail in 1997,[20] there was an individual from the United States who struggled hard for Japan and helped it avoid being partitioned after the war with the United States. The efforts of this "savior" working behind the scenes explain why Japan today is not a divided nation.

This "savior" was Joseph Grew, the U. S. ambassador to Japan at the outbreak of war. As undersecretary of state in the closing stages of the war, and out of concern for Japan's future, Grew strove to give Japan the opportunity to surrender before it could be partitioned as Germany had been, and proposed the idea of issuing the Potsdam Proclamation. In fact, thanks to his efforts, the Potsdam Proclamation was indeed issued. It gave Japan the chance to surrender, and to do so before any battle for the home islands started. It also allowed Japan to escape the tragic fate of becoming a divided nation, and to develop into what it has become today.

The terms of the Potsdam Proclamation were rather severe because they were predicated on an occupation policy that the United States presumably would have imposed upon Japan after a last-ditch battle for the home islands. However, President Roosevelt, who died suddenly on April 12, 1945, had never considered issuing anything like the Potsdam Proclamation to give Japan an opportunity beforehand to surrender. Therefore, if he had survived to lead the war effort, Japan would most probably have been partitioned. Even after Roosevelt died, there was every likelihood that, had it not been for Grew's strenuous efforts, Japan still might have suffered the fate of being partitioned.

Today though, the people of Japan have completely forgotten Joseph Grew, a man whom we should think of as "Japan's savior." This is not because the Japanese people are ungrateful, but because the Foreign Ministry, both publicly and privately, continues to steer matters in this direction.

To recognize Grew's achievements would mean admitting the failure of Japan's prewar diplomacy which led the nation to war with the United States. Without that admission, Grew's achievements can never be acknowledged. Admitting this will be impossible without taking a hard look at the blunder at the Washington embassy which caused the "sneak attack" at Pearl Harbor. Without a thorough examination of the significance of this blunder, there can never be any genuine regret, criticism, or reevaluation of the war with the United States, an extremely tragic confrontation that involved the battle for Okinawa and the dropping of the atomic bombs. The postwar Foreign Ministry, for whom concealing its war responsibility has been a "ministerial imperative" rather than a "national imperative," has had to avoid this thorough examination at all costs. As discussed in chapter 4, Toshikazu

Kase's research on the negotiations between Japan and the United States has been a dogged camouflage operation with this sole purpose in mind.

As mentioned in chapter 1, the Japanese government commemorated its centennial anniversary of relations with the United States in 1960, and sent Joseph Grew an impressive award, the Grand Cordon of the Order of the Rising Sun. At first glance, it seemed Grew had formally been paid every courtesy; but in fact the same award was sent to all former American ambassadors to draw attention away from Grew. To commemorate this century of bilateral relations, Grew should have been presented with the highest of honors. However if Grew alone had been sent the highest award, this would have attracted the attention of the Japanese public. To avoid this, all former American ambassadors received the same level of honors so Grew would not stand out.

Grew passed away on May 25, 1965, at the age of 84. Although Grew should rightly be thought of as "Japan's savior," and most Japanese newspapers reproduced Grew's portrait, they only appended short articles, roughly matchbox-sized, which merely reported his death. Only the *Mainichi Shimbun* published an article in his memory a few days later. Of course, because it was written by private individuals, the article paid little attention to Grew's achievements during the closing stages of the war. However, responsibility for the Japanese people's cool treatment of the death of "Japan's savior" does not lie with the media or the Japanese public. It lies with the Foreign Ministry who would have briefed and given guidance to the press at the time of Grew's death. Both the Foreign Ministry, which continued right until Grew's death to draw attention away from his achievements, and postwar research on diplomatic history, mainly spearheaded by the Foreign Ministry, are responsible.

The postwar Foreign Ministry has conducted diplomacy for itself, and not on behalf of the Japanese people. To preserve its own reputation, the Foreign Ministry has forced the Japanese people to embrace a distorted historical perspective. It tried consistently and persistently to ignore Chiune Sugihara; and when ignoring him was no longer an option, it tried to diminish his stature in every conceivable way. Such actions demonstrate that the Foreign Ministry has conducted diplomacy for its own sake, and has deceived the Japanese people.

Under the Occupation, the Foreign Ministry falsified history by concealing its own war responsibility; because of this, the Japanese people were trapped in a "warped linguistic space." Today, Japan should be voicing the loudest condemnation of the unjustness of the Tokyo Trial, a tribunal that has been criticized by intelligent people around the world; instead, the Foreign Ministry builds upon the social framework that resulted from this court's ruling. Even after the Occupation was lifted, the Foreign Ministry pursued a diplomacy for its own benefit whenever the occasion arose, as if the Japanese people didn't exist. This fundamental trait of the Foreign Ministry becomes obvious to anyone who examines the Ministry's relationship with Chiune Sugihara.

The fact that Chiune Sugihara was not honored when he should have been is a problem created by the Foreign Ministry, an organization which entered the postwar era by concealing its war responsibility and has worked against the interests of the Japanese people. For the postwar Foreign Ministry, which continues to conceal its war responsibility in this way, Chiune Sugihara is precisely the sort of "witness" who threatens its existence and attests to its deplorable past.

The cocklebur is a weed that appears in the fall. Walk through a grassy field, and its pea-sized burs soon stick to your trousers. These burs, lined with countless prickles, are not easily brushed out. These prickles can sometimes pierce the fabric of your trousers, stick into your flesh, and cause an intense stinging pain. The Chiune Sugihara issue is like a cocklebur to the Foreign Ministry. More than Sugihara's personal objectives, which were quite separate from those of the Foreign Ministry, it is his humanitarian actions which the Ministry can't lightly brush off. The harder it tries to brush these burs off, the deeper they get imbedded; and surprisingly they cause intense pain, even through the Ministry's skin. In other words, as long as the postwar Foreign Ministry doesn't try anew to come to terms with how it conducts itself, the Chiune Sugihara issue, unlike a real cocklebur, will gradually grow, thanks to the conscience of the Japanese people. One day this pea-sized problem will become egg-sized; and if despite this the Foreign Ministry continues to ignore it, the problem will before long grow completely out of all proportions. The "bur" may become even sharper and eat deeper into the Foreign Ministry's surprisingly thick hide, and cause even more excruciating pain. One day, the Foreign Ministry might even be permanently crippled.

Endnotes

Abbreviations

BI&C   Sugihara, Seishirō, *Between Incompetence And Culpability*

BNT   Nomura, Kichisaburō, *Beikoku ni tsukaishite*

FRUS   U. S. Dept. of State, *Foreign Relations of the United States*

ISOS   Levine, Hillel, *In Search of Sugihara*

JPPH   Sugihara, Seishirō, *Japanese Perspectives on Pearl Harbor*

KTK   Kase, Toshikazu, *Kaisōroku*

MBPH   U. S. Dept. of Defense, *The "Magic" Background of Pearl Harbor*

NBKS   Kase, Toshikazu, *Nichi-Bei kōshō*

PHA   U. S. Congress Joint Committee, *Pearl Harbor Attack*

RIB   Sugihara, Yukiko, *Rokusen-nin no inochi no biza*

VFL   Sugihara, Yukiko, *Visas for Life*

(See Bibliography for full citations.)

Preface

1. Sugihara, Seishirō, *Nihon no shintō, bukkyo to sai-kyō bunri* [Shinto and Buddhism in Japan and the separation of church and state] (Tokyo: Bunka Shobō Hakubunsha, 1992).

2. Kim, Duk-Hwang, *A History of Religions in Korea* (Seoul: Daeji Moonhwa-sa Publishing Co., 1988), pp. 49–60.

3. Passin, Herbert, *Society and Education in Japan* (New York: Columbia University, 1965), p. 44.

4. Weber, Max, *Shūkyō shakaigaku ronshū* [Collected works on religion and sociology], translated by Ōtsuka, Hisao and Keizō Ikimatsu (Tokyo: Misuzu Shobō, 1972), p. 5.

5. Tamura, Reiko, "Gaimushō 'ketsuzoku–keibatsu' no kenkyū" [Research on 'kinship and intermarriage' in the Foreign Ministry], in *Fōsaito* (September 1994), pp. 120–3.

6. Nitobe, Inazō, *Bushido: The Soul of Japan* (Tokyo: Charles E. Tuttle, 1969), p. 4.

7. *BI&C*, pp. 130–3.

8. Ibid., pp. 114–22. Recently with regard to the Nanking Incident, attention in the United States has focused on Iris Chang's *The Rape of Nanking: The Forgotten Holocaust of World War II* (New York: Basic Books, 1997), however there are serious problems with this book's historical accuracy, and it does not meet the standards required of a historical reference. The most reliable research on the Nanking Incident in Japan is the collaborative work by Asia University's Professor Shūdō Higashinakano and Tokyo University's Professor Nobukatsu Fujioka, which will soon be brought out in English translation. For the original Japanese version, see their *'Za Reipu obu Nankin' no kenkyū: Chūgoku ni okeru 'jōhō-sen' no teguchi to senryaku* [Research on 'The Rape of Nanking': China's tricks and tactics in the 'propaganda war'] (Tokyo: Shōdensha, 1999).

9. *BI&C*, chap. 5.

10. *JPPH*, pp. 9–16; *BI&C*, pp. 75–7.

11. Alperovitz, Gar, *The Decision to Use the Atomic Bomb and the Architecture of an American Myth* (N. Y.: Alfred A. Knopf, 1995), p. 629.

12. *PHA*, part 12, p. 242, Cable 902, pt. 7.

13. *BI&C*, pp. 3–6.

14. Burns, James MacGregor, *Roosevelt: The Soldier of Freedom, 1940–1945* (New York: Harcourt Brace Yovanovich, 1970), p. 409.

15. *BI&C*, chap. 3.

Translator's Note

1. Fralon, José-Alain, *A Good Man in Evil Times,* trans. Peter Graham (Viking, 2000), pp. 66–7, 115. First published as *Le Juste de Bordeaux* (Mollat, 1998).

2. Tokayer, Marvin and Mary Swartz, *The Fugu Plan: The Untold Story of the Japanese and the Jews during World War II* (Paddington Press, 1979). For references to "the Fugu Plan," see pp. 29, 52; Matsuoka's informal complicity, pp. 79, 117, 127, 148; Sugihara's patriotism, p. 31; "administrative punishment," p. 42. Aikawa (a native of Yamaguchi prefecture) is referred to as "Ayukawa" by the authors, and also by many standard references, however this is mistaken. See *Aikawa Yoshisuke sensei tsuisōroku* (Tokyo, 1968).

3. *RIB.* For an English translation, see her *VFL.* The following page references are from the English version: "Jew Hunting" and German reprisals, p. 6; committee meeting, p. 8; consulted Yukiko, p. 17; closed down the consulate, pp. 26–7.

4. Ibid., resentment, p. 116; "that incident in Lithuania," pp. 108–9; "countless hardships" and "rumors," p. 112; Moscow, p. 119; "in good conscience," pp. 124, 128.

5. *ISOS.* "Banal" and "full of light," pp. 14–5; "underground" railroad, p. 208; Japan's "new eyes," p. 126; vital for Berlin (Ōshima), p. 129, Tokyo (Matsuoka), p. 229; *kind* of refugees, p. 252; Sassoon, p. 224; "great value" to Matsuoka, p. 230; Matsuoka Purge, p. 272.

6. Ibid., risks, pp. 253–5; "*what* was going on," pp. 188–95; "old spy instincts," p. 204; "careful falsehood," pp. 259, 284; "hostile," p. 284.

7. Watanabe, Katsumasa, *Shinsō: Sugihara Biza* [The truth about Sugihara's visas] (Tokyo: Taishō Shuppan, 2000), pp. 426–440; Matsuura, Hiroshi, "Netsuzō sareru Sugihara Chiune zō" [Distortion of the Chiune Sugihara image], *Sekai,* September 2000.

8. For "false claims on heroism," *ISOS,* p. 205, Watanabe, *Shinsō,* p. 438.

9. Yoshida, Takashi, "A Battle over History in Japan," in Fogel, Joshua A., ed., *The Nanjing Massacre in History and Historiography* (Berkeley: University of California Press, 2000). See pp. 71 and 114 for his description of "progressives" and "revisionists."

10. For "writing the legend," see *ISOS,* p. 284; "candidate for sainthood," *ISOS,* p. 6.

11. Sakamoto, Pamela Rotner, *Japanese Diplomats and Jewish Refugees: A World War II Dilemma* (Westport: Praeger, 1998). For reference to "only a few like Sugihara," see p. 4; "liberally interpreting them," p. 112; admonishment, pp. 163–4; "bystanders," pp. 45–54, 119–24.

12. *The Economist,* July 1, 2000. Emphasis added.

13. For the reference to Nomura, see Auer, James E., *The Postwar Rearmament of Japanese Maritime Forces: 1945–1971* (Praeger, 1973).

14. In singling out the Foreign Ministry to blame for the folly of Japan's prewar diplomacy, the author minimizes the role played by other instruments of state, notably the military and the imperial household. Progressive critics would certainly take issue with many of his views, especially those which downplay questions of Japan's overall war responsibility and its role as a victimizer *(kagai no mondai).* They might also conclude that self-indulgent dwelling on Japanese victimhood while excluding the suffering of non-Japanese demonstrates "an attitude no different than Japan's wartime racism." See Yoshida, "Battle over history," p. 93.

Chapter 1

1. Iguchi, Takeo, "Maboroshi no 'sensen fukoku' zenbun" [Complete text of illusory "declaration of war"], *This is Yomiuri* (December 1997). See also his "Shinju-wan kishū kōgeki, chū-Bei taishikan ni ochido nashi: Tsūkoku okure wo desaki ni sekinin tenka shita Nihon seifu" [The embassy to the U. S. was not at fault for the surprise attack on Pearl Harbor: The Japanese government pushed responsibility for the notice's delay on its embassy abroad], *Ronza* (January 1997). Iguchi presented the complete text of the "declaration of war" in the Dec. 1997 article as new evidence regarding the Pearl Harbor surprise attack. This "declaration" was later published in the *Yomiuri Shimbun*, Dec. 8, 1997. See also Robert Butow, "Marching off to War on the Wrong Foot: The Final Note Tokyo did not Send to Washington," *Pacific Historical Review*, vol. LXIII (1994), pp. 67–79.

2. *PHA*, part 12, pp. 238–9, Cable 901; *BI&C*, p. 88.

3. Yamagiwa, Akira and Masanori Nakamura, eds., Yoshinosuke Okada, trans., *Shiryō Nihon senryō (I): Tennōsei* [Reference materials on the occupation of Japan. Vol. 1. The emperor system] (Tokyo: Ōtsuki Shoten, 1990), p. 520; *Shūkan shinchō* "Tennō–Ma Gensui kaiken 'Tōjō ni damasareta' ga kamosu butsugi" [The controversy raised by the statement "tricked by Tōjō" at the meeting between the Emperor and General MacArthur] December 18, 1986, pp. 140–3; *BI&C*, p. 142.

4. Ariyama, Teruo. *Senryō-ki media shi kenkyū: jiyū to tōsei, 1945-nen* [Research on the history of the media under the Occupation: Freedom and control, 1945] (Tokyo: Kashiwa Shobō, 1996), p. 184; "Nyū Yōku Taimuzu kisha Kurukkuhōn ni taisuru bunshō ni yoru Okotae (yakubun)" [His Majesty's responses to the question sheet from New York Times reporter Kluckhorn (translated text)]. Takamatsunomiya File. Zaidan Hōjin Shiryō Chōsakai, Tokyo; *BI&C*, p. 143.

5. Shigemitsu, Mamoru, *Zoku Shigemitsu Mamoru shuki* [Mamoru Shigemitsu memoirs, vol. 2] (Tokyo: Chūō Kōronsha, 1998), p. 259.

6. Ibid., p. 253.

7. *NYT*, September 25, 1945. Yamagiwa et al., p. 511.

8. Okumura, Katsuzō, "Heika to Ma Gensui" [His Majesty and General MacArthur], in Yoshida, Shigeru, *Kaisō jūnen* [Reflections of a decade] (Tokyo: Shinchōsha, 1957), p. 106. Note that Okumura's remarks were not included in the English translation *The Yoshida Memoirs*.

9. Readers outside Japan might question this author's assertion that the war between Japan and the United States could have been avoided if Roosevelt had used the information available to him to avoid that war. They might also ask why Roosevelt has to shoulder any responsibility since, regardless of whatever intelligence advantage he may have enjoyed, he could not have been absolutely sure of the Japanese side's intentions; and in any case, the war was initiated by Japan.

We should consider to what extent the act of "provocation" is a crime. In Europe and the United States, where a "procedural" legal sensibility is emphasized, it is easy to hold the side making the first move completely responsible. However in Japan, where considerations of "substance" inform legal perspectives, it is felt that if one side provokes another into making that first move, then it is also partly responsible. (See chap. 5, "More on the Issue of Rescuing Jewish Refugees.")

Even though the United States enjoyed an intelligence advantage over Japan, this does not mean it was completely aware of all Japan's motives and activities. One certainly cannot make that claim. However, it is true the U. S. had a basic awareness of Japan's *overall* motives and activities, so it must be conceded that it knew enough to take appropriate measures to avoid a military confrontation with Japan. The same applies even if, for instance, it was unaware of the Imperial Japanese Navy's plan to attack Pearl Harbor. On the other hand, if it did indeed know of these plans, it would clearly have known how to avoid a military confrontation at this time.

In any case, the American government's intention to "provoke" Japan is clearly recorded in Secretary of War Henry Stimson's diary, in particular regarding the war council meeting of November 25, 1941. (See *BI&C*, pp. 39–40.) Researchers in Japan like myself are frustrated by certain opinions held in the United States on the history of the 1941 Japan-U. S. negotiations. Namely, even though the record is clear that the U. S. (during the closing stages of those negotiations) intended to "provoke" Japan into firing the first shot, nevertheless subsequent historical facts are neither interpreted nor informed by the intention expressed in Stimson's diary. Extant historical materials make it clear American government leaders, including Roosevelt, were waiting for Japan to make the first move, even as they preserved a good record for the American side.

This author naturally does not maintain that Japan, which made the first move, has no responsibility at all. There should be no misunderstanding about this. It is precisely because Japan has an enormous responsibility for making the first move that this book questions the Foreign Ministry's liability for its unequivocal mistakes in conducting Japan's diplomacy. My purpose in writing this book was to hold the Ministry accountable for its incompetence and blunders. Therefore, since this is my original purpose for the book, I would urge readers not to misinterpret my intentions here.

10. Sherwood, Robert E., *Roosevelt and Hopkins: An Intimate History* (New York: Harper, 1948), pp. 695–7.

11. Stimson, Henry, *The Diaries of Henry Lewis Stimson* (Yale University Library, New Haven, 1973). Microfilm. May 8, 1945; Iokibe, Makoto, *Beikoku no Nihon senryō seisaku (ge)* [American policy towards Japan's occupation, vol. 2] (Tokyo: Chūō Kōronsha, 1985), p. 158.

12. Stimson, *Diaries*, May 13, 1945; Iokibe, p. 156.

13. Iokibe, p. 196. For the evolution of the draft for the Potsdam Proclamation, see Yamagiwa, Akira. "Potsudamu sengen no sōan ni tsuite" [Draft of the Potsdam declaration], *Yokohama shiritsu daigaku ronsō* vol. 37, nos. 2–3 (1986), pp. 35–71; Stimson, *Diaries*, July 2, 1945.

14. Takahashi, Hiroshi, *Shōwa tennō hatsugen roku* [Speeches by the Shōwa emperor] (Tokyo: Shōgakkan, 1989), p. 106.

15. Iglehart, C. W., *Kokusai Kirisutokyō daigaku sōritsu shi: Myōnichi no daigaku e no bijon* [International Christian University: An Adventure in Christian Higher Education in Japan] (Tokyo: ICU, 1990), pp. 106, 133.

16. Funayama, Kikuya, *Hakutōwashi to sakura no ki: Nihon wo aishita Josefu Gurū taishi* [The bald eagle and the cherry tree: Ambassador Joseph Grew who loved Japan] (Tokyo: Aki Shobō, 1996).

17. *Mainichi Shimbun*, May 15, 1960.

18. Materials from the investigation are reproduced in Sugihara, Seishirō, *Nichi-Bei kaisen ikō no Nihon gaikō no kenkyū* (Tokyo: Aki Shobō, 1997), pp. 143–83. (For the English translation, see *BI&C*, pp. 85–112.)

19. *JPPH*, p. 9; *Japan Times*, December 5, 1991.

20. For an overview of media reports in both Japan and the United States during the fiftieth anniversary of the attack on Pearl Harbor, see Sugita, Makoto [Seishirō Sugihara], *Sōtenken–Shinju-wan 50-shūnen hōdō: Nani ga doko made wakatta ka* [Overview of reports on the fiftieth anniversary of Pearl Harbor: what and how much is known?] (Tokyo: Morita Shuppan, 1992). (For the English translation, see *JPPH*.)

21. *BI&C*, pp. 73–84.

22. See Iguchi, "Shinju-wan kishū kōgeki." See also note 1, above.

23. Because history involves the problem of how to perceive what has occurred in the past, it incorporates elements and aspects of the social sciences. That is, the manner in which we view perceptions of the past influences the decisions and actions we take over the course of society in the future. This issue will be dealt with more fully in chap. 2, "Teaching Historical Science as a Social Science."

24. Kase, Hideaki, "'Shinju-wan' no gimon ni kotaeru" [Answering questions about 'Pearl Harbor'], *Shokun!* (March 1998), p. 102.

25. See Iguchi, "Shinju-wan kishū kōgeki." See also note 1, above.

26. Shigemitsu, *Zoku Shigemitsu Mamoru shuki*, p. 253.

27. Kase, "Gimon," p. 103.

28. *NYT*, September 25, 1945; Yamagiwa et al., p. 511.

29. In their selected translations from *Taiheiyō sensō e no michi*, James Morley and David Titus refer to a version of Kase's "memoirs" held in the Japanese Defense Agency archives. However upon closer inspection, these materials are extremely brief and remain classified. It is unlikely they are the extensive diaries Kase referred to in his *Journey to the Missouri*. See Morley and Titus, *Japan's Road to the Pacific War*, vol. 5, *The Final Confrontation: Japan's Negotiations with the United States, 1941* (New York: Columbia University Press, 1994), p. 415.

Chapter 2

1. *BI&C*, pp. 75–81. Strictly speaking, the argument that there is no firm evidence Roosevelt had foreknowledge of the "sneak attack" at Pearl Harbor is unreasonable. It does not address the testimony by John A. Burns, then a police officer in Honolulu actively engaged in F.B.I. intelligence activities and later the first governor of Hawaii, who said he was told a few days

beforehand that "we're going to be attacked before the week is out"; nor the statement by Roosevelt, as related by his secretary of labor Frances Perkins at the final cabinet meeting before the attack on Pearl Harbor, that he "knew" where the missing Japanese fleet was. See Toland, *Infamy*, pp. 286, 294. Robert B. Stinnett has recently uncovered documents that show the American side was intercepting radio transmissions by the Imperial Japanese Navy's task force on route to Pearl Harbor, disproving the commonly held notion that the task force had maintained strict radio silence. This largely substantiates the theory that Roosevelt had foreknowledge of the "sneak attack" at Pearl Harbor. See Stinnett, Robert B., *Day of Deceit: The Truth about FDR and Pearl Harbor* (N.Y.: Free Press, 2000).

2. *BI&C*, pp. 21-56. See also chap. 1, n. 9.

3. Kojima, Noboru, *Gosan no ronri* [The logic of miscalculation] (Tokyo: Bungei Shunjū, 1987), p. 229; Stouffer, Samuel A., et al. *Studies in Social Psychology in World War II*, vol. 2, *The American Soldier: Combat and Its Aftermath* (Princeton: Princeton Univ. Press, 1949), pp. 105–91.

4. Funayama, Kikuya, *Hakutōwashi to sakura no ki: Nihon wo aishita Josefu Gurū taishi* [The bald eagle and the cherry tree: Ambassador Joseph Grew who loved Japan] (Tokyo: Aki Shobō, 1996).

5. *BI&C*, pp. 143–87.

6. Kobori, Keiichirō, *Tōkyō saiban–Nihon no benmei* [The Tokyo Trial and Japan's defense] (Tokyo: Kōdansha, 1995), pp. 563–5.

7. *KTK*, vol. 2, p. 96.

8. Jiji Tsūshinsha, *Naigai kyōiku*, Jan. 8, 1988, p. 8.

9. *BI&C*, pp. 114–6, 173–7.

10. *JPPH*, p. 9; *Japan Times*, Dec. 7, 1991.

11. *JPPH*, pp. 19–28.

12. *BI&C*, pp. 143–87.

13. Yoshida, Shigeru, *Kaiso jūnen 1* [Reflections of a decade, vol. 1] (Tokyo: Shinchōsha, 1952), pp. 116–7.

14. *BI&C*, pp. 191–207. For an accessible bilingual account by Japanese scholars of the Nanking Incident, see Takemoto, Tadeo and Yasuo Ohara, *The Alleged Nanking Massacre: Japan's rebuttal to China's forged claims* (Tokyo: Meiseisha, 2000) which critically reviews works by writers such as Iris Chang. For the most completely documented account of the Incident, see Higashinakano, Shūdō, *"Nankin gyakusatsu" no tettei kenshō* [Thorough examination of the "Nanking Massacre"] (Tokyo: Tendensha, 1998).

15. Yamamoto, Masao, ed., *Teikoku Riku-Kaigun masaka monogatari 1* [Astonishing anecdotes of the Imperial Japanese Army and Navy, vol. 1] (Tokyo: Senshi kankōkai, 1990), pp. 9–17; Nakamura, Akira, "Tōjō Rikushō wa saikinsen ni hantai shita–Moto hishokan Imoto Kumao-shi ga shokan de akasu" [Army Minister Tōjō was against biological warfare–As revealed in the correspondence of his former secretary Kumao Imoto], in Shōwashi kenkyūjo, *Shōwashi kenkyūjo hōkoku*, Apr. 10, 1999.

16. Kobori, *Tōkyō saiban*, pp. 563–5.

17. We can see from the way history unfolded after the war that the European colonial powers lacked the grace to voluntarily grant independence to their Asian colonies, even though the time had come for the liberation of these colonized lands. It's clear they were forced to reach this understanding only through the powerful leadership of the United States. Nevertheless, even without America's strong leadership, times had changed and the independence of the Asian nations had to be recognized. This change in global circumstances, including the awakening in the Asian nations themselves, was clearly a product of the war. At the very least, the war hastened the arrival of these changes.

18. "Beikoku jinbun kagaku komondan hōkokusho" [Report of the United States Cultural Science Mission to Japan], in *Nihon jinbun kagaku no atarashii shinro* [The new course ahead for cultural science in Japan] (Tokyo: Kagaku shiryō kankōkai, 1950), p. 8. The original citation is from the Joseph C. Trainor Papers, located at Stanford University.

19. Aristotle, *Eudemosu rinrigaku* [The Eudemian Ethics], in Akitoshi Kaku, trans., *Arisutoteresu: Sekai no meicho 8-kan* [World classics series, vol. 8, Aristotle] (Tokyo: Chūō Kōronsha, 1972), p. 520. Kaku based his Japanese translation on various sources, including Rackham, H., *The Eudemian Ethics* (Loeb Classical Library, 1961); and Solomon, J., *The Works of Aristotle*, vol. 9 (Oxford, 1915). Bracketed [ ] words in the quoted text were inserted by Kaku.

Chapter 3

1. Burns, *Soldier of Freedom*, p. 6; Beard, Charles A., *President Roosevelt and the Coming of the War, 1941: A Study in Appearances and Realities* (Archon Books, 1968), p. 3; Franklin D. Roosevelt, "Campaign Address at Boston, Massachusetts: *We Are Going Full Speed Ahead!* " October 30, 1940, in *Public Papers and Addresses*, vol. 9 (New York: Macmillan, 1941), p. 517.

2. Burns, *Soldier of Freedom*, pp. 249–52.

3. Ibid., p. 94.

4. Japan Foreign Ministry, *Gaimushō no hyakunen (ge)* [The Foreign Ministry's one hundred years, vol. 2], edited by Gaimushō Hyakunenshi Hensan Iinkai [Foreign Ministry centennial history editorial committee] (Tokyo: Hara Shobō, 1969), pp. 546–7; Kase, Toshikazu, "A Failure of Diplomacy," in Cook, Haruko T. and Theodore F. Cook, eds., *Japan at War: An Oral History* (New York: The New Press, 1992), p. 92.

5. Japan Foreign Ministry, *Nihon gaikō nenpyō narabi ni shuyō bunsho* [Chronology and major documents of Japanese foreign relations] (Tokyo: Hara Shobō, 1965), pp. 31–2; *FRUS*, 1941, vol. 4, p. 928.

6. *BNT*, p. 45.

7. Ibid., pp. 45–6.

8. *KTK*, vol. 1, p. 163.

9. See chap. 4, n. 10.

10. Watanabe, Katsumasa, *Ketsudan: Inochi no biza* [Decision: Visas for life] (Tokyo: Taishō Shuppan, 1996), p. 193.

11. Ibid., pp. 193–7.

12. Horinouchi, Kensuke, *Nihon gaikō shi, dai-21 kan, Nichi-Doku-I dōmei: Nisso chūritsu jōyaku* [History of Japanese diplomacy, vol. 21, The Japan-Germany-Italy alliance: The Japan-Soviet neutrality pact] (Tokyo: Kashima Kenkyūjo Shuppankai, 1971), p. 98.

13. *BNT*, p. 50.

14. Iwakuro, Hideo, "Heiwa e no tatakai: 41-nen 1-gatsu–8-gatsu" [Struggle for peace: Jan.-Aug., 1941], *Bungei Shunjū* (Aug. 1966), p. 230.

15. Kase, "Failure of Diplomacy," p. 94.

16. *MBPH*, vol. 1, p. 49, Cable 191, Matsuoka to Nomura, May 3, 1941.

17. Hull, Cordell, *The Memoirs of Cordell Hull* (New York: Macmillan, 1948), vol. 2, p. 997.

18. Ibid., vol. 2, p. 1001.

19. Kase, "Failure of Diplomacy," p. 91; *KTK*, vol. 1, p. 163.

20. *RIB*, pp. 213–4. For a translation of this report, see chap. 5, "Chiune Sugihara, A Gentle and Capable Individual." (This translation does not appear in her *VFL*.)

21. Sanbō Honbu [Army General Staff], *Sugiyama Memō* [The Sugiyama memoranda] (Tokyo: Hara Shobō, 1967), vol. 1, p. 249.

22. Domon, Shūhei, *Sanbō no sensō* [The Army General Staff's war] (Tokyo: Kōdansha, 1987), p. 204.

23. Japan Foreign Ministry, *Gaikō shiryō: Nichi-Bei kōshō kiroku no bu* [Source materials on Japanese foreign relations: Negotiations between Japan and the United States, documents volume] (Tokyo: Hara Shobō, 1946), pp. 96–7; *FRUS, Japan, 1931–1941*, vol. 2, pp. 503–4.

24. For Japanese translations by Iwashima Hisao, an expert on the intelligence war, of the following intercepts, see his *Jōhōsen ni kanpai shita Nihon: Rikugun jōhō "shinwa" no hōkai* [Losing the intelligence war: Destroying the "myth" of Japan's Army General Staff intelligence] (Tokyo: Hara Shobō, 1984), pp. 91–7.

25. *MBPH*, vol. 1, p. 52. Cable 482, Ōshima to Matsuoka, May 3, 1941.

26. Ibid., vol. 1, p. 52. Cable 192, Matsuoka to Nomura, May 5, 1941.

27. Ibid., vol. 1, p. 53. Cable 267, Nomura to Matsuoka, May 5, 1941.

28. For an alternative explanation of how Germany may have discovered the U. S. was intercepting and decoding Japanese diplomatic messages, see Harris, Ruth, "The 'Magic' Leak of 1941," *Pacific Historical Review* (February 1981), pp. 82–6.

29. Emmerson, John K., *The Japanese Thread: A Life in the U. S. Foreign Service* (New York: Holt, Rinehart and Winston, 1978), p. 100; Grew, Joseph, *Ten Years in Japan* (New York: Simon and Schuster, 1944), pp. 414–5; *BI&C*, pp. 49–51.

30. Although there are no extant records of this compromise plan, the gist of it was published in 1991 (to coincide with the 50th anniversary of

the Pearl Harbor attack) by Robert Fearey who also worked under Grew. See Fearey's "Tokyo 1941: Diplomacy's Final Round," *Foreign Service Journal* (December 1991), p. 29; *BI&C*, pp. 8–9.

31. *BI&C*, pp. 42–9.

32. *BNT*, pp. 92–4.

33. Ibid., pp. 101–2. Nomura cites FDR's "wonderful" remark in English.

34. Ibid., p. 111; *JPPH*, p. 88.

35. The author explores this issue in more depth elsewhere. See *BI&C*, pp. 30–4. Japan had already selected its delegation, and even the ship the delegation would travel in. From the very start however, there were no signs at all of such preparations by the U. S. On December 8, 1996, the *Sankei Shimbun* featured the draft of a previously unpublished "declaration of resolve" by Konoe. The draft was prepared by author and Konoe policy consultant Yūzō Yamamoto, and is thought to be the declaration Konoe would have used to address the nation when departing for the summit meeting. It reveals the earnest hopes Konoe had pinned on the summit, for which advanced arrangements had been made.

36. Wedemeyer, Albert C., *Dainiji sekai taisen ni shōsha nashi* [World War II had no winners], translated by Sakutarō Senō (Tokyo: Kōdansha, 1997), vol. 2, pp. 360–6. Originally published as *The Wedemeyer Reports!* (N.Y.: Holt, 1958); Haffner, Sebastian, *Hitorā to wa nani ka* [The meaning of Hitler], translated by Tatsuo Akabane (Tokyo: Sōshisha, 1979), p. 142. Originally published as *Anmerkungen zu Hitler* (München: Kindler, 1978).

37. Japan National Defense Agency, *Senshi sōsho: Hitō kōryaku sakusen* [War history series: Operation to capture the Philippines] (Tokyo: Asagumo Shimbunsha, 1966), pp. 58–61.

38. *FRUS*, 1941, vol. 4, pp. 278–80.

39. *BI&C*, pp. 37–43.

40. *Sankei Shimbun*, Aug. 22, 1999, evening edition; Sugita, *Sōtenken*, pp. 68–71.

41. Sudō, Shinji, "Haru Nōto to Manshū mondai" [The Hull Note and the Manchurian question], in Keiō gijuku daigaku hōgaku kenkyūkai, eds., *Hōgaku kenkyū* vol. 69, no. 11 (1968).

42. *BI&C*, pp. 42–9.

43. Japan National Defense Agency, *Senshi sōsho: Marē shinkō sakusen* [War history series: Operation to occupy Malaysia] (Tokyo: Asagumo Shimbunsha, 1966), pp. 2–3.

44. *Gendaishi shiryō dai 34-kan: Taiheiyō sensō 1* [Source materials for modern Japanese history, vol. 34, The Pacific war, part 1] (Tokyo: Misuzu Shobō, 1968), pp. 600–3; see also n. 46, below.

45. Toland, John, *Infamy: Pearl Harbor and Its Aftermath* (New York: Berkley Books, 1983), p. 313.

46. For more details on Yamamoto Isoroku and the surprise attack on Pearl Harbor, see Konno, Tsutomu, *Shinju-wan kishu: Rūzuberuto wa shitte ita ka* [The surprise attack on Pearl Harbor: Did Roosevelt know?] (Tokyo: Yomiuri Shimbunsha, 1991); and Sugita, *Sōtenken*.

47. Amō, Eiji, "Nichi-Bei kōshō tenmatsu-ki" [An account of the Japan-U. S. negotiations], *Saron* (*rinji zōkangō* [special edition]) (December 1949), pp. 36–9.

48. *BI&C*, pp. 21–56.

Chapter 4

1. *KTK*, vol. 2, pp. 96–7.

2. Jiji Tsūshinsha, *Naigai kyōiku*, Jan. 8, 1988, p. 8.

3. Kase, Toshikazu, *Mizurii gō e no dōtei* [Journey to the Missouri] (Tokyo: Bungei Shunjū, 1951), p. 6; Kase, Toshikazu, *Journey to the Missouri*, ed. David Nelson Rowe (New Haven: Yale University Press, 1950), p. vii.

4. Kase, *Mizurii*, p. 6; Kase, *Missouri*, pp. vii–viii.

5. Kase, *Mizurii*, p. 276; Kase, *Missouri*, pp. 190–1.

6. Kase, *Mizurii*, p. 280; Kase, *Missouri*, p. 192.

7. *KTK*, vol. 2, pp. 96–7.

8. Kase, *Mizurii*, p. 42; Kase, *Missouri*, p. 17.

9. Kase, *Mizurii*, pp. 44–5; Kase, *Missouri*, p. 19.

10. This "Fifth Column" refers to Germany's Nazi period during which German officials and civilians living abroad were brought together into an organized unit; they deeply infiltrated their host nations, and conducted activities aimed at placing those nations under German influence. The Fifth Column's activities were most successful in Japan, and German agents then had deeply infiltrated the ministries for home and foreign affairs, and the army. In September 1940, a foreign observer asked: "[H]ow has it been possible for a proud, courageous and independent people, which has never been conquered by the sword, to allow itself to be thus conquered by [the Fifth Column]?...Only now do...they begin to see...the spectre of the twentieth century Trojan Horse." See Examiner (pseud.), "The Nazi Fifth Column in Japan," *Oriental Affairs*, vol. 14 (Sep. 1940); *BI&C*, pp. 35–6.

11. The delay in delivering the "final notice" occurred not only because the start of work on producing the clean copy in English was delayed, but also because none of the career diplomats, with the rank of counselor, secretary, or above, could type English properly. In accordance with home office instructions ("[I]n the preparation of the aide memoire be absolutely sure not to use a typist or any other person. Be most extremely cautious in preserving secrecy"), the only one that could type at all decently was Katsuzō Okumura, a proverbial "one-finger typist" who couldn't type quickly.

12. *NBKS* and *KTK*.

13. *NBKS*, pp. 80–1.

14. Iwakuro, Hideo, *Iwakuro Hideo shi danwa sokkiroku: Watakushi ga sanka shita Nichi-Bei kōshō* [The stenographic records of a conversation with Mr. Hideo Iwakuro: The Japan-United States Negotiations I participated in], p. 280. Located in Japan's National Diet Library, Modern Japanese Political History Materials Room.

15. *KTK*, vol. 1, p. 175.

16. *NBKS*, pp. 81–4.

17. Kase, "Failure of Diplomacy," p. 93.

18. Japan Foreign Ministry, *Gaimushō no hyakunen*, vol. 2, p. 554.

19. Konoe, Fumimaro, "Dainiji daisanji Konoe Naikaku ni okeru Nichi-Bei kōshō no keika (sōkō)" [Progress of the Japan-U. S. negotiations during the second and third Konoe cabinets (draft)], in *Konoe Nikki* [Konoe diary] (Tokyo: Kyōdō Tsūshinsha Kaihatsukyoku, 1968), p. 212.

20. *KTK*, vol. 2, p. 97.

21. Iwashima, *Jōhōsen ni kanpai shita Nihon*, pp. 91–6.

22. *KTK*, vol. 1, pp. 20–1.

23. Ibid., vol. 1, pp. 196–7. Furthermore, Eiji Amō, vice foreign minister during the third Konoe cabinet, also stated that Japan was decoding America's diplomatic cables, and that information obtained from these contributed to Matsuoka's ousting from the cabinet. See Amō, "Nichi-Bei kōshō tenmatsu-ki," p. 32.

24. Amō, "Nichi-Bei kōshō tenmatsu-ki," pp. 36–9.

25. Kase, "Gimon," pp. 100–1.

26. Hull, *Memoirs*, vol. 2, p. 1096.

27. *PHA*, vol. 12, p. 238, Cable 901 (pilot message).

28. Ibid., vol. 12, p. 248, Cable 907.

29. Ibid., vol. 12, p. 248, Cable 908.

30. Iwakuro, *Sokkiroku*, p. 292.

31. Kase, *Mizurii*, p. 6; Kase, *Missouri*, p. viii.

32. *NBKS*, p. 326.

33. Kase, Toshikazu, *Yoshida Shigeru no yuigon* [The last words of Shigeru Yoshida] (Tokyo: Yomiuri Shimbunsha, 1967).

34. *BI&C*, pp. 85–112.

35. Hora, Tomio, *Nitchū Sensō-shi shiryō 8: Nankin jiken 1* [Materials on the Japan-China War, part 8: The Nanking Incident, vol. 1] (Tokyo: Kawade Shobō Shinsha, 1973), pp. 382–3.

36. Ibid., pp. 180–7.

37. *RIB*, p. 109.

38. Shillony, Ben-Ami, *The Jews and the Japanese: The Successful Outsiders* (Tokyo: Charles E. Tuttle, 1991), p. 190; Shillony, Ben-Ami, *Yudayajin to Nihonjin–Seikō shita nokemono* [Jewish people and Japanese people: Successful outcasts], translated by Jun'ichi Nakayama (Tokyo: Nihon Kōhō, 1993), pp. 305–11.

39. Watanabe, *Ketsudan*, p. 277.

40. *RIB*, p. 17; *VFL*, p. 4.

41. Warhaftig, Zorach, *Nihon ni kita Yudaya nanmin* [Jewish refugees who came to Japan], translated by Takigawa Yoshito (Tokyo: Hara Shobō, 1992), p. 347. Originally published in Hebrew as *Palit Vesarid* [Refugee and survivor] (Jerusalem: Yad Vashem, 1984).

42. *Sankei Shimbun*, March 30, 1998.

43. Inuzuka, Kiyoko, *Yudayajin mondai to Nihon no kōsaku* [Japan's activities on the Jewish issue] (Tokyo: Nihon Kōgyō Shimbunsha, 1982),

pp. 76–9; Shino, Teruhisa, *Yakusoku no kuni e no nagai tabi* [Long journey to the promised land] (Riburio Shuppan, 1988), pp. 136–9.
44. *BI&C*, pp. 123–4.
45. These files are kept under *Minzoku mondai kankei zakken: Yudayajin no bu* [Miscellaneous files on ethnic questions: The Jews].
46. *BI&C*, pp. 104–5.
47. Grew, Joseph, *Tai-Nichi Jūnen* [Ten years in Japan], trans. Kin'ichi Ishikawa (Tokyo: Mainichi Shimbunsha, 1984), vol. 2, p. 166; Grew, *Ten Years in Japan*, p. 415; See also *BI&C*, pp. 49–51.
48. See note 10. (Nazi Fifth Column.)
49. Kase, Toshikazu, *Nihon gaikō wo shikaru* [Reproving Japanese diplomacy] (Tokyo: TBS Britannica, 1997).
50. Ibid., pp. 22–3.
51. Kase, *Mizurii*, pp. 44–5; Kase, *Missouri*, p. 19.
52. Owada, Hisashi, "Kokuren taishi wo oete: Nihon gaikō–Watashi no teigen" [Finishing up as U. N. Ambassador: My suggestions for Japanese diplomacy], *Bungei Shunjū* (February 1999), pp. 206–17.
53. Kase, *Shikaru*, p. 46.
54. Ibid., p. 50.

Chapter 5

1. *ISOS*. Translated into Japanese by Kiyoshi Suwa and Teruhisa Shino as *Chiune: Ichiman-nin no inochi wo sukutta gaikōkan Sugihara Chiune no nazo* [Chiune: The enigma of Chiune Sugihara, the diplomat who saved 10,000 lives] (Tokyo: Shimizu Shoin, 1998).
2. Shimada, Masahiko, "Sugihara Chiune: Mōze ni natta Nihonjin" [Chiune Sugihara: A Japanese Moses], *Yomiuri Shimbun*, May 15, 1999, evening edition.
3. *ISOS*, p. 4; Levine, *Ichiman-nin*, pp. 8–9.
4. Yukiko Sugihara mentions in her book that she was not allowed to help issue the visas, and this agrees with testimony from other consular staff. *VFL*, p. 23; *RIB*, pp. 33, 37.
5. Watanabe, *Ketsudan*, pp. 65–8.
6. Ibid., p. 135.
7. Warhaftig, *Yudaya nanmin*, p. 105.
8. *VFL*, p. 9; Tokayer and Swartz, *Fugu Plan*, p. 30.
9. Warhaftig, *Yudaya nanmin*, p. 94.
10. Watanabe, *Ketsudan*, p. 132; Japan Foreign Ministry, "Minzoku mondai zakken: Yudayajin no bu" [Miscellaneous files on ethnic questions: The Jews], file 10, p. 0638. Diplomatic Records Office, Tokyo.
11. Japan Foreign Ministry, "Yudayajin no bu," file 10, p. 0638; *RIB*, p. 207 (Note: this does not appear in her English version, *VFL*.)
12. *ISOS*, p. 259; Levine, *Ichiman-nin*, p. 430.
13. *ISOS*, p. 259; Levine, *Ichiman-nin*, p. 430.
14. Chiune Sugihara thought he could allow the Jewish refugees to escape first from Lithuania. *VFL*, p. 17; *RIB*, pp. 31–2.

15. Shiraishi, Masaaki, "Iwayuru 'inochi no biza' hakkyū kankei kiroku ni tsuite" [Documents regarding issuing the so-called 'visas for life'], *Gaikō shiryō kanpō* [Journal of the Diplomatic Record Office] no. 9 (1996), p. 67. Although the original cables show the date as August 1, this is in fact mistaken.

16. *ISOS*, p. 174; Levine, *Ichiman-nin*, p. 278.

17. Watanabe, *Ketsudan*, p. 301.

18. Tokudome, Kinue, "Sugihara Chiune no isan wo tadashiku uketsuida ka" [Are we correctly carrying on the legacy of Chiune Sugihara?], *Ronza* (September 1998), p. 211.

19. Saotome, Katsumoto, *Seimei wo mitsumeru: Sugihara Ryōji to Rērochika no pan* [Gazing at life: Consul Sugihara and Lerochka's bread] (Tokyo: Kusanone Shuppankai, 1998), pp. 59–78. The title of this book refers to Lerochka, a 3-year-old Leningrad girl who died in February 1942. A piece of bread, apparently her last meal, was preserved as part of a memorial to 600,000 people who perished from starvation due to the conflict in Leningrad in 1941–1942.

20. Chūnichi Shimbun Shakaibu, *Jiyū e no tōsō: Sugihara biza to Yudayajin* [Flight to freedom: Sugihara's visas and the Jews] (Tokyo: Tōkyō Shimbun Shuppankyoku, 1995), pp. 29, 43.

21. Ganor, Solly, *Nihonjin ni sukuwareta Yudayajin no shuki* [Recollections of Jews saved by a Japanese], translated by Ōtani Kenjirō (Tokyo: Kōdansha, 1997), pp. 74–80. Originally published as *Light One Candle: A Survivor's Tale from Lithuania to Jerusalem* (New York: Kodansha International, 1995).

22. See note 20.

23. Watanabe, *Ketsudan*, p. 61.

24. Ibid., p. 68.

25. Ibid., pp. 73–5.

26. Chūnichi Shimbun Shakaibu, *Jiyū e no tōsō*, pp. 142–4.

27. *RIB*, pp. 213–4. (Note: this cable does not appear in her English version, *VFL*.)

28. Onodera, Yuriko, *Baruto-kai no hotori ni te: Bukan no tsuma no Dai Tō-A sensō* [Near the Baltic Sea: The Greater East Asian War through the eyes of a military attaché's wife] (Tokyo: Kyōdō Tsūshinsha, 1985), p. 132; *Sankei Shimbun*, September 12, 1987. It appears that Chiune Sugihara was in contact with Makoto Onodera. See Chūnichi Shimbun Shakaibu, *Jiyū e no tōsō*, pp. 142–4.

29. Shino, *Yakusoku no kuni*, p. 138.

30. *Gaimushō shitsumu hōkoku: Amerika-kyoku* [Released Documents of the Ministry of Foreign Affairs: American Affairs bureau] 3 vols., 1939–1942 (Tokyo: Kress, 1994), vol. 3, pp. 228–9.

31. Chūnichi Shimbun Shakaibu, *Jiyū e no tōsō*, pp. 63–5.

32. Ibid., pp. 69–71.

33. Miyazawa, Masanori, "Jinshū byōdō wo tsuranuita Nihon no Yudayajin seisaku" [The racial equality permeating Japan's Jewish policy],

Nihon Kaigi, ed., *Nihon no ibuki* (September 1998), pp. 6–8.
34. *VFL*, p. 61; *RIB*, p. 79.
35. Chiune Sugihara frequently admitted that the visas he issued were in fact dubious. Warhaftig, *Yudaya nanmin*, p. 105.
36. Shino, *Yakusoku no kuni*, p. 82. Apparently Saburō Nei acted out of respect for Chiune Sugihara, and there are also examples of transit visas issued by Nei. See Chūnichi Shimbun Shakaibu, *Jiyū e no tōsō*, p. 58.
37. Warhaftig, *Yudaya nanmin*, p. 204.
38. Watanabe, *Ketsudan*, p. 195.
39. Levine, Hillel, "Kyūshutsu no wa hirogeta 'zen'i no inbō'" [The 'conspiracy of goodness' which widened the circle of rescued], *Tōkyō Shimbun*, September 5, 1998, evening edition.
40. *ISOS*, p. 8; Warhaftig, *Yudaya nanmin*, p. 12.

Chapter 6
1. *RIB*, p. 150. For a slightly abridged translation of this passage, see also her *VFL*, pp. 108–9.
2. Hosaka, Masayasu, "Gaimushō gojū-nen no kashitsu to taiman" [Fifty years of mistakes and negligence in the Ministry of Foreign Affairs], *Bungei Shunjū* (December 1991), p. 190.
3. Ibid., pp. 190–1.
4. Author's interview with Yukiko Sugihara, May 14, 1999. See also *VFL*, p. 124; *RIB*, p. 171.
5. *VFL*, p. 109; *RIB*, p. 151.
6. Warhaftig, *Yudaya nanmin*, pp. 100–2.
7. Watanabe, Katsumasa, "Waseda no hokori: Sugihara Chiune" [The pride of Waseda: Chiune Sugihara], Waseda Daigaku Kōyūkai, eds., *Waseda gakuhō* (June 1999), p. 11; For Watanabe's book, see *Ketsudan: Inochi no biza* [Determination: Visas for life] (Tokyo: Taishō Shuppan, 1996).
8. *VFL*, p. 24; *RIB*, p. 39.
9. Chūnichi Shimbun Shakaibu, *Jiyū e no tōsō*, p. 40.
10. Author's interview with Yukiko Sugihara, May 14, 1999.
11. Author's interview with Yukiko Sugihara, May 14, 1999. The characters for Consul Sugihara's first name could conceivably be pronounced either way, but he generally introduced himself as "Senpo" to Jewish visitors at the consulate because they found this easier to pronounce.
12. Dambmann, Gerhard, *Koritsu suru Taikoku Nippon* [Japan, The Isolated Power], translated by Tetsuya Tsukamoto (Tokyo: TBS Britannica, 1981), pp. 220–1. Originally published in German as *25mal Japan: Weltmacht als Einzelgänger* (Munich & Zurich: Piper, 1979).
13. Ibid., pp. 220–1.
14. At present it is still not clear exactly how many Jews were saved by Chiune Sugihara's visas. We don't know how many people actually used these visas, nor is it clear how many used each visa. He also issued visas that weren't recorded, while those forged by Jozef Szimkin can also be thought of as a by-product of Sugihara's visas; Sugihara also issued more

visas during his next posting in Prague. Therefore, we cannot know exactly how many visas he issued, nor exactly how many refugees were saved.

15. Shino, *Yakusoku no kuni*, p. 122.

16. These minutes can be found in *RIB*, pp. 226–7. Because this is only an excerpted passage, there is no explicit reference to the government spokesperson interrupting the foreign minister, and answering for him.

17. *Sankei Shimbun*, May 7, 1998, evening edition.

18. Fujiwara, Nobuo, "Sugihara Chiune wa han-seifu no eiyū ni arazu" [Chiune Sugihara was no anti-government hero], interview in Nihon Kaigi, ed., *Nihon no ibuki* (September 1999), pp. 6–7.

19. Tokudome, "Sugihara Chiune no isan," p. 210.

20. *BI&C*, chap. 1.

Glossary

Abe Shintarō 安倍晋太郎
Akihito 明仁
Amō Eiji 天羽英二
Asano Takuminokami 浅野内匠頭
Aikawa [Ayukawa] Yoshisuke 鮎川義介
bakuhan 幕藩
bushidō 武士道
Chiang Kai-shek 蒋介石
*Chiune: Ichiman-nin no inochi wo sukutta gaikōkan Sugihara Chiune
    no nazo* 『千畝・一万人の命を救った外交官杉原千畝の謎』
Chosŏn 朝鮮
Chu Yüan-chang 朱元璋
Chūshingura 『忠臣蔵』
Daihon'ei renraku kaigi 大本営連絡会議
Domon Shūhei 土門周平
Dōra 銅鑼
Fujiwara Nobuo 藤原宣夫
fukuzatsu kaiki 複雑怪奇
Funayama Kikuya 船山喜久弥
Funayama Sadakichi 船山貞吉
"Genka kokusai jōsei ni shosuru Teikoku taigai hōshin"
    「現下国際状勢二処する帝国対外方針」
hakkō ichiu 八紘一宇
Hidaka Shinrokurō 日高信六郎
Hiranuma Kiichirō 平沼騏一郎
Hirohito 裕仁
Hirota Kōki 広田弘毅

Hu Wei-yung 胡惟庸
Hyōdō Nagao 兵藤長雄
Iguchi Sadao 井口貞夫
Iguchi Takeo 井口武夫
Ikawa Tadao 井川忠雄
ikkun banmin byōdō 一君万民平等
Itagaki Seishirō 板垣征四郎
Itō Hirobumi 伊藤博文
Iwakuro Hideo 岩畔豪雄
"Jikyoku ni tomonau Yudayajin taisaku"
　　「時局ニ伴フ猶太人対策」
jison jiei 自存自衛
Jiyū e no tōsō: Sugihara biza to Yudayajin
　　『自由への逃走・杉原ビザとユダヤ人』
kagai no mondai 加害の問題
kamikaze 神風
kanji 漢字
Kase Hideaki 加瀬英明
Kase Toshikazu 加瀬俊一
keibatsu 閨閥
kenkyūkai 研究会
Kira Kōzukenosuke 吉良上野介
Komura Jutarō 小村寿太郎
Konoe Fumimaro 近衛文麿
Koritsu suru Taikoku Nippon 『孤立する大国ニッポン』
Koryŏ 高麗
Kurusu Saburō 来栖三郎
Kusakawa Shōzō 草川昭三
Lan Yü 藍玉
Matsui Iwane 松井石根
Matsuoka Yōsuke 松岡洋右
Miyazawa Kiichi 宮沢喜一
Miyazawa Masanori 宮沢正典
Nakano Naoya 中野直也
Nakasone Yasuhiro 中曽根康弘
Nei Saburō 根井三郎
Nichi-Bei kōshō 『日米交渉』
Nihon gaikō wo shikaru 『日本外交を叱る』
Niizeki Kin'ya 新関欽哉
Nitobe Inazō 新渡戸稲造
Nomura Kichisaburō 野村吉三郎

Oda Nobunaga 織田信長
Ōhashi Chūichi 大橋忠一
Ōishi [Kuranosuke] 大石内蔵助
Okazaki Katsuo 岡崎勝男
Ōkubo Toshimichi 大久保利通
Okumura Katsuzō 奥村勝蔵
Onodera Makoto 小野寺信
Ōoka sabaki 大岡裁き
Ōshima Hiroshi 大島浩
Rokusen-nin no inochi no biza 『六千人の命のビザ』
rōnin 浪人
Saitō Ototsugu 斉藤音次
Sakamoto Mizuo 阪本瑞男
sakoku 鎖国
Sei-I Taishōgun 征夷大将軍
Shigemitsu Mamoru 重光葵
Shino Teruhisa 篠輝久
shinryaku 侵略
shinshutsu 進出
shinzui 真髄
Shiratori Toshio 白鳥敏夫
"Sobieto Renpō kokumin keizai taikan"「ソビエト連邦国民経済大観」
sonnō jōi 尊王攘夷
Sugihara Chiune [Senpo] 杉原千畝
Sugihara Seishirō 杉原誠四郎
Sugihara Yukiko 杉原幸子
Suzuki Kantarō 鈴木貫太郎
Suzuki Muneo 鈴木宗男
taisei hōkan 大政奉還
Tan'gun 檀君
Tennō no tame ni 天皇のために
tennō-sei 天皇制
Terasaki Hidenari 寺崎英成
Terasaki Tarō 寺崎太郎
Tōgō Shigenori 東郷茂徳
Tōjō Hideki 東条英機
Tokudome Kinue 徳留絹枝
Tokugawa Ieyasu 徳川家康
Tokugawa Yoshinobu 徳川慶喜
Toyoda Teijirō 豊田貞次郎

Ushiba Tomohiko　牛場友彦
Watanabe Katsumasa　渡辺勝正
Watanabe Michio　渡辺美智雄
Yakusoku no kuni e no nagai tabi　『約束の国への長い旅』
Yamamoto Isoroku　山本五十六
Yamamoto Kumaichi　山本熊一
Yamato　大和
Yi Sŏng-gye　李成桂
yi-hsing ke-ming　易姓革命
Yokota Kisaburō　横田喜三郎
Yoshida Shigeru　吉田茂
"Yudayajin taisaku yōkō"　「猶太人対策要綱」
Yūki Shirōji　結城司郎次

Bibliography

Alperovitz, Gar. *The Decision to Use the Atomic Bomb and the Architecture of an American Myth*. N. Y.: Alfred A. Knopf, 1995.

Amō, Eiji. "Nichi-Bei kōshō tenmatsu-ki" [An account of the Japan-U. S. negotiations]. *Saron* (*rinji zōkangō* [special edition]) (December 1949).

Aristotle. *Eudemosu rinrigaku* [The Eudemian Ethics]. In *Arisutoteresu: Sekai no meicho 8-kan* [World classics series. Vol. 8. Aristotle]. Translated by Akitoshi Kaku. Tokyo: Chūō Kōronsha, 1972.

Ariyama, Teruo. *Senryō-ki media shi kenkyū: jiyū to tōsei, 1945-nen* [Research on the history of the media under the Occupation: Freedom and control, 1945]. Tokyo: Kashiwa Shobō, 1996.

Auer, James E. *The Postwar Rearmament of Japanese Maritime Forces: 1945–1971*. Praeger, 1973.

Beard, Charles A. *President Roosevelt and the Coming of the War, 1941: A Study in Appearances and Realities*. Archon Books, 1968.

Burns, James MacGregor. *Roosevelt: The Soldier of Freedom, 1940–1945*. New York: Harcourt Brace Yovanovich, 1970.

Butow, Robert. "Marching off to War on the Wrong Foot: The Final Note Tokyo did not Send to Washington." *Pacific Historical Review*, vol. LXIII (1994).

Chang, Iris. *The Rape of Nanking: The Forgotten Holocaust of World War II*. New York: Basic Books, 1997.

Chūnichi Shimbun Shakaibu. *Jiyū e no tōsō: Sugihara biza to Yudayajin* [Flight to freedom: Sugihara's visas and the Jews]. Tokyo: Tōkyō Shimbun Shuppankyoku, 1995.

Dambmann, Gerhard. *Koritsu suru Taikoku Nippon* [Japan, The Isolated Power]. Translated by Tetsuya Tsukamoto. Tokyo: TBS Britannica, 1981.

Domon, Shūhei. *Sanbō no sensō* [The Army General Staff's war]. Tokyo: Kōdansha, 1987.

Emmerson, John K. *The Japanese Thread: A Life in the U. S. Foreign Service*. New York: Holt, Rinehart and Winston, 1978.

Examiner (pseud.) "The Nazi Fifth Column in Japan." *Oriental Affairs*, vol. 14 (September 1940).

Fearey, Robert. "Tokyo 1941: Diplomacy's Final Round." *Foreign Service Journal* (December 1991).

Fralon, José-Alain. *A Good Man in Evil Times*. Translated by Peter Graham. Viking, 2000.

Fujiwara, Nobuo. "Sugihara Chiune wa han-seifu no eiyū ni arazu" [Chiune Sugihara was no anti-government hero]. *Nihon no ibuki* (Sep. 1999).

Funayama, Kikuya. *Hakutōwashi to sakura no ki: Nihon wo aishita Josefu Gurū taishi* [The bald eagle and the cherry tree: Ambassador Joseph Grew who loved Japan]. Tokyo: Aki Shobō, 1996.

Ganor, Solly. *Nihonjin ni sukuwareta Yudayajin no shuki* [Recollections of Jews saved by a Japanese]. Translated by Ōtani Kenjirō. Tokyo: Kōdansha, 1997. Originally published as Light One Candle: *A Survivor's Tale from Lithuania to Jerusalem*. N.Y.: Kodansha International, 1995.

Gendaishi shiryō dai 34-kan: Taiheiyō sensō 1 [Source materials for modern Japanese history. Vol. 34. The Pacific war, part 1]. Tokyo: Misuzu Shobō, 1968.

Grew, Joseph. *Tai-Nichi Jūnen* [Ten years in Japan]. 2 vols. Translated by Kin'ichi Ishikawa. Tokyo: Mainichi Shimbunsha, 1984.

———. *Ten Years in Japan*. New York: Simon and Schuster, 1944.

Haffner, Sebastian. *Hitorā to wa nani ka* [The meaning of Hitler]. Translated by Tatsuo Akabane. Tokyo: Sōshisha, 1979. Originally published as *Anmerkungen zu Hitler*. München: Kindler, 1978.

Harris, Ruth. "The 'Magic' Leak of 1941." *Pacific Historical Review* (February 1981).

Higashinakano, Shūdō. *"Nankin gyakusatsu" no tettei kenshō* [Thorough examination of the "Nanking Massacre"]. Tokyo: Tendensha, 1998.

Higashinakano, Shūdō and Nobukatsu Fujioka. *'Za Reipu obu Nankin' no kenkyū: Chūgoku ni okeru 'jōhō-sen' no teguchi to senryaku* [Research on 'The Rape of Nanking': China's tricks and tactics in the 'propaganda war']. Tokyo: Shōdensha, 1999.

Hora, Tomio. *Nitchū Sensō-shi shiryō 8: Nankin jiken 1* [Materials on the Japan-China War. Part 8. The Nanking Incident. Vol. 1]. Tokyo: Kawade Shobō Shinsha, 1973.

Horinouchi, Kensuke. *Nihon gaikō shi, dai-21 kan, Nichi-Doku-I dōmei: Nisso chūritsu jōyaku* [History of Japanese diplomacy. Vol. 21. The Japan-Germany-Italy alliance: The Japan-Soviet neutrality pact]. Tokyo: Kashima Kenkyūjo Shuppankai, 1971.

Hosaka, Masayasu. "Gaimushō gojū-nen no kashitsu to taiman" [Fifty years of mistakes and negligence in the Ministry of Foreign Affairs]. *Bungei Shunjū* (December 1991).

Hull, Cordell. *The Memoirs of Cordell Hull.* 2 vols. N.Y.: Macmillan, 1948.

Iglehart, C. W. *Kokusai Kirisutokyō daigaku sōritsu shi: Myōnichi no daigaku e no bijon* [International Christian University: An Adventure in Christian Higher Education in Japan]. Tokyo: ICU, 1990.

Iguchi, Takeo. "Maboroshi no 'sensen fukoku' zenbun" [Complete text of illusory "declaration of war"]. *This is Yomiuri* (December 1997).

———. "Shinju-wan kishū kōgeki, chū-Bei taishikan ni ochido nashi: Tsūkoku okure wo desaki ni sekinin tenka shita Nihon seifu" [The embassy to the U.S. was not at fault for the surprise attack on Pearl Harbor: The Japanese government pushed responsibility for the notice's delay on its embassy abroad]. *Ronza* (January 1997).

Inuzuka, Kiyoko. *Yudayajin mondai to Nihon no kōsaku* [Japan's activities on the Jewish issue]. Tokyo: Nihon Kōgyō Shimbunsha, 1982.

Iokibe, Makoto. *Beikoku no Nihon senryō seisaku (ge)* [American policy towards Japan's occupation. Vol. 2]. Tokyo: Chūō Kōronsha, 1985.

Iwakuro, Hideo. "Heiwa e no tatakai: 41-nen 1-gatsu–8-gatsu" [Struggle for peace: January-August, 1941]. *Bungei Shunjū* (August 1966).

———. *Iwakuro Hideo shi danwa sokkiroku: Watakushi ga sanka shita Nichi-Bei kōshō* [The stenographic records of a conversation with Mr. Hideo Iwakuro: The Japan-United States Negotiations I participated in]. Japan National Diet Library, Modern Japanese Political History Materials Room.

Iwashima, Hisao. *Jōhōsen ni kanpai shita Nihon: Rikugun jōhō "shinwa" no hōkai* [Losing the intelligence war: Destroying the "myth" of Japan's Army General Staff intelligence]. Tokyo: Hara Shobō, 1984.

Japan Foreign Ministry. *Gaikō shiryō: Nichi-Bei kōshō kiroku no bu* [Source materials on Japanese foreign relations: Negotiations between Japan and the United States, documents volume]. Tokyo: Hara Shobō, 1946.

———. *Gaimushō no hyakunen (ge)* [The Foreign Ministry's one hundred years. Vol. 2]. Edited by Gaimushō Hyakunenshi Hensan Iinkai [Foreign Ministry centennial history editorial committee]. Tokyo: Hara Shobō, 1969.

———. *Gaimushō shitsumu hōkoku: Amerika-kyoku* [Released Documents of the Ministry of Foreign Affairs: American Affairs bureau]. 3 vols., 1939–1942. Tokyo: Kress, 1994.

———. "Minzoku mondai zakken: Yudayajin no bu" [Miscellaneous files on ethnic questions: The Jews]. Diplomatic Records Office, Tokyo.

———. *Nihon gaikō nenpyō narabi ni shuyō bunsho* [Chronology and major documents of Japanese foreign relations]. Tokyo: Hara Shobō, 1965.

Japan National Defense Agency. *Senshi sōsho: Hitō kōryaku sakusen* [War history series: Operation to capture the Philippines]. Tokyo: Asagumo Shimbunsha, 1966.

———. *Senshi sōsho: Marē shinkō sakusen* [War history series: Operation to occupy Malaysia]. Tokyo: Asagumo Shimbunsha, 1966

Kagaku shiryō kankōkai, eds. "Beikoku jinbun kagaku komondan hōkokusho" [Report of the United States Cultural Science Mission to Japan]. In *Nihon jinbun kagaku no atarashii shinro* [The new course ahead for cultural science in Japan]. Tokyo: Kagaku shiryō kankōkai, 1950.

Kase, Hideaki. "'Shinju-wan' no gimon ni kotaeru" [Answering questions about 'Pearl Harbor']. *Shokun!* (March 1998).

Kase, Toshikazu. "A Failure of Diplomacy." In Cook, Haruko and Theodore Cook, eds. *Japan at War: An Oral History.* N.Y.: New Press, 1992.

————. *Journey to the Missouri.* Edited by David Nelson Rowe. New Haven: Yale University Press, 1950.

————. *Kase Toshikazu Kaisōroku* [Memoirs]. 2 vols. Tokyo: Yamate Shobō, 1986.

————. *Mizurii gō e no dōtei* [Journey to the Missouri]. Tokyo: Bungei Shunjū, 1951.

————. *Nihon gaikō shi, dai-23 kan, Nichi-Bei kōshō* [History of Japanese diplomacy. Vol. 23. Negotiations between Japan and the United States]. Tokyo: Kashima Kenkyūjo Shuppankai, 1970.

————. *Nihon gaikō wo shikaru* [Reproving Japanese diplomacy]. Tokyo: TBS Britannica, 1997.

————. *Yoshida Shigeru no yuigon* [The last words of Shigeru Yoshida]. Tokyo: Yomiuri Shimbunsha, 1967.

Kim, Duk-Hwang. *A History of Religions in Korea.* Seoul: Daeji Moonhwasa Publishing Co., 1988.

Kobori, Keiichirō. *Tōkyō saiban–Nihon no benmei* [The Tokyo Trial and Japan's defense]. Tokyo: Kōdansha, 1995.

Kojima, Noboru. *Gosan no ronri* [The logic of miscalculation]. Tokyo: Bungei Shunjū, 1987.

Konno, Tsutomu. *Shinju-wan kishu: Rūzuberuto wa shitte ita ka* [The surprise attack on Pearl Harbor: Did Roosevelt know?] Tokyo: Yomiuri Shimbunsha, 1991.

Konoe, Fumimaro. "Dainiji daisanji Konoe Naikaku ni okeru Nichi-Bei kōshō no keika (sōkō)" [Progress of the Japan-U. S. negotiations during the second and third Konoe cabinets (draft)]. In *Konoe Nikki* [Konoe diary]. Tokyo: Kyōdō Tsūshinsha Kaihatsukyoku, 1968.

Levine, Hillel. *Chiune: Ichiman-nin no inochi wo sukutta gaikōkan Sugihara Chiune no nazo* [Chiune: The enigma of Chiune Sugihara, the diplomat who saved 10,000 lives]. Translated by Suwa, Kiyoshi and Teruhisa Shino. Tokyo: Shimizu Shoin, 1998.

————. *In Search of Sugihara: The elusive Japanese diplomat who risked his life to rescue 10,000 Jews from the Holocaust.* N.Y.: Free Press, 1996.

————. "Kyūshutsu no wa hirogeta 'zen'i no inbō' " [The 'conspiracy of goodness' which widened the circle of rescued]. *Tōkyō Shimbun* (September 5, 1998, evening edition).

Matsuura, Hiroshi. "Netsuzō sareru Sugihara Chiune zō" [Distortion of the Chiune Sugihara image]. *Sekai* (September 2000).

Miyazawa, Masanori. "Jinshū byōdō wo tsuranuita Nihon no Yudayajin seisaku" [The racial equality permeating Japan's Jewish policy]. Nihon Kaigi, ed. *Nihon no ibuki* (September 1998).

Morley, James and David Titus. *Japan's Road to the Pacific War*. Vol. 5. *The Final Confrontation: Japan's Negotiations with the United States, 1941*. New York: Columbia University Press, 1994.

Nakamura, Akira. "Tōjō Rikushō wa saikinsen ni hantai shita–Moto hishokan Imoto Kumao-shi ga shokan de akasu" [Army Minister Tōjō was against biological warfare–As revealed in the correspondence of his former secretary Kumao Imoto]. *Shōwashi kenkyūjo hōkoku* (Apr. 10, 1999).

Nitobe, Inazō. *Bushido: The Soul of Japan*. Tokyo: Charles E. Tuttle, 1969.

Nomura, Kichisaburō. *Beikoku ni tsukaishite: Nichi-Bei kōshō no kaiko* [On a mission to the United States: Reflections on negotiations between Japan and the United States]. Tokyo: Iwanami Shoten, 1946.

"Nyū Yōku Taimuzu kisha Kurukkuhōn ni taisuru bunshō ni yoru Okotae (yakubun)" [His Majesty's responses to the question sheet from New York Times reporter Kluckhorn (translated text)]. Takamatsunomiya File. Zaidan Hōjin Shiryō Chōsakai, Tokyo.

Okumura, Katsuzō. "Heika to Ma Gensui" [His Majesty and General MacArthur]. In Yoshida, Shigeru. *Kaisō jūnen* [Reflections of a decade]. Tokyo: Shinchōsha, 1957.

Onodera, Yuriko. *Baruto-kai no hotori ni te: Bukan no tsuma no Dai Tō-A sensō* [Near the Baltic Sea: The Greater East Asian War through the eyes of a military attaché's wife]. Tokyo: Kyōdō Tsūshinsha, 1985.

Owada, Hisashi. "Kokuren taishi wo oete: Nihon gaikō–Watashi no teigen" [Finishing up as U. N. Ambassador: My suggestions for Japanese diplomacy]. *Bungei Shunjū* (February 1999).

Passin, Herbert. *Society and Education in Japan*. New York: Columbia University, 1965.

Roosevelt, Franklin D. "Campaign Address at Boston, Massachusetts: *We Are Going Full Speed Ahead!*" (October 30, 1940). In *Public Papers and Addresses*. Vol. 9. New York: Macmillan, 1941.

Sakamoto, Pamela Rotner. *Japanese Diplomats and Jewish Refugees: A World War II Dilemma*. Westport: Praeger, 1998.

Sanbō Honbu [Army General Staff]. *Sugiyama Memō* [The Sugiyama memoranda]. Tokyo: Hara Shobō, 1967.

Saotome, Katsumoto. *Seimei wo mitsumeru: Sugihara Ryōji to Rērochika no pan* [Gazing at life: Consul Sugihara and Lerochka's bread]. Tokyo: Kusanone Shuppankai, 1998.

Sherwood, Robert E. *Roosevelt and Hopkins: An Intimate History*. New York: Harper, 1948.

Shigemitsu, Mamoru. *Zoku Shigemitsu Mamoru shuki* [Mamoru Shigemitsu memoirs. Vol. 2]. Tokyo: Chūō Kōronsha, 1998.

Shillony, Ben-Ami. *The Jews and the Japanese: The Successful Outsiders*. Tokyo: Charles E. Tuttle, 1991.

———. *Yudayajin to Nihonjin–Seikō shita nokemono* [Jewish people and Japanese people: Successful outcasts]. Translated by Jun'ichi Nakayama. Tokyo: Nihon Kōhō, 1993.

Shimada, Masahiko. "Sugihara Chiune: Mōze ni natta Nihonjin" [Chiune Sugihara: A Japanese Moses]. *Yomiuri Shimbun* (May 15, 1999, eve. ed.)

Shino, Teruhisa. *Yakusoku no kuni e no nagai tabi* [Long journey to the promised land]. Riburio Shuppan, 1988.

Shiraishi, Masaaki. "Iwayuru 'inochi no biza' hakkyū kankei kiroku ni tsuite" [Documents regarding issuing the so-called 'visas for life']. *Gaikō shiryō kanpō* [Journal of the Diplomatic Record Office], no. 9 (1996).

Shūkan shinchō. "Tennō–Ma Gensui kaiken 'Tōjō ni damasareta' ga kamosu butsugi" [The controversy raised by the statement "tricked by Tōjō" at the meeting between the Emperor and General MacArthur]. Dec. 18, 1986.

Stimson, Henry. *The Diaries of Henry Lewis Stimson.* Yale University Library, New Haven, 1973. Microfilm.

Stinnett, Robert B. *Day of Deceit: The Truth about FDR and Pearl Harbor.* N.Y.: Free Press, 2000.

Stouffer, Samuel A., et al. *Studies in Social Psychology in World War II.* Vol. 2. *The American Soldier: Combat and Its Aftermath.* Princeton: Princeton University Press, 1949.

Sudō, Shinji. "Haru Nōto to Manshū mondai" [The Hull Note and the Manchurian question]. In Keiō gijuku daigaku hōgaku kenkyūkai, eds. *Hōgaku kenkyū* vol. 69, no. 11 (1968).

Sugihara, Seishirō. *Between Incompetence And Culpability: Assessing the Diplomacy Of Japan's Foreign Ministry From Pearl Harbor to Potsdam.* Translated by Norman Hu. Lanham: University Press of America, 1997.

————. *Japanese Perspectives on Pearl Harbor: A Critical Review of Japanese Reports on the Fiftieth Anniversary of the Pearl Harbor Attack.* Translated by Theodore McNelly. H.K.: Asian Research Service, 1995.

————. *Nichi-Bei kaisen ikō no Nihon gaikō no kenkyū* [Research on Japanese diplomacy since the outbreak of the Japan-U. S. war]. Tokyo: Aki Shobō, 1997.

————. *Nihon no shintō, bukkyo to sai-kyō bunri* [Shinto and Buddhism in Japan and the separation of church and state]. Tokyo: Bunka Shobō Hakubunsha, 1992.

Sugihara, Yukiko. *Rokusen-nin no inochi no biza* [Visas for 6,000 lives]. Tokyo: Taishō Shuppan, 1993.

————. *Visas for Life.* San Francisco: Edu-Comm. Plus, 1995.

Sugita, Makoto [Seishirō Sugihara]. *Sōtenken–Shinju-wan 50-shūnen hōdō: Nani ga doko made wakatta ka* [Overview of reports on the fiftieth anniversary of Pearl Harbor: what and how much is known?]. Tokyo: Morita Shuppan, 1992.

Takahashi, Hiroshi. *Shōwa tennō hatsugen roku* [Speeches by the Shōwa emperor]. Tokyo: Shōgakkan, 1989.

Takemoto, Tadeo and Yasuo Ohara. *The Alleged Nanking Massacre: Japan's rebuttal to China's forged claims.* Tokyo: Meiseisha, 2000.

Tamura, Reiko. "Gaimushō 'ketsuzoku–keibatsu' no kenkyū" [Research on 'kinship and intermarriage' in the Foreign Ministry]. *Fōsaito* (Sep. '94).

Tokayer, Marvin and Mary Swartz. *The Fugu Plan: The Untold Story of the Japanese and the Jews during World War II.* Paddington Press, 1979.

Tokudome, Kinue. "Sugihara Chiune no isan wo tadashiku uketsuida ka" [Are we correctly carrying on the legacy of Chiune Sugihara?] *Ronza* (September 1998).

Toland, John. *Infamy: Pearl Harbor and Its Aftermath.* New York: Berkley Books, 1983.

U. S. Department of Defense. *The "Magic" Background of Pearl Harbor.* 8 vols. U.S.G.P.O., 1977-1978.

U. S. Department of State. *Foreign Relations of the United States: Diplomatic Papers.* Washington, D.C.: G.P.O., various years.

———. *Foreign Relations of the United States: Japan, 1931–1941.* 2 vols. Washington, D.C.: G.P.O., 1943.

U.S. Congress. Joint Committee on the Investigation of the Pearl Harbor Attack. *Pearl Harbor Attack: Hearings before the Joint Committee on the Investigation of the Pearl Harbor Attack.* 79th Cong., 1st sess., 39 parts. Washington, D.C.: G.P.O., 1946.

Warhaftig, Zorach. *Nihon ni kita Yudaya nanmin* [Jewish refugees who came to Japan]. Translated by Takigawa Yoshito. Tokyo: Hara Shobō, 1992. Originally published in Hebrew as *Palit Vesarid* [Refugee and survivor]. Jerusalem: Yad Vashem, 1984.

Watanabe, Katsumasa. "Waseda no hokori: Sugihara Chiune" [The pride of Waseda: Chiune Sugihara]. *Waseda gakuhō* (June 1999).

———. *Ketsudan: Inochi no biza* [Decision: Visas for life]. Tokyo: Taishō Shuppan, 1996.

———. *Shinsō: Sugihara Biza* [The truth about Sugihara's visas]. Tokyo: Taishō Shuppan, 2000.

Weber, Max. *Shūkyō shakaigaku ronshū* [Collected works on religion and sociology]. Translated by Ōtsuka, Hisao and Keizō Ikimatsu. Tokyo: Misuzu Shobō, 1972.

Wedemeyer, Albert C. *Dainiji sekai taisen ni shōsha nashi* [World War II had no winners]. Translated by Sakutarō Senō. Tokyo: Kōdansha, 1997. Originally published as *The Wedemeyer Reports!* New York: Holt, 1958.

Yamagiwa, Akira. "Potsudamu sengen no sōan ni tsuite" [Draft of the Potsdam declaration]. *Yokohama shiritsu daigaku ronsō* vol. 37, nos. 2–3 (1986).

Yamagiwa, Akira and Masanori Nakamura, eds. Yoshinosuke Okada, trans. *Shiryō Nihon senryō (I): Tennōsei* [Reference materials on the occupation of Japan. Vol. 1. The emperor system]. Tokyo: Ōtsuki Shoten, 1990.

Yamamoto, Masao, ed. *Teikoku Riku-Kaigun masaka monogatari 1* [Astonishing anecdotes of the Imperial Japanese Army and Navy. Vol. 1]. Tokyo: Senshi kankōkai, 1990.

Yoshida, Shigeru. *The Yoshida Memoirs: The Story of Japan in Crisis.* Translated by Kenichi Yoshida. Westport: Greenwood Press, 1961.

Yoshida, Shigeru. *Kaiso jūnen 1* [Reflections of a decade. Vol. 1]. Tokyo: Shinchōsha, 1952.

Yoshida, Takashi. "A Battle over History in Japan." In Fogel, Joshua A., ed. *The Nanjing Massacre in History and Historiography.* Berkeley: University of California Press, 2000.

Index